BEYOND STATE FAILURE AND COLLAPSE

BEYOND STATE FAILURE AND COLLAPSE

Making the State Relevant in Africa

Edited by
George Klay Kieh Jr.

LEXINGTON BOOKS

A division of
ROWMAN & LITTLEFIELD PUBLISHERS, INC.
Lanham • Boulder • New York • Toronto • Plymouth, UK

LEXINGTON BOOKS

A division of Rowman & Littlefield Publishers, Inc.
A wholly owned subsidiary of The Rowman & Littlefield Publishing Group, Inc.
4501 Forbes Boulevard, Suite 200
Lanham, MD 20706

Estover Road
Plymouth PL6 7PY
United Kingdom

British Library Cataloguing in Publication Information Available

Library of Congress Cataloging-in-Publication Data

Beyond state failure and collapse : making the state relevant in Africa / edited by George Klay Kieh.
p. cm.
Includes bibliographical references.
ISBN-13: 978-0-7391-0892-5 (cloth : alk. paper)
ISBN-10: 0-7391-0892-1 (cloth : alk. paper)
1. Africa—Politics and government—1960- 2. Democracy—Africa. 3. Africa—Social conditions—1960- I. Kieh, George Klay, 1956–
JQ1875.B48 2007
320.1096—dc22 2006032212

Printed in the United States of America

∞™ The paper used in this publication meets the minimum requirements of American National Standard for Information Sciences—Permanence of Paper for Printed Library Materials, ANSI/NISO Z39.48–1992.

Contents

Figures and Tables

Preface

UNDOUBTEDLY, THE AFRICAN PEOPLE'S hopes and aspirations for a democratic, stable and prosperous post-independence era have been shattered. Clearly, after more than four decades of independence, the postcolonial project has been enveloped in a multidimensional crisis of underdevelopment—cultural, ecological, economic, political, social, and so forth. Perpetuating this crisis, illegitimate regimes and ethnic entrepreneurs have manipulated primordial differences; water, land and the air have been polluted; Africans have some of the lowest standards of living in the world; both civilian and military despots have repressed and suffocated society; and basic human needs have not been met.

Accordingly, these horrendous conditions have made the state distant and irrelevant to the needs of the vast majority of African peoples. In other words, the popular collective mirror image that the African masses have of the state is that of a brutal, repressive, predatory and anti-people apparatus.

Significantly, despite the irrelevance of the postcolonial state in Africa, the reality is that it has been, is, and will continue to be in the foreseeable future the single most dominant architecture in the lives of the peoples of Africa. Accordingly, it is imperative for the state in Africa to be re-fashioned so that it can fulfill the high hopes that the peoples of Africa entertained during the dawn of the independence era. In short, it has already been established that the postcolonial state in Africa is irrelevant to the needs of the vast majority of the African peoples. So, the critical problem is how to make the state in Africa relevant. It is against this backdrop that this book is conceived.

Clearly, the book would not have been possible without the immense interest and generous support of the Ford Foundation. The Foundation provided a one-year grant in early 2000 both for the holding of an international conference on "Beyond State Failure and Collapse: Making the State Relevant in Africa," in Monrovia, Liberia, in March 2000, and for the conduct of the subsequent research that resulted in this book. The research project involved scholars from various African states, those who participated in the conference, as well as those who joined the project after the holding of the conference. I am grateful to Professor Julius Ihonvbere, former Program Officer, Governance and Civil Society Unit at the Ford Foundation, who is currently serving as Special Advisor to the President of the Federal Republic of Nigeria for Policy, for working with me in helping to translate the idea of the project into reality. Specifically, Professor Ihonvbere provided suggestions at the various stages of the project. Also, many thanks to Ms. Celeste Dado, the former Grants Administrator at the Ford Foundation, for her assistance and usual kind understanding.

I am indebted to the researchers who generously devoted their energies to the project. Without their invaluable contributions, the idea for the project would have remained on the "conceptual drawing board."

In Liberia, I am thankful to the Liberia Democracy Watch, especially Nathaniel Kwarbo, the former Executive Director, and Augustus Toure, the former Deputy Executive Director, for coordinating the project, particularly for hosting the international conference. Similarly, my gratitude goes to the National Forum for Public Policy and Development for cohosting the International Conference. Particularly, Yanquoi Kargbo, the then-Chair of the Board of Directors, Alaric Tokpa, a Member of the Board of Directors, and Abraham B. Mitchell, the then–Executive Director, are deserving of commendation for their contributions to the success of the project.

At Lexington Books, I am grateful to Rebekka Brooks Istrail, my former acquisitions editor, for her patience, understanding and cooperation, especially as my family and I dealt with the tragic death of our son, Frederick. Also, Rebekka worked with me through the various production phases of the book.

George Klay Kieh Jr.

I

BACKGROUND

1

Introduction: The Terminally Ill Berlinist State

George Klay Kieh Jr.

THERE IS A GENERAL CONSENSUS in the scholarly literature that the Berlinist state in Africa is irrelevant to the lives of the vast majority of the African people. After the euphoria that greeted the wave of "flag independence" subsided, the venal underbelly of the postcolonial state became exposed. The African people came to the disappointing realization that the postcolonial state was the continuation of its Berlinist progenitor. That is, although "flag independence" occasioned the formal end of colonial rule, the state architecture designed by the imperialists remained deeply ensconced on the post-independence landscape. In essence, the Berlinist state that was fashioned by the colonial powers was bequeathed to the African local ruling classes. Regrettably, the African local ruling classes retained the features of the Berlinist state. Operationally, the Berlinist state retained the albatross of oppression, repression, exploitation, marginalization, divisiveness and underdevelopment. Exasperated by the failure of the Berlinist state to transform and improve their material conditions and thus their standard of living, the African people have detached themselves from the Berlinist state and ostracized the state from their lives. Accordingly, enveloped in a cocoon of illegitimacy, the Berlinist state has become terminally ill and irrelevant. Claude Ake provides a poignant analysis of the *causa movens* for the "illness" and subsequent irrelevance of the Berlinist state in the postcolonial era:

> The state in Africa is plagued by a crisis of legitimacy because of its external dependence, the decision of the political class to inherit the colonial socioeconomic

> system instead of transforming it; the massive state violence to de-radicalize the nationalist movement and impose political monolithism in the face of deep-rooted social pluralism, and the use of force to repress a rising tide of resentment against the failures of the nationalist leadership, especially the mismanagement of development, and the impoverishment of the masses.[1]

So, after more than four decades, the postcolonial Berlinist state has experienced monumental failure and engendered multifaceted crises of underdevelopment. Against this background, the purpose of this chapter is threefold. First, there will be a brief discussion of indigenous African state systems prior to the contact with Europe. Second, the chapter will examine the development of the Berlinist state in Africa, including its nature, character and mission. Third, the failure of the Berlinist state and its attendant multifaceted crises of underdevelopment will be deciphered.

Indigenous African State Systems

Prior to European contact, various types of indigenous state systems existed in Africa. On the one hand, as Vincent Khapoya notes, "Africans were able to build large and complex states in different times and places."[2] On the other hand, Africans constructed small and simple state systems. Significantly, some of the indigenous African state systems like ancient Egypt, Mali, Songhay, Ibo, Yoruba and Ashanti were quite renowned for the lessons they provided in statecraft.

Like in Europe and elsewhere, there were variations of state-society relations. In some of the indigenous African state systems, state-society relations were generally adversarial due to the authoritarian nature of the state. In other state systems, state-society relations were good because the citizens of those states were involved in making the decisions that affected their lives. In short, state-society relations were dictated, by and large, by the texture of the governance system. For example, in the democratic indigenous African state systems, the state was relevant to the lives of the majority of its citizens. And this was reflected in several areas. At the political level, there was the rule of law; checks and balances were provided by councils; there were debates in policy-making circles and citizens contributed to the policy-making process through various fora. Economically, the state, inter alia, provided opportunities for citizens to earn a livelihood. Socially, both formal and informal state institutions provided education and healthcare. In the security realm, the state provided a stable domestic environment and protected the body politic from external aggression.

The Berlinist State: Evolution, Nature, Character, Mission, and Political Economy

Unfortunately, colonialism aborted the process of indigenous state formation, expansion and consolidation. Not only did the European imperialists and colonialists truncate and destroy indigenous state development, but they introduced and subsequently imposed values that undermined democracy. Under the aegis of the Berlin Conference of 1884–1885, the European imperialists fashioned a totalitarian state that was subsequently imposed on their respective colonies in Africa. Although there were nuances in the operations of the incipient colonial Berlinist state in the Belgian, British, French, German and Portuguese colonies, there were shared intrinsic characteristics. For example, as Washington Okumu argues, "European colonial rule [in general] was, at its root, brutal and oppressive."[3] So, it did not matter which colonial power was in control of particular colonies, the fact of the matter was that all of the colonial states had a Berlinist core—they were all creatures and handmaids of European colonialism and imperialism.

In terms of its nature, the Berlinist state is European imperial construct, whose formation negated and disregarded the objective conditions in various indigenous African states. In other words, in designing the Berlinist state, the European imperialists and colonialists were guided by the imperatives of the colonial and imperialist project. Principal among which was the acquisition of wealth. As Robert Rotberg posits, "[European] peoples and their statesmen dreamed of wealth and glory that African victories might bring."[4] Similarly, as Robert July observes, "Africa had resources that were important to Western commercial and industrial development."[5] Toward this end, as Warren Halliburton postulates, "The [European] forces took advantage of Africa's great mineral deposits, its fertile land and its low cost of labor to develop their own nations' wealth."[6] In short, as Carlene Edie argues, "The [Berlinist] state was created in response to both the internal and external needs of the colonial powers."[7]

The nature of the Berlinist state was central to defining the asymmetrical relationship between the colonizers and the colonized. At the vortex of this relationship was the belief that the Berlinist state's primary preoccupation was the creation of an enabling environment in which the various colonial powers could extract primary products to help feed their industro-manufacturing multiplexes. Specifically, the colonizers had no sense of responsibility to provide the basic human needs of the colonized. In fact, the colonizers felt that the colonized owed them gratitude for the so-called civilizing mission of the colonial project. Hence, the colonized lived at the periphery of the colonial society: They were governed by draconian laws that they did not participate in formulating; their views were inconsequential in the formulation of policies; and they had no access to quality education, health care, housing and employment. The only exception was the small cadre of compradors, who were given special treatment by the colonizers in exchange for their services in promoting the colonial project. At the other end of the lopsided relationship, the colonized were, inter alia, required to provide cheap labor and other resources for the colonizers' accumulation of wealth project.

During the colonial era, the Berlinist state had a multidimensional character —absolutist, violent, predatory and negligent, among others. Depending on the particular set of circumstances and situation, one or a combination of the aspects of the Berlinist state's character was ascendant. Carlene Edie provides an apt description of the general character of the Berlinist state:

> All colonial states in Africa had certain characteristics: they were conceived in violence and issued from conquest; they established imperial sovereignty on the conquered territories; they were all centralized and coercive; they all created a bureaucratic elite; they dominated economic activities; they employ racist ideologies; they all sought to integrate the economy of the colony into the imperial economy.[8]

As an absolutist construct, the Berlinist state was extremely expansive in terms of its scope and the dynamics of its operations. That is, the Berlinist state's functions covered virtually all aspects of colonial life. At the economic level, the Berlinist state decided who could participate in the production process. In other words, the Berlinist state was the sole determinant of the companies and individuals that could invest in the colonial economy and the sectors in which such private investments could be made. This was in addition to the Berlinist state's own ubiquitous role in the colonial economy. Also, the Berlinist state played a pivotal role in the establishment and regulation of the pricing structure. Similarly, the colonial Berlinist state had a monopoly over the ownership and distribution of land. In that vein, it decided who could own land, in what quantity and the location. Cumulatively, the Berlinist state was the hegemon in the economic realm. Bruce Berman provides an apt description of the economic omnipotence of the Berlinist state thus:

> The state in colonial Africa, within the broader context of the intrusion of capitalist modernity, was the central institutional force in the organization, production and distribution of social resources. It also shaped the accompanying changes in the social criteria for access to those resources; and the resulting social differentiation between individuals and communities.[9]

Culturally, the Berlinist state desecrated traditional African institutions and values by demonizing them as paganistic and uncivilized. Alternatively, the

Berlinist state introduced new cultural institutions and values. Among the new values introduced by the Berlinist state were rugged individualism and private ownership. The Berlinist state manufactured ethnic identities in order to promote the colonial project. For example, the Belgian colonialists and imperialists transformed Hutu and Tutsi from social classes into ethnic groups with their accompanying engineered antagonisms. At the political level, the bureaucracy of the Berlinist state exercised total control over the body politic. Also, it promulgated draconian laws that were designed to coerce Africans into total submission. These laws, among other things, stipulated behavior that was acceptable and the penalties for aberrations. In essence, by authoritatively defining rules of behavior that specified for Africans what was required, prohibited and permitted, the colonial state structured the choices of individuals by constructing social, economic and political situations.[10]

The Berlinist state was also quite violent. It used brute force to enforce its illegitimate and undemocratic laws and to asphyxiate democracy. For example, there were occasions when entire villages were decimated for allegedly violating the colonial penal code. Similarly, Africans were beaten, maimed and murdered for an assortment of violations of colonial legal rules. For example, the German imperialists in Southwest Africa—the land of the Herero, Ovambo and Nama people—had something of a record in cruelty.[11]

Another feature of the Berlinist state was its predatory proclivity. Beginning with the stealing of land at the onset of the colonial project, the Berlinist state plundered and pillaged African resources in the interest of the imperial project throughout the course of colonialism. Additionally, Africans were exploited and cheated at the individual level, whether they were farmers or workers. For example, African resources were siphoned off by the colonialists and the imperialists to help create wealth in the metropole while simultaneously occasioning underdevelopment in Africa. Besides its direct predatory acts, the Berlinist state served as an instrumentarium for private capital, by creating an enabling environment in which private companies from the colonial power could rob and exploit Africans and their resources.

The Berlinist state was quite negligent. It made no effort to address the basic human needs of Africans. In those instances in which the Berlinist state invested in socioeconomic structures, the primary purpose was to promote the colonial project. For example, as Claude Ake argues, "[The Berlinist state] went into the business of education to ensure that workers could do the jobs they were required to perform and would remain steadfast in the performance of their often tedious and disagreeable tasks."[12] Overall, the Berlinist state had absolutely no interest in human development in Africa.

Clearly, given its development, nature and character, the mission of the Berlinist state during the colonial era was to serve the interests of the colonial and imperialist powers and their merchant princes. Specifically, the Berlinist state's mission was to contribute to the creation of wealth in the colonial power and to serve the geopolitical interests of the imperial power. Accordingly, the various African colonies were simply instruments for the achievement of the aforementioned twin objectives.

Briefly, the resultant political economy of the Berlinist state during the colonial era had several general features. A colonial bureaucracy consisting of a chief administrative officer and a coterie of staff officers, who performed an assortment of functions, governed each Berlinist state. Executive and legislative powers were fused in the chief colonial officer. The judiciary was used as a vehicle for providing legal justifications for the heinous and despicable activities and acts of the Berlinst state and its functionaries. Laws were capriciously legislated by the colonial bureaucracy without the participation of Africans. In turn, the laws were enforced through the use of brute force. The human rights of the colonized Africans were routinely violated with impunity, against the backdrop of the dominant and pervasive view among the colonizers that Africans were barbarians and less human. African civil society organizations that were opposed to colonialism were violently suppressed. Customarily, protests and demonstrations organized to demand social justice were met with violent responses from the Berlinist state. Similarly, those who dared to criticize the Berlinist state and its functionaries were targets of vitriolic abuses, including imprisonment, torture, banishment and death. Economically, the Berlinist state was anchored on a peripheral capitalist mode of production. Each colonial Berlinist state specialized in the production of a commodity as determined by the colonial power. In other words, the colonialists and the imperialists transformed Africa into a network of monocratic economies. The commodity produced by each colony was sold and the proceeds were deposited into the account of the colonial bureaucracy. The colonial economy was disarticulated. That is, the various sectors of the economy were not linked. Instead, each performed an assigned role. There were classes on the basis of wealth and income. Generally, the colonial state managers and the merchant princes occupied the upper stratum of the class structure. The middle tier comprised businesspeople from the colonial power and the African compradors, who served the interests of the colonial powers. The colonized Africans occupied the lowest sphere. Essentially, the major function of the Berlinst state was to facilitate the accumulation of capital by the state and private individuals (the citizens of the colonial powers resident in the various colonies). The Berlinist state performed this function, among other things, by the maintenance of conditions most favorable to the expansion of capitalism and plunder in Africa.[13]

The Postcolonial Era and State Failure

The collapse of European colonialism in Africa was greeted by the African people with relief, hope and optimism for a prosperous, stable and democratic future for all. Jeffress Ramsay provides a captivating synopsis of the state of ecstasy that engulfed the African continent in the 1960s:

> The times were electric. In country after country, the flags of Britain, Belgium, and France were replaced by the banners of the new states, whose leaders offered idealistic promises to remake the continent and the world. Hopes were high, and the most ambitious of goals [seemed] obtainable. Even Africans spoke of the resource-rich continent as being on the verge of a development take-off. Some of the old, racist myths about Africa were [at] last being questioned.[14]

Regrettably, "political independence" has failed to bear the fruits of democracy and peace: The African ruling classes have betrayed the trust and confidence of their peoples.[15] Contrary to the expectation of the African peoples, the African local ruling classes failed to reconstitute the Berlinist state so that it could be made relevant to the lives of the vast majority of the peoples. Instead, the Berlinist state was kept intact: By its nature, it remained a European construct divorced from the objective conditions prevailing in each independent African state. In terms of character, the postcolonial Berlinist state remained absolutist, violent, predatory and negligent. The mission of the Berlinist state remained as the facilitation of the private accumulation process in the interests of international finance capital and multinational corporations. The peripheral capitalist economy and its attendant dynamics remained unchanged. Against this background, the Berlinist state has occasioned state failure (cultural, economic, political, security and social) and its associated crises of underdevelopment in Africa.

Cultural Failure

From its inception, the Berlinist state failed to forge the bonds of nationhood in Africa's various multiethnic societies. Instead, in a number of countries like Nigeria, ethnicity became the foundation stone of the postcolonial political architecture. For example, under Nigeria's postcolonial federal state system, the country was divided into various regions based on ethnic suzerainty in each region. The North was designed as Huasa and Fulani terrain, the West as Yoruba land and the East as the Ibo sphere. The resultant political dynamics shaped the character and operations of the ethnically based federal system.

Even when Nigeria replaced the regions with states, ethnicity still remained the fulcrum of the state-based federal arrangement. Even the various political parties that were established immediately after independence were ethnically based. Since then, ethnicity has become a pervasive feature of Nigerian life. Consequently, three major problems have ensued. It has become quite a challenge to build various national organizations across the ethnic spectrum. Another problem is that ethnic entrepreneurs have used and continue to use ethnicity as a weapon for prosecuting their various personal agendas—political and otherwise. A third problem is that ethnicity has undermined class solidarity especially among the subaltern classes. This is because ethnicity has created interethnic suspicions and mistrust, thereby making it very difficult for members of the subordinate classes from divergent ethnic backgrounds to collaborate and wage a class struggle against Nigeria's ruling class.

Similarly, in several African states, regimes that have been entrapped in the web of illegitimacy have resorted to "playing the ethnic card." This has assumed the form of the regime playing ethnic groups against one another in the classic tradition of the British "divide and rule" colonial policy. This strategy has been quite successful in diverting the attention of the African people away from the failure of these regimes to address their basic needs. Instead, energy is needlessly wasted on internecine squabbles. In fact, on various occasions, these squabbles have degenerated into full-scale civil wars.

Economic Failure

The economic failure of the Berlinist state during the postcolonial era in Africa can be captured at various levels. Structurally, the economies of African states are monocratic. That is, each African state relies on a single commodity as the lifeblood of its economy. For example, Mauritius gets 90 percent of its earnings from groundnuts and groundnut oil exports.[16] The preponderant reliance on a single commodity as the engine of the economy makes these African states vulnerable to the vicissitudes of the global capitalist system: Changes in the prices of the commodities as dictated by the core states determine the economic health of the various African states. The various peripheral capitalist economies lack industrial base: They do not have the capacity to manufacture products. Thus, these peripheral capitalist economies are simply export enclaves for the production of raw materials—agricultural and mineral—to help feed the industrial and manufacturing complexes of the core states. There are no intersectoral linkages between and among the various sectors of the economies of African states. One of the consequences is that technological development in one sector does not spillover into the other sectors. African states have dual economies. The urban area is analogous to the local core and serves as the linchpin of the monetized section of the economy. Virtually all of the major economic activities, social services and infrastructure are concentrated in the urban area. On the other hand, the rural area, the local periphery, exists on the fringes of the domestic economy. Its principal role is to supply the urban area akin to the way in which the peripheral capitalist economies of African states serve and supply the core states.

In terms of performance, the peripheral capitalist economies have done quite poorly. For example, the number of poor people in sub-Saharan Africa rose from 242 million in 1990 to 290 million in 1998.[17] In 1995, 32 of the 47 least developed countries in the world were in Africa.[18] Dismal economic policies and strategies have occasioned over dependence and reliance on external borrowing and precipitated debt bondage. For example, in 1997, debt servicing stood at $35 billion or 31 percent of goods and services exported by African countries.[19] Debt bondage has made African states vulnerable to virulent exploitation by Western industrialized states and their commercial banks as well as the Bretton Woods Institutions—the International Monetary Fund and the World Bank. For example, between 1981 and 1985, Western private banks, official sources and international financial institutions siphoned off about $26.8 billion in the form of profits and debt servicing.[20] Similarly, in 1986, some sixteen African countries transferred 350 percent more money to the IMF than they received from it in 1985.[21]

Political Failure

Despite the wave of optimism that swept across Africa in 1990, concerning the emergence of the "third wave of democratization" and the associated withering away of authoritarianism, the Berlinist state remains in the throes of political failure in most parts of the continent. For example, by the close of the 1990s, only nine African countries—Benin, Cape Verde, Mali, Malawi, Mauritius, Namibia, Sao Tome, Precipe and South Africa—had made significant progress in terms of political democratization.[22] Twenty-six countries had made medium-level strides in democratizing politically.[23] Unfortunately, more than half of the countries—twenty-eight states—are still in the throes of authoritarianism.[24] These countries constitute the category Freedom House refers to as "not free."[25]

Specifically, in terms of some of the indices of political democratization, the Berlinist state has performed poorly. For example, political rights and civil liberties are still being violated in several African states. This is reflected in the muzzling of freedoms of speech, of the press, of association, of assembly, of thought and of movement. Politics have not been institutionalized. There are still major challenges to the establishment of the sanctity of the rule of law. Political parties, by-and-large, are trappings around the personalities of various ambitious compradors. In other words, political parties have not transcended the personalities of their leaders. Several countries like Libya and Egypt remain resistant to political democratization. There is still the lack of transparency in the conduct of public affairs.

Security Failure

Security failure in postcolonial Africa is a by-product of cultural, economic, political and social failure; state failure in these spheres has generated tensions, suspicions, mistrust, crisis and conflict (including civil wars and military coups d'etat). For example, by the end of the first decade of the post-independence era, more than thirty civil wars had been fought in Africa.[26] During the 1990s, Africa was torn by nine wars, numerous other instances of large-scale violent conflicts and a kaleidoscope of coups and demonstrations.[27] In the new millennium, civil wars continued to rage in the Sudan and Senegal.

Another indicator of security failure is the illegal seizure of political power by the military. From 1952 to 2000, thirty-three Africa countries experienced coups d'etat. West Africa has been the most coup-prone region in the continent: of the region's sixteen countries, only Cape Verde and Senegal have not experienced coups. Amid state failure, the military in various African countries has routinely intervened in politics and arrogated unto itself the role of governor. The horrendous performance of various military regimes has in turn generated other coups.

Social Failure

The Berlinist state has failed to address the social needs—education, health and sanitation needs—of its people. For example, in 1990, the literacy rate in Africa stood at a dismal 51 percent.[28] During the same period, only 48 percent of the population of African states had access to health care;[29] 32 percent had access to sanitation;[30] 40 percent had access to safe drinking water;[31] and the under-five mortality rate was 175.[32]

Social failure has, inter alia, led to the prevalence of diseases. Scores of Africans have even died from preventable and curable diseases. The lack of public investment in the construction of quality hospitals and other health facilities; the inadequacy of medical personnel; and the lack of equipment and supplies have precipitated a health crisis throughout most parts of the continent.

State Collapse

State collapse has been caused by state failure in Africa. That is, the inability and unwillingness of the state to address the various needs—cultural, economic, political, security, social and so on—of the vast majority of the people have set into motion the process of state collapse. Although virtually all of the Berlinist states in Africa have experienced state failure, not all of them have experienced state collapse. The major reason is that some states have developed various mechanisms for managing and suppressing the vagaries of state failure. Clearly, those states that have experienced either partial or full collapse have lost their capacity to suppress the pivots of state collapse. For example, after more than two decades of chronic state failure and the Mobutu regime's ability to prevent actual state collapse, the Congolese state finally experienced actual state collapse in 1996 as the result of a civil war.

State Reconstitution

Failed and collapsed states are often confronted with the reconstitution conundrum. Based on the African experience, three general trajectories have emerged. Some states have reverted to the same authoritarian path that helped precipitate their failure and/or collapse in the first place. Other states have taken steps to democratically reconstitute along the liberal path. Some have experienced the phenomenon of non-reconstitution.

Clearly, there is no doubt development, democracy and stability can only be obtained if the failed and/or collapsed states in Africa are democratically reconstituted. That is, the states must address the pantomimes of state failure and make themselves relevant to the lives of the vast majority of the African peoples.

Conceptual Issues

This volume employs three distinct but interrelated concepts. *State failure* entails the inability or unwillingness of the state to address the needs—cultural, economic, political, social and so on—of its citizens. Using I. William Zartman's conceptual framework, *state collapse* is defined as a "situation where the structure, authority (legitimate power), law, and political order have fallen apart and must be reconstituted in some form old or new."[33] *State relevance* is the ability and willingness of the state to address the needs—cultural, economic, political, social—of its citizens. In essence, this volume is anchored on the argument that, contrary to the popular notion in the scholarly literature, state failure and state collapse are not interchangeable. Instead, they are two distinct but interrelated concepts. State failure may lead to state collapse. But state failure does not mean state collapse.

The Foci of the Book

The book is concerned with three major interrelated issues. The first major concern is to examine the manifestations and causes of state failure in nine African countries—Burundi, the Democratic Republic of the Congo, Ethiopia, Kenya, Nigeria, Sierra Leone, Somalia, South Africa and Uganda. In all of these countries, the Berlinist state has failed to address the cultural, economic, political, social and other needs of the vast majority of the peoples. Accordingly, the state has become distant from ordinary citizens and inconsequential to their daily struggles for survival.

The second task is to decipher the state failure–state collapse nexus in five of the case studies—Democratic Republic of the Congo, Ethiopia, Sierra Leone, Somalia and Uganda. Of the nine case studies, these five countries have experienced both state failure and collapse while the other four have not yet experienced collapse. What are the linkages between state failure and state collapse? What factors have prevented state collapse in Burundi, Kenya, Nigeria and South Africa? What factors have occasioned state collapse in the Democratic Republic of the Congo, Ethiopia, Sierra Leone, Somalia and Uganda?

The final objective is to examine the efforts that are being made to make the state relevant and to suggest ways in which the various failed and/or collapsed states that are covered in this volume can be democratically reconstituted, so that they can become relevant to the lives of the vast majority of their citizens. Importantly, these prescriptions would provide lessons from which the other failed and/or collapsed African states not covered in this volume could draw.

The Organization of the Book

The book is divided into thirteen chapters. In chapter 1, George Klay Kieh Jr. sets the context for the volume by historicizing the development of the so-called modern state in Africa. He posits that traditional African societies had a variety of state systems, prior to the imposition of colonialism by the imperialist powers. The incipient "Berlinist state" was then bequeathed to Africa beginning at the dawn of the wave of "flag independence" that swept through the continent. Kieh argues that unfortunately the neocolonial African compradors, who inherited the "Berlinist state," did not democratically reconstitute it. Thus, after more than four decades of political independence, the "Berlinist state" has failed woefully to address the cultural, economic, political, security and social needs of the vast majority of African peoples. Accordingly, the "Berlinist state" became terminally ill and thus ripe for failure and collapse. Kieh then discusses the conceptual issues and the foci of the book.

Chapter 2 seeks to provide the theoretical foundations of the book. In this vein, Kieh examines the various theoretical frameworks that have been employed by the contributors to the volume. Specifically, he identifies three theoretical models—federalist, institutional and eclectic—and discusses their basic tenets.

In chapter 3, Pita Ogaba Agbese examines the politico-economic nature and dynamics of the African state. Using human rights reports as empirical referents, Agbese argues that the African state in its current form is an anathema to democracy and development; thus, it is imperative that the African state be reconstituted. In his assessment of the undercurrents of state failure and state collapse in Africa, he asserts that the genesis of the twin phenomena can be traced to the character of the postcolonial state in Africa. Agbese further postulates that the failed postcolonial state in Africa is a composite of several tendencies—rentier, prebendal, extractive, personalized, weak, underdeveloped, neopatrimonial and so forth. He then maintains that a particular tendency of the African state may be ascendant at particular historical intervals depending on various conjunctural factors. He concludes by positing that the state in Africa can be made relevant by a reconstitution process that emphasizes mass inclusion, accountability, transparency and political and economic reconfiguration that stress development rather than the personal accumulation of wealth.

Chapter 4 focuses on the Burundian state. Leonce Ndikumana begins the chapter by discussing the causes and manifestations of state failure, and the risk of state collapse in Burundi. On the causes of state failure, he identifies the poor performance of the main institutions in Burundi—educational, the military and the judiciary—as the principal taproots. He observes that the poor-performance problematic is exacerbated by ethnic discrimination and the regional monopolization of power by the Tutsi elites. According to Ndikumana, over time, ethnic exclusion has alienated the majority of the Burundian people from state institutions. This is because these state institutions have become the exclusive domain of a few, thereby making these institutions unable to perform their required functions—the maintenance of law and order, promoting social justice, ensuring individual security and the equitable distribution of wealth. In terms of the risk of state collapse, Ndikumana argues that the Burundian elites have managed the risk by using what he calls "dampening factors" at each level of the process of state collapse. He then maps out ways in which the state could be made relevant. Among the ways are the creation of a developmental state, the provision of good leadership, the development and functioning of a robust civil society and the implementation of institutional reform.

In chapter 5, Musifiky Mwanasali examines the taproots of state failure and state collapse in the Democratic Republic of the Congo. He begins by analyzing the failures of the Mobutu regime and the efforts to democratize the Congolese state. He then deciphers the collapse of the state, including the Mobutu regime and the subsequent emergence of the Laurent Kabila regime. Mwanasali then briefly discusses the travails of the Kabila regime, including the outbreak of the third civil war and the assassination of President Laurent Kabila. He then proffers ways in which the Congolese state could be made relevant to the lives of the majority of its people. Specifically, he asserts that political stability must be established. That is, the current civil war must end. This must be followed by the setting into motion of the process of establishing a democratic political order that provides space to the important role of traditional political systems and the decentralization of power.

Kidane Mengisteab examines Ethiopia's ethnic federalist strategy of state-building, and proffers ways in which the Ethiopian state could be made inclusive and relevant to the lives of the majority of the citizens—these are the foci of chapter 6. He begins the chapter by historicizing the development of the Ethiopian state. He argues that the modern Ethiopian state is the by-product of internal expansion. Unfortunately, the expansionist strategy did not develop mechanisms for the consolidation of state-building. The shortcomings of the state-building project were reflected in the performance of the state under various regimes. He laments that the two military regimes that dislodged the monarchy failed to take advantage of the opportunity to give Ethiopia a "fresh start" at building an ethnically neutral state that serves the interests of all ethnic groups. He then offers several prescriptions for consolidating the state-building project and for making the state relevant to the lives of the majority of the Ethiopians: (1) The need for dialogue among Ethiopia's various ethnic groups and regions; (2) the development of a process-led constitutional order; (3) the establishment of an ethnically neutral state; (4) the promotion of internal economic integration; (5) democratic governance; (6) the decentralization of power; (7) safeguarding political and civil liberties; and (8) catering to the socioeconomic needs of the citizens.

In chapter 7, Godwin Murunga examines the failure of the Kenyan state and its consequent loss of legitimacy. He identifies the misuse of state power and poor economic performance as the fulcrums of state failure in Kenya. Murunga begins his analysis with a discussion of the evolution and performance of the state during the colonial and postcolonial eras. He maintains that the Kenyatta regime established the foundation for state failure during the postcolonial era, through, among other things, the institutionalization of authoritarianism and the "cult of the presidency." Building on the foundation of the "Kenyattan state," the "Moi state" continued on the authoritarian path and exacerbated the socioeconomic failure of the state. He then discusses the rise of the new Kibaki regime, especially its efforts at state reconstitution. Murunga then outlines several suggestions for making the Kenyan state relevant: (1) The formulation of a new social contract based on the rule of law; (2) a committed leadership; (3) the establishment of a strong, developmental and democratic state; (4) the need for efficiency, accountability and transparency; (5) the reduction of poverty; (6) the improvement of the standard of living; (7) the protection of local industries; and (8) a change in attitude in the international system regarding the pretense of "knowing all."

Toure Khazah-Toure in chapter 8 discusses the tragedy of state failure in Nigeria and offers some prescriptions for getting out of what he terms the "quagmire." Toure begins his analysis by discussing the origins of state failure in Nigeria, beginning with the colonial era. He then deciphers the horrendous performance of the postcolonial state, which has been dominated by authoritarian and predatory military rule. He then argues that the preconditions for making the state relevant in Nigeria rest on: (1) The existence of real democracy; (2) the guaranteeing of group and collective rights; (3) the development of mechanisms for addressing violent ethnic and religious problems and conflicts; (4) the need for a true multiparty system based on pluralism; (5) the establishment of representative democratic structures and institutions; (6) addressing the critical issues of the ownership, control and distribution of resources; and (7) addressing the issue of citizenship.

In chapter 9, Hashim Gibrill examines the problem of the violent disintegration of the Sierra Leonean state and the post-conflict efforts to reconstitute the state. He begins the discussion by analyzing the evolution of the Sierra Leonean state. He then discusses the process of state failure and collapse, including the identification of the array of internal and external factors and actors. Among the factors that were responsible for state failure and collapse, Gibrill examines the role of authoritarianism, the crisis of socioeconomic underdevelopment, the militarization of the political process and the criminal misappropriation and exploitation of natural resources. Gibrill then outlines the trajectory for making the state relevant in Sierra Leone: (1) The establishment of political stability; (2) the promotion of self-reliance; (3) the promotion of national reconciliation; (4) the restructuring of state institutions, so as to make them democratic; (5) the promotion of good governance; (6) post-conflict reconstruction and development; (7) the development of a viable economy; (8) the provision of social services—education, health care and so on; and (9) the promotion of gender equality.

Alice B. Hashim posits that federalism is the sine qua non for making the state relevant in Somalia in chapter 10. She begins the discussion by examining the causes of state failure and collapse in Somalia. Specifically, she probes the role of British, French and Italian colonialism in laying the foundation for state failure and collapse. Specifically, she insists that colonialism disrupted the traditional Somali way of life and fostered regional divide. Hashim then examines the horrendous performance of the postcolonial state, beginning with the parliamentary era (1960–1969). She argues that the parliamentary system bequeathed to Somalia was based on exclusion; that it was nonparticipatory, evidenced by the fact that the constitution was not debated; and that it failed to address the critical issue of justice. Hashim then examines the performance of the state during the Barre regime. She argues that the Barre regime was initially committed to the reconstitution of the state; but, overtime, the state became repressive and out of touch with the concerns of the vast majority of the Somali people. Hashim then suggests the establishment of a federal system of state as the architecture for making the state relevant in Somalia. The proposed federal system would draw on traditional Somali experiences. Specifically, the new state would be based on delegating powers to a central government in the areas of defense, foreign affairs and postal matters. The constituent units would engage in shared decision-making in economic, educational, social and other matters.

In chapter 11, Owen Sichone discusses the failure of the apartheid state in South Africa and the efforts by the ANC-led regime to democratically reconstitute it. Sichone begins the discussion by deciphering the undemocratic nature of the apartheid state that dominated the South African landscape from 1948 to 1994. He argues that the apartheid state was based on racial discrimination and preferential treatment of European settlers in all areas of human development. Consequently, Whites enjoyed a high standard of living, while more than 50 percent of the Black population lived in abject poverty. Sichone then examines the efforts of the ANC-led government to democratically reconstitute the South African state, so that it can become relevant to the lives of the majority of South Africans. Specifically, he discusses the efforts to dismantle the infrastructure of racial discrimination and to establish the basis for equal access to social and economic resources. Sichone concludes by suggesting that state relevance in South African would be attained if several critical issues were addressed: (1) education; (2) basic services; (3) the high unemployment rate among Blacks; (4) poverty; (5) the culture of violence; and (6) the establishment of legitimate state authority.

Paul Omach discusses the tragedy of state failure and collapse in Uganda and the efforts by the Museveni regime to reconstitute the state. He begins his analysis by examining the development of the Ugandan state from the colonial period. He argues that colonialism provided the *terra firma* for state failure and collapse. The colonial state developed the idea of administrative duality. Also, it fostered class inequalities, regional disparities, and ethnic and religious conflicts. Building on the colonial state, the postcolonial successor developed a constitutional order that failed to address critical issues such as the distribution of power and regional autonomy. Similarly, the postcolonial state under the Obote regime weakened national institutions, engendered conflicts between the central government and the traditional political systems. For example, in 1966, the Obote regime precipitated a constitutional crisis by abolishing Uganda's federal system of state. The Obote regime also fostered ethnic conflicts by favoring some ethnic groups over others. To make matter worse, the Obote regime continued the tradition of authoritarianism and its attendant vagaries of repression, oppression and exclusion. The Amin regime worsened the conditions of the state, especially through its murderous rule. Successive interim regimes after Amin were short-lived because they could not deal with the ills of state failure. Eventually, the Ugandan state collapsed under the weight of a civil war. The Museveni regime that emerged after the civil war promulgated a ten-point program designed to reconstitute the state. Unfortunately, according to Omach, the Museveni formula has engendered, inter alia, insecurity in the northern portion of the country, and continued the tradition of political repression and dependence on external forces. Omach then offers some prescriptions for making the state relevant in Uganda: (1) The need to address the issue of state system—unitary versus federal; (2) the need to establish a clear system of government—presidential, parliamentary, mixed; (3) the establishment of a clearly defined role for traditional political systems; (4) the promotion of political pluralism; (5) the promotion of the respect for human rights; (6) the revitalization of state institutions; (7) the creation of a stable political order, including ending the civil war; (8) the building of a viable economic system that transcends the parameters of neoliberal economic policies; (9) the reduction of external dependence; and (10) the promotion of ethnic and regional pluralism.

In chapter 13, George Klay Kieh Jr. draws on the lessons provided by the various chapters in this volume. Specifically, he maps out the modalities for making the state relevant in Africa. He identifies several areas of state relevance —cultural, economic, political, religious, security and social. Within each genre, Kieh then discusses specific issues of state relevance.

Notes

1. Claude Ake, ed., "The State in Contemporary Africa," in *Political Economy of Nigeria* (London: Longman, 1985), 2.
2. Vincent Khapoya, *The African Experience: An Introduction*, 2nd ed. (Upper Saddle River, NJ: Prentice Hall, 1998), 68.
3. Washington Okumu, *The African Renaissance* (Trenton, NJ: Africa World Press, 2002), 78.
4. Robert Rotberg, *A Political History of Tropical Africa* (New York: Harcourt, Brace and World, Inc., 1965), 244.
5. Robert July, *A History of the African People* (Prospect Heights, IL: Waveland, 1992), 264.
6. Warren Halliburton, *Africa's Struggle for Independence* (New York: Crestwood House, 1992), 7.
7. Carlene Edie, *Politics in Africa: A New Beginning?* (Belmont, CA: Wadsworth/Thomas Learning, 2003), 48.
8. Edie, *Politics in Africa*, 48.
9. Bruce Berman, "Ethnicity, Patronage and the African State: The Politics of Uncivil Nationalism," *African Affairs* 97, no. 388 (July 1998): 313.
10. Berman, "Ethnicity, Patronage and the African State."
11. Mai Palmberg, *The Struggle for Africa* (London: Zed Press, 1983), 18.
12. Clauke Ake, *Democracy and Development in Africa* (Washington DC: The Brookings Institution, 1996), 2.
13. Seew, *How Europe Underdeveloped Africa* (Washington, DC: Howard University Press, 1982), 164.
14. Jeffress Ramsey, "Africa: The Struggle for Development," in *Africa*, 8th edition (Guilford, CT: McGraw-Hill/Dushkin, 1999), 3.
15. George Klay Kieh Jr., "Democratization and Peace in Africa," *Journal of Asian and African Studies* 31, nos. 1–2 (1996): 99.
16. See Kofi Hadjar, *On Transforming Africa* (Trenton, NJ: Africa World Press, 1987), 9.
17. See David Dollar and Aart Kraay, "Growth Is Good for the Poor," in *The Globalization Reader*, ed. Frank J. Lechner and John Boli (Malden, MA: Blackwell Publishing, 2004), 189.
18. See *People's Democracy* (June 18, 1995): 1.
19. See United Nations Economic Commission for Africa, *The African Debt Crisis* (Addis Ababa, Ethiopia: UNECA, 1999), 5.
20. See Frederick Clairmonte and John Cavanagh, "Impossible Debt on the Road to Global Ruin," *Guardian* (January 9, 1987): 1.
21. Ramsey, "Africa: The Struggle for Development," 6.
22. See George Klay Kieh Jr., "Democratization in Africa: A Balance Sheet," in *Preparing Africa for the Twenty-first Century*, ed. John Mukum Mbaku (Brookfield, VT: Ashgate, 1999), 108–9.
23. Kieh, "Democratization in Africa."

24. Kieh, "Democratization in Africa."

25. For detailed data on political democratization in Africa, see Freedom House's annual survey *Freedom in the World* (New York: Freedom House).

26. See Conflict Watch, "Conflict Trends" (Pretoria, South Africa: African Center for the Constructive Resolution of Disputes, 2001), 1.

27. Raymond Copson, "Peace in Africa," in *Conflict Resolution in Africa*, ed. Francis Deng and I. William Zartman (Washington, DC: The Brookings Institution, 1991), 20.

28. See United Nations Development Program, Human Development Report (New York: Oxford University Press, 1991), 135.

29. United Nations Development Program, Human Development Report, 131.

30. United Nations Development Program, Human Development Report, 147.

31. United Nations Development Program, Human Development Report, 131.

32. United Nations Development Program, Human Development Report, 135.

33. I. William Zartman, ed., *Collapsed States* (Boulder, CO: Lynne Rienner Publishers, 1995), 1.

2

Making the State Relevant: Theoretical Models

George Klay Kieh Jr.

THERE IS AN EMERGING CORPUS OF ACADEMIC LITERATURE on various theoretical frameworks on state relevance. These frameworks are ostensibly designed to serve as intellectual compasses for navigating the terrain of making the state relevant. The purpose in this chapter is not to address all of these theoretical frameworks but to examine those that are germane to the chapters in this volume.

Against this background, the purpose of this chapter is to examine four theoretical frameworks on state relevance: The ethnic federalist, the institutionalist, the state deconstruction and integrative models. Specifically, the basic contours of each model will be summarized and deciphered.

The Ethnic Federalist Model

With various states plagued with an assortment of conflicts—communal, regional and others—the federalist model has emerged as the dominant theoretical framework for making the state relevant in divided or conflictual societies. Adherents to the ethnic federalist model argue that it provides the best option for accommodating and reconciling the differences that underlie various societal conflicts. As Eghosa Osaghae observes "Of all of the attempts to resolve ethnic problems by constitutional means, federalism stands out clearly as the most prescribed option for divided societies."[1] The model is anchored on several contours. The base premises revolve around several postulates. At the core is the argument that ethnic nationalism is not antithetical to the state-building project. In other words, the clamor by ethnic groups for involvement in the body politic fosters long-term stability. Conversely, if the state and its custodians are impervious to ethnic claims, this may then generate conflict and even ignite secessionist fervor. The historical experiences of the polity, especially the nature and dynamics of interethnic and state-society relations must dictate the texture of the federal design. Also, the various ethnic claimants must be committed to peaceful coexistence with other ethnic groups in the body polity and to the overall preservation of the state. The state must be a democratic polity. This is because dictatorship, with its one-party government and its denial of free election, is incompatible with the working of the federal principle. Federalism demands forms of government that have the characteristics usually associated with democracy or free government. There is a wide variety in the forms which such government may take, but the main essentials are free elections and a party system with its guarantee of a responsible opposition.[2]

Another postulate concerns the structural layers. There are two major tiers of such layers: the central tier consisting of the national level that must be ethnically neutral. That is, the center must not be aligned with or dominated by any one particular ethnic group. The local tier consists of regional, state or provincial administration. Within the local tier, there are ethnically based territorial administrations that are specifically designed as the bastions of the various ethnic poles.

The systemic powers of the state are divided between a central government and various local units representing ethnic groups. Generally, the central government has exclusive powers in the areas of foreign affairs, defense, the postal service and the minting of currency. The local level may also have certain exclusive powers in a number of policy areas. Both levels may have concurrent or shared powers in areas such as lawmaking, taxation, etc. Importantly, as Mihailo Markovic notes, "the [local levels] must be relatively autonomous."[3] Notwithstanding, there must be a satisfactory level of coordination within the system as a whole.[4]

Both the center and the local levels must derive their power from the constitution. The constitution must clearly delineate the powers and attendant functions of the central level and those of the local levels. The main purpose is to help protect the autonomy and existence of the local units. As Michael Burgess and Alain Gagnon posit, "constitutional autonomy is paramount."[5]

The state must have a democratic political culture that is based on pluralism, mutual respect, consultation, negotiation and accommodation. Operationally, the national decision-making processes must include all of the multiple centers of power, including their inherent right to articulate their views freely and openly. The various actors at the center and local levels must demonstrate respect for one another, even amid disagreements over policies. The associated requirement is that debates and discussions must reflect the mutual recognition that all sides are inherently interested in the overall well-being of the larger body politic. Also, there must be regular consultation between the center and the local levels and among the local levels. This is critical to the promotion of the esprit de corps that is exigent for the smooth operation of the polity. Similarly, through regular consultation, issues would be clarified and the potential for violent conflicts would be minimized. Negotiation must be one of the major tools of the decision-making processes at the national and local levels. The various parties in each instance must be willing to listen to each other's views and to make the necessary adjustments and changes in their positions based on the strength of a position or positions of other parties. Ultimately, the parties must demonstrate a willingness and commitment to be accommodative by engaging in tradeoffs and the attendant recognition and acceptance of the fact that they will not get everything they want at all times.

The polity must have institutionalized conflict management mechanisms that are used to address disagreement over issues. The collective purpose of these mechanisms is to peacefully resolve conflicts within the context of the political-legal-constitutional order. Donald Horowitz identified five conflict reducing mechanisms: the proliferation of the points of power; the generation of intraethnic competition; the generation of interethnic cooperation; the encouragement of the alignment of nonethnic issues; and the reduction of the disparities between regions through redistribution.[6]

The Institutionalist Model

The institutionalist model is hoisted on several pillars. The major centerpiece is the argument that a reconstituted state needs public institutions that are effective and efficient. Generally, the institutions are the executive, legislature and the judiciary. These institutions must justly conduct the business of the state efficaciously. The rationale is that institutional atrophy is a precipitant of conflicts that could disrupt the body politic. In other words, the inefficiency of public institutions and their overall poor performance could engender discontent from segments of the public—and the discontent could escalate into violent conflict and its disruptive consequences.

Another caveat is that the various public institutions perform their assigned functions. Generally, the executive is responsible for the enforcement of the law; the legislature performs lawmaking functions; and the judiciary has the responsibility for the adjudication of the law. The overall collective function of these institutions, as Leonce Ndikumana argues, is "economizing, reducing risks and uncertainty, and distributing wealth."[7]

The smooth operation of institutions and the state in general is dependent upon the effective functioning of a body of rules. The rules can be embodied in a constitution and various statues. The rules must clearly delineate the acceptable parameters within which the various institutions function and relate to the larger society. The rules must be flexible and remain open to periodic political contestation and reform.[8]

Another tenet is the importance of interinstitutional relationships. The relationships should revolve around two major issues: the distribution of power and competition. Each institution has assigned roles; these roles are designed in ways that permit a balance of power among the various institutions. The goal is to help ensure that no institution becomes hegemonic. Linked to the distribution of power is the issue of intra- and interinstitutional competition for resources and influence in the policy-making arena. However, the competition must be designed to help improve the efficiency and effectiveness of the totality of the system, and not simply to pander to institutional chauvinism and its concomitant particularistic agenda.

The various institutions must be accountable to one another and to the society as a whole. In the case of the former, the system must have built-in checks that would allow the various institutions to hold one another accountable for policy and other actions. Similarly, the society at large must have various tools such as fora and elections to help assess the performance of the various institutions and their custodians on a regular basis.

Also, transparency must be the cornerstone of the operations of the various institutions. That is, at every level and stage of their operations (besides classified matters), the various institutions must conduct their functions openly.

The State Deconstruction Model

The base premise of the state deconstruction model is that the state, especially in Africa, cannot be made relevant within the context of its current neocolonial form. In other words, the neocolonial state is—by its very nature, character and mission—repugnant to state relevance. Accordingly, the neocolonial demon must be exorcised from the core of the African state's tapestry.[9]

Another tenet is the rethinking process. This involves the reconceptualization of the nature, character and mission of the reconstituted state. In essence, this process is analogous to the formulation of an architectural design that seeks to create a desired construct.

The reconstitution phase is the operational dimension of the relevance project. Briefly, it involves the implementation of the design formulated at the rethinking stage. Specifically, this would entail several issues. One central matter is the ushering in of a new constitutional order that would, inter alia, delineate power relations. Also, class relations must be reconstructed so as to mitigate against exploitation and inequities. Linked to the aforementioned is the fundamental restructuring of the peripheral capitalist economy and its relations of production. The purpose must be to change the state's traditional role from serving as an export enclave in the interest of international finance capital to the creation of a diversified economic system that primarily serves the national interests. The state must provide the basic needs of its citizens—health, education, housing, etc. Importantly, the reconstituted state must have what Makau Mutua calls "moral legitimacy."[10] That is, the actions of the custodians of the state must be pro-people, in order for the state to win the respect and support of its citizens.

The Integrative Model

The central argument of the integrative model is that state relevance is a multidimensional phenomenon involving various elements. Accordingly, the integrative model attempts to weave together the various contours of the ethnic federal, institutionalist and state deconstruction models. In short, according to the integrative model, all of the postulates proffered by the various models are essential and germane to describing and explaining state relevance.

Against this background, as an amalgam of the caveats of the various models on state relevance, the integrative model contains several elements. The state in postcolonial regions like Africa needs to be deconstructed. Since the state in postcolonial societies was bequeathed to them as part of the colonial legacy and has not been transformed, the state retains its colonial *raisons d'etre* in terms of its nature, character and mission. By its nature, the postcolonial state is a European imperialist construct that reflects the realities and interests of European neocolonialism and imperialism. Accordingly, the design of the postcolonial state did not reflect the objective conditions prevailing in postcolonial societies. Hence, by its nature, the postcolonial state does not reflect the realities of postcolonial societies; hence, it cannot serve the interests of the peoples in those postcolonial societies.

In terms of its character, the state is a "multiheaded" hydra that is authoritarian, exploitative, divisive, absolutist, prebendal, negligent, criminalized, privatized, neopatrimonial and predatory, among others. One or more dimensions of the state's character is usually dominant, depending on the specific set of circumstances. In short, the demonstration of a particular feature or features of the postcolonial state's character is contingent upon the environment and its dynamics. For example, in serving the interests of metropolitan-based multinational corporations, the authoritarian and exploitative features of the postcolonial state tend to be ascendant. This is because providing service to the multinational corporations usually requires the suppression of the liberties of workers—including the right to strike—and the exploitation of the workers, as reflected in the comparatively low wages that they receive for their labor.

The mission of the postcolonial state is to serve the interests of the dominant powers and their multinational corporations and businesses. This is reflected, among other things, in the custodians of state (the compradors) using the power of the state to suppress the rights of workers and to enable multinational corporations to siphon off a country's wealth and repatriate it to the core. Against this background, the postcolonial state must be cleansed of these maladies. The new mission must involve serving the interest of the state and its citizens.

The deconstruction process must then be followed by the rethinking project. Specifically, this would involve the designing of the elements of the to-be-reconstituted state, including structures, processes and policies. Specifically, this phase of the state-relevance process must seek to address the critical issue of the development of institutions, modalities and policies—cultural, economic, political—that would cater to the interests of all stakeholders within the state. Significantly, the rethinking project must take into consideration the objective conditions of the state under consideration. That is, while its is important to learn and draw from the experiences of other postcolonial states, the design must be based on the objective local realities. To do otherwise would be tantamount to replacing one foreign construct devoid of the affected state's historical circumstances with another foreign construct.

Generally, the operationalization of the elements of the reconstituted state involves the practicalization of the state design. The elements of the design of the reconstituted state must be comprehensive: They must cover the cultural, economic, political, social and other dimensions. At the cultural level, in a multiethnic society, the state must promote ethnic, racial and overall communal tolerance and peaceful coexistence among all of the groups. Economically, the state must be productive in helping to create the conditions for wealth creation; the state must reduce poverty and address class inequalities and the attendant disparities in wealth and income; and it must seek to improve the standard of and conditions of living for all of its citizens. At the political level, there must be a process-led constitution, the respect for human rights, the sanctity of the rule of law, the institutionalization of politics, the holding of free, fair and regular elections and a vigorous civil society, among others. Socially, the state must provide quality health care, education, housing and other basic needs for all of its citizens, irrespective of their stations in life.

Also, it is important that the reconstituted state must be anchored on several major foundational pillars: holistic democracy; constructive, enlightened and regular dialogue among the various stakeholders; and state legitimacy. Holistic democracy must be the cornerstone of the reconstituted state. It must embrace the totality of life. Dialogue among the stakeholders is critical as a vehicle for facilitating communication, a tool for managing conflict, and an instrument for regularly assessing the performance of the state, with the intention of correcting problems. State legitimacy entails that the stakeholders accord the state their respect, support, loyalty and cooperation.

In multiethnic societies, it is critical to promote pluralism. Specifically, this would entail that each ethnic group recognizes and be sensitive to, and respectful of, the cultures of the other ethnic groups. That is, ethnic groups and their members should have the right to engage in various cultural activities as long as they do not violate the rights and sensitivities of other ethnic groups.

Importantly, the state must be ethnically neutral. That is, the interests of one ethnic group must not dominate the institutions and policies of the state. Instead, both state institutions and policies must reflect the national interests, including those of the various ethnic groups. In the event that a particular ethnic group is aggrieved in terms of the treatment it is receiving from the state and its institutions, concrete steps should be taken to respond to such grievances, and the state must design the requisite architecture that would address those situations. Depending on the nature of an ethnic group or group's grievances, an ethnic federal construct may provide an option. The ethnic federal construct is the best arrangement because it allows for the redesigning of the state in ways that give ethnic groups autonomy in the conduct of their affairs. This is because each of the local units is linked to an ethnic group. The center provides an opportunity for the various ethnic groups to work collectively for the national interests.

Also, multiethnic societies require a democratic political system that is based on a culture of pluralism, negotiation and compromise. The state's decision-making processes must reflect the multiplicity of the stakeholders. In the making of public policies, the stakeholders must demonstrate commitment and willingness to dialogue with one another as a way, in part, of understanding the agendas of the other stakeholders. Similarly, the stakeholders must take notice of the fact that in a pluralistic decision-making setting, no side ever gets all it wants and desires at all times. The outcome must be the embodiment of the stakeholders' willingness to subordinate their proposals to the preferences of the majority on any given public policy.

Another element is the salience of vibrant and efficient state institutions. The state must have various institutions to formulate and implement polices in the collective interest of its citizens. Generally, the institutions should be the executive and its associated agencies, the legislature and the judiciary.

Each state institution must be assigned specific functions—rule making for the legislature, rule enforcement for the executive and rule adjudication for the judiciary. These functions must be performed effectively and efficiently so that the state can earn the respect and support of its citizens. In other words, the ultimate objective of each institution must be to provide public goods and services to the citizens of a state at an affordable and reasonable cost and in an effective and efficient manner, including the expeditious delivery of these goods and services.

The various public agencies need to cooperate so that the state can operate smoothly in meeting its obligations to its citizens. In other words, the delineation of institutional functions by the law should not inhibit interinstitutional cooperation. This is because the various functions that the institutions perform are interlinked and intertwined. Hence, cooperation among them is epicentral to the success of the performance of their individual and collective responsibilities and functions. The ambit of cooperation spans information sharing and the routine establishment of interinstitutional working groups to address issues that are common to the functions of the various state institutions. This would promote the economy of scale by helping to reduce duplication and transaction cost.

Both intra- and interinstitutional competition are essential for promoting efficiency. An enabling environment should be created so that functionaries within the same institution and those in various institutions can compete, especially in terms of proffering suggestions for the design of national policies. This should transcend the usual bureaucratic cutthroat "zero sum game" that stifles creativity and initiative in the interest of narrow institutional turfs. Within each state institution, mechanisms should be designed so that the functionaries in the various sections can be encouraged to participate in the policy-making process by providing various policy proposals. Similarly, the functionaries within various agencies should be encouraged to proffer various options for designing and implementing a public policy. Overall mechanisms should then be created both within and across institutions for assessing the various options and for choosing the best policy course of action.

The various responsibilities of state functionaries must be clearly delineated in the laws—the constitution and the statues. These laws must clearly specify the distribution of powers and must have built-in checks, so as to ensure that a state agency does not become dominant. It is important that the functional design attempts as much as possible to reduce the duplication of functions. This would help to minimize the occurrence of interinstitutional conflicts.

In the performance of their functions, state institutions must demonstrate transparency. That is, the ways they conduct business must be made open to the citizenry. Apart from classified information that is critical to the national security of the state, state institutions should freely and regularly provide information to the citizens regarding the performance of their responsibilities at various stages.

Similarly, state institutions and their custodians must be accountable to the citizens for their actions, especially the manner in which the conduct the business of the state. There should be various mechanisms that would enable the citizens to hold the custodians of the state responsible for their actions. One of the major mechanisms is the holding of regular, free and competitive elections.

Conclusion

This chapter has attempted to provide the theoretical crucibles in which the various chapters in this volume are located. Toward this end, the chapter examined the basic contours of four theoretical models that are used to describe, explain and predict state relevance: the ethnic federalist, the institutionalist, the state deconstruction and the integrative theoretical models. The crux of the ethnic federalist model is the provision of a road map for designing and operating a culturally heterogeneous society with its attendant multiple ethnic units that are clamoring for autonomy. As for the institutionalist model, its emphasis is on the designing of public institutions that would function efficiently and effectively in the performance of their responsibilities. The state deconstruction model is based on the central argument that the postcolonial state cannot be relevant because its nature, character and mission make it intrinsically anti-people and anti-democratic. Accordingly, the state deconstruction model posits the need to strip the postcolonial state off its colonial heritage, to rethink the design of a new democratic state and to bring to realization a functioning new and reconstituted state. The integrative model views state relevance as a multidimensional phenomenon; hence, its theoretical postulates are an amalgam of the major arguments of the ethnic federalist, institutionalist and state deconstruction models.

Finally, the application of the various theoretical models to the country case studies in the following chapters tend to reflect the circumstances of state failure, state collapse and state reconstitution in each of the countries. As indicated in chapter 1, some of the countries covered in this volume have experienced state failure without state collapse—Kenya, Nigeria, Burundi and South Africa. On the other hands, countries like Sierra Leone, Somalia and Uganda have experienced both state failure and collapse. Notwithstanding, in all of the countries, some form of state reconstitution is taking place. In short, the contributors have attempted to tailor the theoretical model to the specificities of the countries under study.

Notes

1. Eghosa Osaghae, "Federalism and the Ethnic Question in Africa," in *Ethnicity and Governance in the Third World*, ed. John Mukum Mbaku et al. (Aldershot, UK: Ashgate Publishing Co., 2001), 33.
2. J. A. Corry, "Constitutional Trends and Federalism," in *Canadian Federalism: Myth or Reality*, ed. Peter Meekinson (New York: Methuen, 1968), 15.
3. Mihailo Markovic, "The Federal Experience in Yugoslavia," in *Rethinking Federalism: Citizens, Markets and Governments in a Changing World*, ed. Karen Knop et al. (Vancouver, BC, Canada: University of Vancouver Press, 1995), 3.
4. Markovic, "The Federal Experience in Yugoslavia."
5. Michael Burgess and Alain Gagnon, "Introduction: Building on Traditions and Transitions," in *Comparative Federalism and Federation*, ed. Michael Burgess and Alain Gagnon (Toronto, Ont., Canada: University of Toronto Press, 1993), 5.
6. See Donald Horowitz, cited in Osagahe, "Federalism and the Ethnic Question in Africa," 53.
7. Leonce Ndikumana, "Institutional Failure and Ethnic Conflicts in Burundi," *African Studies Review* 41, no.1 (April 1998): 39.
8. See Bruce Magnusson, "Testing Democracy in Benin: Experiments in Institutional Reform," in *State, Conflict and Democracy in Africa*, ed. Richard Joseph (Boulder, CO: Lynne Rienner Publishers, 1999), 234.
9. For an analysis of the centrality of stripping the African state of its neocolonial core, see George Klay Kieh Jr., "Constitutionalism and the Reconstitution of Collapsed States in Africa," paper delivered at the International Conference on Constitutionalism and Society in Africa, Ohio University, Athens, Ohio, November 6–8, 2000, p. 18.
10. See Makau Mutua, "Breaking Barriers: Radical Constitutionalism in the Next African Century," paper presented at the International Conference on Constitutionalism in Africa, Kampala, Uganda, October 5–8, 1999, p. 1.

3

The Political Economy of the African State

Pita Ogaba Agbese

IT HAS BECOME A WELL-ESTABLISHED TRADITION for international nongovernmental organizations such as Amnesty International and Human Rights Watch to issue annual or periodic reports on how states around the world treat their citizens. In these reports, states' treatment of their citizens is frequently measured by their adherence or lack of adherence to basic human rights provisions. Such reports have become an important barometer for gauging and evaluating the general conduct of states. Evaluating state behavior through the publication of human rights reports provides a very useful mechanism for passing moral judgements on the states and their custodians. At the same time, reports on human rights practices constitute an empirical basis for comparative examination of the nature and character of states and the states' relationship with their citizens. Human rights reports are also essential tools for assessing how one state performs relative to either its own benchmarks on human rights or its international obligations, including treaty obligations, on fundamental rights of their citizens. Reports on human rights practices also serve as mechanisms for determining acceptable and unacceptable state behavior within the context of an increasingly integrated global system.

In Africa, local and international human rights crusaders and political activists frequently use indictments contained in human rights reports issued by both private and public organizations as fodder in their struggle against state brutality, arbitrariness and repression. In such cases, the reports are often cited as evidence of the unacceptability of particular African states' behavior by the international community. Governments in the United States and

Western Europe have increasingly found the practice of issuing annual reports on human rights practices a useful device for drawing the attention of third world states to their responsibilities on human rights under international law. The failure of some African states to meet international minimum standards on human rights has resulted in ostracization and the imposition of mild economic sanctions. Independent scrutiny of state behavior, which is embedded in human rights reports, has thus acquired a new measure of importance and acceptability in the contemporary global system. This derives largely from a recognition that in an increasingly interdependent global system, states can no longer hide behind vague notions of sovereignty to violate their citizens' rights with impunity. In its annual report for the year 2000, Human Rights Watch, a New York–based human rights advocacy group, indicted several African governments for their wanton and wholesale violation of their citizens' rights. It is worth quoting, and at length, the observations that the organization made on several African states. For the Democratic Republic of the Congo (DRC), the report noted that the country

> [e]ntered its third year under the autocratic rule of President Laurent Kabila, and struggled . . . to find a negotiated settlement to a devastating year-long war. . . . The government's attempts to intimidate the political opposition, the free press, and the country's dynamic civil society and human rights movements led to severe restriction on the freedoms of expression and association. Government security agencies routinely used the broad accusation of partaking in "political activism" to arbitrarily arrest and detain scores of mid- and local-level opposition activists. Fifteen UDPS members arrested on May 28 during a gathering of their party were made to undress at the police station and were whipped. Similar crackdowns occurred in Lubumbashi, the second largest city, where several leaders of the UDPS regional chapter were detained in the last week of July. Others who were freed after shorter detention periods from police and military lockups reported that they were subjected to daily whippings and other forms of cruel, inhuman, or degrading treatment and torture. Prominent leaders of the opposition were effectively reduced to silence after long periods of harsh and degrading detention.

Lest Liberians begin to chuckle that these ample examples of governmental high-handedness are taking place in a country far from the shores of Liberia and that such practices may be unknown in their country, the report's assessment on Liberia does not paint a flattering picture at all. In the opinion of Human Rights Watch, the same abysmal state of affairs with respect to human rights violations that occurs on a regular basis in the Democratic Republic of the Congo and in several other African countries was also typical of contemporary state practices in Liberia during the Taylor regime. Thus, lawlessness and gross violations of human rights, which tend to characterize states in which guns pave the way to power for their leaders, seem to be replicated in abundance in Liberia. In the words of the 2000 Human Rights Watch's annual report:

> Liberians were subjected to human rights abuses by government police and security forces as well as violence at the hands of Liberian rebels in an incursion from Guinea and armed groups in a spill-over from the Sierra Leonean conflict. Growing violence and insecurity threatened to reverse the tenuous peace established since 1997 after the end of the brutal seven-year civil war. Two years after the United Nations–sanctioned election that brought former warring faction leader Charles Taylor to power, the peace situation in Liberia remained fragile. The incomplete implementation of the peace accords, particularly with regard to demobilization; a general amnesty to faction fighters for egregious abuses committed "in the course of actual military engagements"; and the wholesale enrollment of fighters from Taylor's former faction into the country's restructured police and security forces contributed to make this situation increasingly more volatile. Liberians continued to report regular harassment, extortion, mistreatment, and torture by the police and armed forces.

Human Rights Watch contends that several other African countries had virtually the same poor human rights records as cited above for Liberia and the Democratic Republic of the Congo. For example, Zambia was roundly castigated for its human rights violations. As the Report notes:

> With a persistent background of political polarization and economic problems, Zambia's human rights record remained poor. The independent media came under attack and human rights nongovernmental organizations (NGOs) and political opposition parties came under threat of deregistration.

In light of well-documented evidence that the Kenyan government did not respect the fundamental rights of its people, it may be no surprise that its human rights practices came under sharp criticism by Human Rights Watch in its annual report for 2000. It observes:

> Kenya remained in a state of worsening political and economic crisis as the government continued to stall on promises of reform that would have brought greater democratization. While some cosmetic changes were made by the government of President Daniel arap Moi, little or no genuine progress was achieved in diminishing the absolute power enjoyed by the executive branch. For the fourth year in a row, the standard of living for the average Kenyan dropped. In the political arena, the government adeptly derailed the grassroots constitutional reform lobby that threatened its monopoly by dividing the reform constituency and reducing its momentum. The government selected ruling party and opposition politicians to serve on an Inter-Parties Parliamentary Group (IPPG) with

> responsibility for constitutional change, while excluding the broad-based National Convention Executive Council (NCEC), a pro-democracy coalition of opposition parties, human rights, religious, and nongovernmental groups, from participation in the reform process. President Moi continued to push for a less consultative constitutional review process through the Parliament, which he led through his party's majority there. Throughout 1999, the reform crisis remained unresolved and the year was characterized by distrust, infighting, and a lack of consensus on the constitutional reform process.

Against this background, I shall contend that the unflattering portraits of African states as clearly depicted in the several human rights reports for the year 2000 provide eloquent testimony to the imperative of reconstructing the African state. I shall suggest that the troubled relationship between state and citizens on the continent point to the reality that the African state as presently constituted cannot advance the material interests of African peoples. This chapter will also argue that by analyzing the relationship between the state and the citizen, one can accumulate important material evidence for teasing out the character and essence of the African state. I shall also argue that the genesis for state collapse or state failure can be inferred from the character of the postcolonial states in Africa. Furthermore, I shall contend that unidimensional depictions of the African state that conceptualize the state as a "rentier," "prebendal," "extractive," "personalized," "weak," or "overdeveloped" state do not capture the true essence of the African state. A more robust understanding of the African state, I contend, can be derived from viewing the typical African state as a composite of several tendencies or characteristics. I shall argue that the ascendancy of any particular tendency is a function of numerous conjunctural factors. Thus, at several historical moments, some tendencies are clearly more dominant while at other times, those same tendencies, while far from the political surface, do not completely disappear from the political arena. The type of challenge faced by the state is also a function of the dominant tendency at any given time. Since the state is an arena for social struggles, the scope and intensity of such struggles tend to be reflected in the ascendancy or decline of particular tendencies.

This chapter is structured on the basis of a series of propositions distilled from scholarly works on the African state. The propositions reflect issues of general agreement on the African state. They are articulated and elaborated upon in this chapter to synthesize what we currently know about the character of the African state and the relationship between state characteristics and state failure and state collapse in Africa.

A central question which underpins the analysis in this chapter but which was not directly answered is this: What legitimate state forms can best deal with Africa's myriad political and economic problems?

Propositions on the African State

Propositions are used here in the ordinary dictionary meaning as "anything stated for the purposes of discussion." Nonetheless, I believe that most, if not all, students of the African state would be in general agreement with my general characterizations of what we currently know about the state in Africa. I have deliberately stated these in the form of propositions.

The Post-Colonial African State Is a Product of Imperialism/Colonialism

There is a general understanding within the literature on the African state that it is a product of European colonial and imperial rule in Africa. Ibbo Mandaza notes that it was the colonial state that in most cases carved and defined the form and content of a given emergent postcolonial state; this had to be sustained within a system that, while it rejected colonialism for what it was, nevertheless adopted the very elements that held the territory together. The achievement of unity and stability became the overriding objective of the new nation, regardless of how this might run counter to the democratic process that was inherent in the struggle for national independence.[1]

European states established the colonial state in Africa as a tool to enhance the exploitation of Africa. During the colonial era, the essential role of the state consisted of ensuring the extraction of resources from Africa to Europe. The colonial state was not designed to maximize the welfare of Africans. On the contrary, being an illegitimate entity, its creators intended that it would visit maximum brutality on the African peoples to ensure optimum exploitation. No serious limitations were thus placed on the colonial state. Even the little social services which it provided were designed to enhance its capacity to extract and transfer African resources to the countries of Western Europe. For instance, roads, rail networks and other infrastructure of the colonial era were not designed and built to make life easier for Africans but as mechanisms for facilitating rapid transportation of the continent's riches to Europe.

At political independence, African inheritors of political power largely retained the structures of the inherited colonial state apparatus. In many cases, even when new laws were enacted by the new leaders of Africa, the antecedents of the laws derived from colonial laws. For instance, press control measures adopted by African governments after flag independence had their origins in colonial restrictions on the press. Sometimes the legacies of colonial rule are reflected in silly injunctions. For instance, the utterly ridiculous prohibition in some African countries against the use of red ink in signing "official" documents.[2] It is true that the postcolonial state retains all the trappings of colonial rule but at the same time, a fuller understanding of the postcolonial state requires the recognition of the fact, as clearly postulated by Achie Mafeje, that the postcolonial state even as an heir to the colonial state is also a product of anti-colonialism.[3] Thus, while colonial origins of the postcolonial state are obviously in evidence, some attributes of the anti-colonial struggles are reflected, even if more mutely, in the African state. The colonial origins of the African state have a number of fundamental consequences on the nature of politics and political praxis in contemporary Africa.

For African States to Advance Beyond the Ravages of Colonial Rule, the Colonial State Must Be Transformed

Amilcar Cabral reflected the prevailing opinion, particularly in radical circles in Africa in the era of de-colonization, that the postcolonial system would have no use for the structures of the colonial state. As Cabral put it, "we are not interested in the preservation of any structures of the colonial state. It is our opinion that it is necessary to totally destroy, to break, to reduce to ash, all aspects of the colonial state in our country to make everything possible for people."[4] Cabral's stand that the postcolonial leaders would have no use for the colonial state stemmed from a belief that the same structures that had been used to oppress and de-humanize African peoples could not be turned into an instrument for their emancipation. In effect, it was felt that the very logic and rationale of the colonial state were antithetical to the quest for African liberation.

Ironically, even as African leaders recognized the imperative of a fundamental restructuring of the inherited colonial state, they began to adopt measures that consolidated, rather than diminished the significance of the inherited structures. Without exception, every African country has expanded the frontiers of the postcolonial state. New state institutions in the form of bureaucracies or parastatals were established shortly after independence. In particular, the coercive arm of the state has been greatly expanded. Other African countries may not be able to beat Rwanda's record of increasing the size of its armed forces from seven thousand in 1989 to more than thirty thousand in 1994,[5] but everywhere in Africa, there has been a phenomenal growth in the size and composition of the bureaucracy in general and of the armed forces in particular. The expansion of the state's coercive capacity has increasingly been followed by general repression and wanton violations of human rights. In addition, the strong emphasis on coercive structures of the state has had a debilitating impact on other public institutions. For African states under military rule, budgetary allocations to the coercive institutions usually take the lion's share of public resources.

Several factors shaped the phenomenal growth of the state in Africa. For one thing, with the state's central role in the private capital accumulation process, an enlarged state guarantees access to more members of the dominant classes to literally feed at the public trough. Second, state expansion was necessitated by the new economic responsibilities that the emergent postcolonial states took upon themselves. Third, access to foreign aid facilitated the state expansionism by funding new structures and programs. The establishment of the single-party political system was also a major impetus behind the emergence of the bloated state. Finally, the centralization of political power, particularly under military dictatorships, was a factor that shaped the swelling of the postcolonial structure.

To Comprehend the Nature and Character of the African State, it Is Essential to Understand the Characteristics of Africa's Ruling Classes

Unmasking the African state in order to understand its specificities and characteristics requires a holistic comprehension of the nature, character and composition of the political elites that control the state in Africa. Several works on social classes in Africa have vividly demonstrated the weaknesses of Africa's dominant classes and the implications that these weaknesses have for state and society in Africa. It is also generally understood that the ruling classes have no firm footing in the productive sectors of the national economies. Hence, state power becomes the principal means to private capital accumulation. Control of state power enables state officials and their cronies to acquire and extend their individual ownership of public property on a private basis.

The linkage between the state and dominant classes has been underscored by Robert Fatton, who aptly observes:

> The study of the state presupposes the analysis of classes, in particular the degree of hegemony the ruling class has attained. It is hegemony, or the lack of it, that determines the nature of the state and the scope of its autonomy. . . . In reality, the state is neither a balloon floating freely in midair nor an omnipotent, autonomous organization. It is grounded in class processes and practices, ligatured to the exercise of class domination. This is particularly so in Africa, where an intense and accelerated process of class formation is taking place. While still fragile and weak, African ruling classes are clearly discernible. Their conspicuous lifestyles and life chances distinguish them from the vast majority living in poverty.[6]

The weaknesses of Africa's ruling classes in the economic sphere are a direct outcome of the marginalization from economic activities which Africans suffered in the colonial era. Colonial rule excluded Africans from the commanding heights of the economy. While African labor produced the resources, the logic of colonial domination excluded Africans from owning the fruits of their labor. Thus, at independence, no indigenous bourgeois class had emerged. Even after political independence, foreign bourgeoisie continued to control the economy and to foreclose easy entry into the major arenas of economic activities to Africans. The inheritors of state power at independence felt they had to resort to using political power as an instrument for capital accumulation.

As Richard Joseph sees this in relation to state and capital accumulation in Nigeria, "continued foreign penetration and domination of the economy after political independence, together with the constraints to peripheral capitalist industrialization in the world economy, meant that access to the state remained disproportionately important in the struggle for resources for upward mobility."[7] Africa's ruling classes tend to accumulate capital on a private basis essentially through the instrumentality of state power. In short, access to state power ensures capital accumulation while a corresponding loss of privileged access to the state almost entails permanent destitution. Thus, those who exercise the levers of state grant themselves the power to extract resources from the state for their own material benefits.

Robert Fatton's description of the ruling classes is instructive in this respect. As he contends:

> The absence of a hegemonic African bourgeoisie grounded in a solid and independent economic base and successfully engaged in the private accumulation of capital has transformed politics into a material struggle. In a context of great or increasing scarcity, state power is the foundation on which class power rests. Once an incipient ruling class takes over the state, it monopolizes the state for its exclusive material gains and uses it for the violent exclusion of potential rival groups.[8]

Similarly, John Makumbe contends, "The state in Africa has largely been privatized or personalized by incumbent rulers to the extent that decentralization, however defined, has meant very little empowerment of people at the local level—the grassroots."[9]

In a major analysis of the Nigerian political economy, Claude Ake observes how the desire to use the state for private capital accumulation has extended the reach of the Nigerian state to virtually every sphere of socioeconomic life in the country. Writing in 1981 at the height of political competition in Nigeria's Second Republic, Ake contends:

> The crux of the problem of Nigeria today is the overpoliticization of social life. We are intoxicated with politics; the premium on political power is so high that we are prone to take the most extreme measures to win and to maintain politi-

> cal power. . . . As things stand now, the Nigerian state appears to intervene everywhere and to own virtually everything including access to status and wealth. Inevitably a desperate struggle to win control of state power ensues since this control means for all practical purposes being all-powerful and owning everything. Politics became warfare, a matter of life and death.[10]

The state of affairs described above has enormous implications for development, democracy and stability. For one thing, the utilization of state power as a mechanism for private enrichment imbues a life-and-death struggle over competition for political power. Second, the little resources available to the state which could be used for economic growth and development are instead corruptly appropriated by members of the dominant classes. Third, the resultant corrupt enrichment and the utter neglect of the socioeconomic needs of the majority of citizens alienate ordinary people from the state. In effect, the state loses its legitimacy and is increasingly compelled to mediate its relationship with its citizens through the instrumentality of force and repression.

Ake is one of the African scholars who clearly recognizes the linkages between the weaknesses of Africa's dominant classes and the dysfunctionality of the African state. As he notes:

> The lack of autonomy of the state makes political struggle within the class intense and normless and the premium on power exceptionally high (since there is no mechanism to mediate conflict between fractions of the class and contradictions between particular capitals); the class constantly endangers itself by engaging in a ceaseless struggle in which all seek power without limitation as to means and exercise whatever power they have without restraint except that arising from self-interest.[11]

John Harrington has drawn attention to the devastating consequences of concentrating too much in the hands of the state. He contends that if Rwanda can be said to be an example of a failed state, it is certainly not because the state was weak or ineffectual; if anything, the state became so powerful and efficient that it crushed or overwhelmed Rwandan society completely.[12]

The Hope Reposed in the African State at Independence to Spearhead Economic Development Has Not Materialized

In the wake of the end of colonial rule in Africa, it was generally assumed that the emergent states would be transformed into "developmental states" that would help to mobilize domestic and international resources for economic development. For instance, Harrington has observed that "in the two decades after independence, particularly following upon the Arusha Declaration of 1967, the

Tanzanian state engaged in what may be termed a developmentalist program."[13] When formal colonial rule ended, lofty goals were earmarked for the African state. Such goals included fostering national unity, ensuring economic development and safeguarding Africa's independence and sovereignty. But rather than becoming developmentalist states, African states have played major roles in the economic decline of the continent. Instead of spearheading self-reliance and sovereignty, they have increased the dependence of Africa on the global capitalist system. Most states in Africa can be described as states that generally fail to meet the basic needs of their people. It was the inability of the African state to engender economic growth that led John Mbaku to contend that by the late 1970s, the state in Africa had seized to be productive and protective. Like its colonial counterpart, it had become an agent of exploitation and plunder, employed by the ruling elite to enrich themselves at the expense of the general population. The results were pervasive poverty and deprivation.[14]

In a major indictment of the African state, derived from his analysis of Rwanda, Timothy Longman laments:

> The record of the independent African state has been abominable. It has tolerated little freedom, grossly violated human rights, applied excessive force, encouraged ethnic and regional divisions, and redistributed wealth from the African masses to a limited domestic and international elite. In the international arena, the independent African state has facilitated the export of wealth from the continent, amassed crippling debts, and imported armaments that have contributed to destabilization.[15]

Similarly, William Reno declares,

> [M]any African countries appear to be states in names only. Their sovereignty is virtually a political fiction; their control over economic flows across their boundaries, effectively minimal; their lapses from public security into political violence, fostered by foreign arms dumping; their retreat in practice from public welfare institutions, internationally sanctioned; their proliferation of state salariat frequently foreign-aid driven.[16]

Intolerance, incompetence, corruption and gross mismanagement of natural resources have become major characteristics of the postcolonial era in Africa. Few people would object to a characterization that sees the African state as one of the primary sources of many of the ills afflicting Africa. African states either through commission or omission have placed millions of Africans in jeopardy. The failures of the African state can be measured in terms of decaying infrastructure, collapse of the educational and health systems, deterioration in living standards, mass poverty and ethnic tensions.

The failures of African states are so glaring that if one were to use the standard Weberian characteristics of states as entities—that exercise unchallenged control of territory, have monopoly over legitimate use of violence, demonstrate ability to extract resources and rely on impersonal or rational rule—one would be hard-pressed to argue that most African states satisfy these criteria. In fact, for many African states, their very existence is at issue. Even states with vaunted human and material resources such as Nigeria cannot take their survival as a single sovereign country for granted.

Almost Without Exception, African States Have Relied Largely on Crude Force, Brutality, and Repression as Instruments of Governance

As noted earlier, reports of human rights advocates paint a dreary picture of the state of human rights in the continent. From the evidence of human rights violations, African states may be described as entities "dressed in uniforms of brutality" as the legendary reggae musician, Bob Marley, would put it. Arrest, detention and general harassment of political opponents have become the hallmark of governance in many African countries. The following description of the state of affairs in contemporary Guinea can be replicated for many other African countries. Bram Posthumus has contended that not long after taking over from the French, Sekou Toure ordered the execution of his first political opponents. His reign went from the harsh to the despotic, as he chased well over a million Guineans out of the country. His favorite ploy was to "uncover plots." There were fourteen in all, each of them resulting in bloody purges.[17]

Repressive, corrupt, administratively incompetent and extractive predators are also common phrases often used to characterize African states. It can be argued that for most Africans, the state is simply an instrument of brutality, oppression and exploitation. One can even go so far as to contend that the African state portends physical danger and health hazards to its own citizens. In Cameroon as in other African states, the state is alienated from ordinary people. Even the ritual of meaningless elections does not provide real contact between the state and citizens as the president is shielded from the public even during elections. As Frances Nyamajoa has correctly observed:

> The president can stay in power and be "re-elected" repeatedly, without ever having to go out personally to campaign. For, under the system of regional or ethnic balance, presidential elections are seldom about voting for the president as such, but more about testing the popularity of the party elites in various regions. This explains why, at every election, the central committee of the CPDM sends its leaders back to their regions and villages to campaign.[18]

Unwillingness to tolerate political opposition was demonstrated in the immediate aftermath of the formal end to colonial rule. Opposition political parties were outlawed and, in many cases, their leaders were thrown into jail or even assassinated. Such tactics were rationalized on several grounds: first, that the new nations were too fragile to permit a multiparty political system; second, that multiparty political competition would create ethnic conflicts, as people would choose their representatives purely on the basis of ethnic or other primordial affiliations. Prime Minister Abubakar Tafawa Balewa's strident condemnation of multiparty competitive system is quite instructive. He contends that "we are not ripe for a system of government in which there is a fully-fledged opposition. In Nigeria, no party can agree to be in opposition for long. A political opposition in the western sense is a luxury we cannot afford."[19] It was largely this logic that was used to defend the establishment of the single-party system in many African countries. This was why it was defended on the ground that it would become a vehicle for popular participation and promotion of national unity.

On the other hand, the multiparty system was condemned as a source for disunity, instability and chaos. Since, in reality, the single-party system was used to preclude political opposition from gaining access to state power, the state, party and national leader became fused. This may be why Leonardo Villalon and Phillip Huxtable have observed that in Africa, "the state, the regime, the party, and even individual personalities have been closely intertwined in the vast majority of African countries, and are not easily disentangled."[20] By clinging to political power as life presidents, many African rulers made their states the monopoly of a few rich people from particular regions, religious persuasion or ethnic groups. The political exclusion that this arrangement has fostered has led to charges of ethnic or regional marginalization and inequality.

In a speech about a decade ago condemning his erstwhile military colleagues, then-General (now President) Olusegun Obasanjo lamented the perpetual state of crisis that seems to envelope his country, Nigeria. As he notes, "Nigeria is a country perpetually potentially great, almost permanently in crisis, regularly threatened with disintegration, prolongingly devoid of democracy, and economically plundered or mismanaged, forever talking about democracy but retreating from democracy."[21]

While Obasanjo directed his frustration in the above speech to Nigeria, it can be contended that his observation can equally apply to other African states. As was the case in Liberia, Zambia and the Democratic Republic of the Congo, even when erstwhile strongmen such as Samuel Doe, Mobutu Seseseko and Kenneth Kaunda respectively fell from power, the states which they had hitherto ruled with iron fists were reconstituted but without any fundamental restructuring.

Despite the Current Travails of African States, It Is Important to Recognize that States Are Central to Politics and the Political Process

While it is true that the deplorable record of African states has made them objects of loathing, apprehension and suspicion, there is no denying the imperative of having a democratic, efficient and responsible state in Africa. As cogently expressed by William Munro:

> The state is pivotal to the political future of African countries. Even in the most abject cases of political chaos in Africa, some institutional form of political and administrative organizations exist which calls itself, and is recognized as, the state.[22]

In this same vein, Bayo Olukoshi has contended:

> The presence of effective and legitimate state structures is essential to the construction of stable and sustainable democratic systems; indeed, there is a sense in which state rehabilitation is at this historical juncture, a central part of the African democratization project and should be more fully factored into our conceptual apparatuses.[23]

The African State as a Composite of Several Tendencies

As noted above, the African state has been variously described as "rentier," "prebendal," "extractive," "collapsed," "failed" and "overdeveloped" state. Reno refers to the contemporary Sierra Leonean state as a "shadow state" by which he means networks and structures that sustain the illegal mining of diamonds and other valuable minerals in Sierra Leone.[24] Rene Lemarchand identifies five types of polities in Africa. These are ethnic or regional hegemonies, totalizing polities, neopatrimonial rulerships, factionalized state systems and liberalized/transitional polities.[25] Villalon and Huxtable have identified five aspects of the African state as follows: a client status, a personalized identity, a centralized or overdeveloped morphology, a prebendal or rentier nature, and an extractive impulse. These terms do indeed describe some attributes of the African state, but the identification of African states along these characteristics creates the impression that these are distinct and mutually exclusive categories. Instead, all African states to a smaller or larger extent, exhibit these tendencies. These tendencies are present all the time even though historical conjunctions such as the end of the Cold War, the interplay of inter- and intraclass struggles and the character of the incumbent ruler may give ascendancy at a particular time to some of these tendencies than others. Thus, it is more useful to view the African state as a composite of an *oppressor*, a *terrorist*, a *criminalized entity*, a *criminal enterprise*, and a *beggar* or *client of a foreign power*. Which of these tendencies is more dominant at any given time is a function of several factors. It is best not to view terminologies such as "rentier," "extractive," or "prebendal" as depicting different kinds of states, but rather as attributes or tendencies that characterized African states as a group. The fact that these tendencies can be used for virtually all African states strongly suggests the systemic nature of the problematique of the African state.

Conclusion

Given the reality that the African state as presently constituted does not advance the material well-being of its citizens and given the declining capacity of the state in social provisioning, several suggestions have been put forward on how the state can be made more efficient, democratic and stable. Along these lines, the World Bank has urged African governments to improve their institutional capacity–building; but as Kidane Mengisteab and Cyril Daddieh have aptly noted, such efforts by the Bank were "largely aimed at insulating policymakers from popular pressures in order to enable the state to promote adjustment."[26] Mengisteab and Daddieh have identified two imperatives for putting state-building in Africa at the top of the political agenda. They contend that it is essential to focus on state-building, first, to demonstrate the positive roles of the state and, second, as a way of avoiding the tragedy associated with state collapse in Liberia, Somalia, Rwanda and elsewhere. In their opinion, if the state apparatus is strengthened, the state could be placed in a better position to address the welfare of its citizens.[27] Mengisteab and Daddieh recognize the reality that the state "simultaneously expresses several contradictory tendencies." However, they maintain that the state in essence is an "organization of citizens and is capable, depending on the balance of power between the state and civil society and within civil society, to serve as a corporate actor or as an agency for promoting the common good."

As in other parts of the world, in Africa the state is not beyond the influence of social forces. State formation in Africa was part of a larger process of integrating Africa into the global capitalist system. The frequent recourse to violence or brute force reflects the inability of Africa's ruling classes to effect ideological control over the populace. African states are marked by capricious exercise of political power.

It is imperative to fundamentally reconstitute the African state on the basis of equality, democracy and accountability. Unlike the era of independence in which the vast majority of Africans were excluded from the process of de-colonization, it must be realized that viable, efficient, democratic and responsible structures of governance cannot be engendered without the active participation of the masses. As an African diplomat says,

"Africa's renaissance will not happen, nor can its transformation begin unless, and until, the principle of accountability is entrenched in Africa's leadership and societal culture."

Notes

1. Ibbo Mandaza, "The One-Party State and Democracy in Southern Africa: Towards a Conceptual Framework," in *The One-Party State and Democracy: The Zimbabwe Debate*, ed. Ibbo Mandaza and Lloyd Sachikonye (Harare: SAPES Books, 1991), 25.

2. I was astonished a few years ago when, on arrival at the Accra Airport in Ghana, the immigration official politely rejected my immigration arrival form on the ground that it had been filled out in red ink. I understand that this practice dated to the colonial days when only the governor of a colony could use red ink on an "official" document.

3. Achie Mafeje, "Theory of Democracy and the African Discourse: Breaking Bread with My Fellow Travelers," in *Democratization Processes in Africa: Problems and Prospects*, ed. Eshetu Chole and Jibrin Ibrahim (Dakar, Senegal: CODESRIA Book Series, 1995), 20.

4. Amilcar Cabral as quoted in *African Colonial State in Comparative Perspective*, Crawford Young (New Haven, CT: Yale University Press, 1994).

5. Timothy Longman, "State, Civil Society, and Genocide in Rwanda," in *State, Conflict, and Democracy in Africa*, ed. Richard Joseph (Boulder, CO: Lynne Rienner, 1999), 339–58.

6. Robert Fatton Jr., *Predatory Rule: State and Civil Society in Africa* (Boulder, CO: Lynne Reinner, 1992), 27–28.

7. Richard Joseph, *Democracy and Prebendal Politics in Nigeria: The Rise and Fall of the Second Republic* (Ibadan: Spectrum Books Limited, 1991), 55.

8. Robert Fatton Jr., *Predatory Rule*, 28.

9. John Mw Makumbe, *Democracy and Development in Zimbabwe: Constraints of Decentralization* (Harare: SAPES Books, 1998), 1.

10. Claude Ake, presidential address to the annual conference of the Nigerian Political Science Association, 1981. For a full text of this address, see *West Africa* (May 25, 1981): 1162–63.

11. Claude Ake, "The Present Crisis in Africa: Economic Crisis or a Crisis of the State?" in *The Political Economy of Crisis and Underdevelopment in Africa: Selected Works of Claude Ake*, ed. Julius Ihonvbere (Lagos: JAD Publishers, 1989), 46.

12. Helen M. Hintjens, "Explaining the 1994 Genocide in Rwanda," *Journal of Modern African Studies* 37, no. 2 (1999): 245.

13. John A. Harrington, "Between the State and Civil Society: Medical Discipline in Tanzania," *Journal of Modern African Studies* 37, no. 2 (1999), 221.

14. John Mukum Mbaku, "A Balance Sheet of Structural Adjustment in Africa: Towards a Sustainable Development Agenda," in *Preparing Africa for the Twenty-First Century: Strategies for Peaceful Coexistence and Sustainable Development*, ed. John M. Mbaku (Aldershot, UK Ashgate, 1999), 119.

15. Timothy Longman, "Rwanda: Chaos from Above," in *The African State at the End of the Twentieth Century: Parameters of the Critical Juncture*, ed. Lenardo Villalon and Phillip A. Huxtable (Boulder, CO: Lynne Rienner, 1998), 86.

16. Richard Werbner, "Multiple Identities, Plural Arenas," in *Post-Colonial Identities in Africa*, ed. Richard Werbner and Terence Ranger (London: Zed Books Ltd., 1996), 5.

17. Bram Posthumus, "In Conte's Fortress," *West Africa* (February 7–13, 2000): 20.

18. Frances B. Nyamajoa, "Cameroon: A Country United by Ethnic Ambition and Difference," *African Affairs* 98, no. 390 (January 1999): 106.

19. Abubakar Tafawa Balewa as quoted in Trevor Clark, *A Right Honorable Gentleman: The Life and Times of Alhaji Abubakar Tafawa Balewa* (Zaria: Hudahuda Publishing Company, 1991), 789.

20. Villalon and Huxtable, eds., *The African State at the End of the Twentieth Century*, 9.

21. Olusegun Obasanjo, "Keynote Address," in *Nigeria: The State of the Nation and the Way Forward*, ed. Abdullahi Mahadi, George Amale Kwanashie and Alhaji Mahmood Yakubu (Kaduna: Arewa House, 1994), 19.

22. William Munro, "Power, Peasants and Political Development: Reconsidering State Construction in Africa," *Comparative Studies in Society and History* 38, no. 1 (1996): 113.

23. Bayo Olukoshi, "State, Conflict, and Democratization in Africa: The Complex Process of Renewal," in *State, Conflict and Democracy in Africa*, ed. Richard Joseph, 5.

24. William Reno, *Corruption and State Politics in Sierra Leone* (New York: Cambridge University Press, 1995).

25. Rene Lemarchand, "Uncivil States and Civil Societies: How Illusions Became Reality," *Journal of Modern African Studies* 30, no. 2 (1992): 177–91.

26. Kidane Mengisteab and Cyril Daddieh, "Why State Building is Still Relevant in Africa and How It Relates to Democratization," in *State-Building and Democratization in Africa: Faith, Hope and Realities*, ed. Kidane Mengisteab and Cyril Daddieh (Westport, CT: Praeger, 1999), 1.

27. Mengisteab and Daddieh, "Why State Building is Still Relevant in Africa," 3.

28. Agwu Ukiwe Okali. "Accountablity and Africa's Renaissance," *West Africa* (February 14–20, 2000): 19.

II

CASE STUDIES

4

Making the State Relevant in Burundi

Leonce Ndikumana

A leader is best when people barely know that he exists.[1]

The final test of a leader is that he leaves behind him in other men the conviction and the will to carry on.[2]

THE PEACE NEGOTIATIONS BETWEEN THE BURUNDIAN GOVERNMENT and the opposition, which started in 1998, have exposed not only entrenched extremisms on the part of leaders on both sides of the ethnic map, but also the greed of individual leaders. Leaders often appear to be motivated by personal or sectarian material and political interests. Political maneuvering by leaders tends to blur party and ethnic lines as ad hoc and opportunistic coalitions are created and dismantled continuously. Opportunism is also illustrated by the repeated internal coups within parties and armed factions. To some extent negotiations have become a career for the leaders, yielding sizeable windfall income, while protecting the leaders' existing positions.[3]

The protracted civil war has severely undermined state capacity. The large majority of the population can no longer count on the state for protection. This is true for both the Tutsi population despite the monolithic nature of the government army as well as the Hutu who are caught between the animosities of the frustrated government military and the armed Hutu opposition. For the international community and regional leaders, the Burundian state has lost credibility. This loss of trust by international leaders can be seen in the impatience shown by negotiation facilitator, former South African President Mandela, who repeatedly voiced his indignation with regard to the attitude of the Burundian leadership from all sides. Mandela accused Burundian leaders of lack of vision, accusing them of having betrayed the Burundian people and soiled the image of the African leadership.

The evidence from the post-independence history of Burundi shows that the Burundian state has failed to perform its usual functions of enforcing the rule of law, protecting individual and property rights, enforcing the rules of fair social exchange, administering justice for all, and redistributing national wealth. Despite such failings, the state has not (yet) collapsed as has been the case in other countries plagued by ethnic antagonisms (like Somalia). This is mainly because the state erected institutions that serve the role of barricades or fences in shielding the central authority from pressure from civil society. However, unless the protracted civil war is peacefully resolved, the risk of state collapse is substantial.

This chapter examines the causes and manifestations of state failure in Burundi and discusses the risk of state collapse. The chapter discusses the ways in which the Burundian state can become relevant or meaningful for the people. The chapter argues that, to be relevant, the state must be inclusive, promote the people's interests, and create an enabling environment for civil society activities and private investment and trade. New institutions must evolve and existing ones must be overhauled to establish a "developmental state" that can maximize the country's economic potential and distribute the country's wealth equitably among the population.

The analysis in this chapter deliberately emphasizes internal factors of state failure and internal strategies for making the state relevant. The chapter does not underestimate the role of external factors of state failure, such as the Belgian colonial legacy or the complacent attitude of post–Cold War international powers, but rather focuses on issues that Burundians can address on their own. After all, it is the responsibility of Burundians, not of the Belgians, to undo the colonial legacy of *divide et impera*. The cries of the Burundian people are deafening and the suffering must stop—or else the very existence of the nation is in jeopardy.

Autopsy of State Failure

State failure is understood as a situation where the institutions of the state chronically perform their functions poorly.[4] Poor performance is the outcome of both endogenous disintegration of the institutions as well as the pressure arising from purely exogenous factors, that is, factors outside of the control of state leadership. In the case of Burundi, by endogenous disintegration of state institutions, we mean the process by which institutions failed due to their exclusive and oppressive nature. The main institutions in Burundi, the military, the educational system, and the judiciary, have inherited the practice of ethnic exclusion from the Belgian colonial administration. This has been compounded by regional monopolization of power by the southern Tutsi elite. Over time, ethnic exclusion has alienated the majority of the population from state institutions and rendered these institutions unable to perform their expected functions, namely the protection of law and order, justice for all, protection of individual and property rights, and redistribution of national wealth.

Failure to Provide Law and Order

The state is expected to provide law and order to allow orderly interactions among social actors. In the case of Burundi, the state has failed on this account, as evidenced by the chronic incidences of violence throughout the post-independence era (see appendix A for a selective chronology of main political events since the 1960s). Violence has often followed incidences of Hutu uprising against government oppression and exclusion, followed by excessive military repression, spreading beyond the areas involved in the uprising and continuing even after the army regained control of the situation.

The civil war that followed the bloody October 1993 military coup differs from the previous conflicts in various ways. The main difference is that the current war opposes armed factions, namely the rebellion against the government army. The war has exposed the inability of the state to protect the population against rebel armies and organized militias. Clearly, a monolithic army is not an insurance for the minority Tutsi against attacks by the Hutu rebellion. At the same time, the war has demonstrated the ethnic bias of the government's military, which uses Hutu civilians as ransom. The war has shown that an ethnically dominated military cannot serve the functions of a national army.

Failure to Administer Justice for All

The Burundian judiciary has failed to enforce the fundamental principles of justice for all. Two of the most visible proofs of this failure are the culture of impunity that has prevailed with respect to crimes against humanity and the arbitrary treatment of the suspects of ethnic crime.

Why Did the Justice System Fail? Diverging Views

Political leaders in Burundi have diverging views about the reasons why the justice system failed.[5] For the Buyoya government, the failure of the system is attributable to shortage of manpower and scarcity of resources. This would explain, according to the Buyoya government, why up to 75 percent of political prisoners languish in detention cells without charges and why so many persons are arbitrarily arrested by the army and security forces without due process. The government claims that there are technically no political prisoners in Burundi.[6]

According to the leaders of Tutsi opposition parties, an important cause of the failure of the legal system is that the legal system is used by the government to undermine the opposition. By mounting accusations against opposition leaders, the government is able to distract public opinion from serious political issues and divide the opposition. The views of the Tutsi opposition converge with those of Buyoya's government in condemning crime only against the Tutsi, while treating all Hutu prisoners and Hutu opposition leaders indiscriminately as "génocidaires." This is an unfortunate globalization of crime, which runs the risk of granting de facto amnesty to those who are truly guilty of ethnic crime. This attitude also overlooks the fact that genocide has taken place and continues to take place on both sides. Selective memory continues to permeate the debate over ethnic crime, whereby each side exonerates the crimes of members of its kinship while exaggerating and globalizing crime by members of the other ethnic group.

The Hutu opposition denounces the use of the legal system by the Buyoya government and past regimes to deliberately oppress the Hutu in order to perpetuate the control of power by the southern Tutsi elite. Hutu leaders denounce the deliberate tolerance of crime by the Tutsi and the relentless manhunt against the Hutu. For example, the justice system has been unable to complete its prosecution of those involved in the assassination of the late President Ndadaye. Subaltern soldiers were condemned in hasty proceedings orchestrated with blatant legal irregularities, while some embarrassing witnesses have "disappeared" in obscure circumstances.

While none of the three views give a complete account for the causes of the failure of the legal system, each is at least partially correct, and each is also fundamentally wrong in some important aspects. Buyoya's view is fundamentally truncated. While the shortage of manpower can partially explain the presence of large numbers of prisoners who are unlawfully incarcerated today, this argument fails to explain the unlawful oppression against the Hutu elite throughout the post-independence era. President Buyoya has no good arguments to justify the ethnic and regional monopolization of the justice system. The Tutsi opposition leaders recognize that it is wrong for a government to confiscate the rights of political association and freedom of speech, but they fail to recognize that this is wrong also when it is applied against the Hutu. The views of Hutu opposition leaders are counterproductive when they deny all individual responsibilities because this amounts to a globalization of guilt. This attitude plays squarely in the hands of the forces of destruction that portray all Hutu people as guilty of genocide against the Tutsi (whether in Burundi or in Rwanda). The leadership must seek to find truth, not to exonerate guilt by promoting negative solidarities.

Redistributive and Allocative Failure

Another function of the state is to redistribute national wealth through taxation and provision of public infrastructure and services. The failure of the state in its redistributive function is illustrated by inefficiencies in tax collection and the misallocation of public resources. While these features are common to most African countries, they tend to be exacerbated in countries that are ruled by ethnically biased regimes.

The ability of a government to collect taxes depends, among other things, on three important factors: the capacity to levy tax, the incentives to collect tax, and the incentives to pay tax. It is the latter two factors that are most affected by ethnic bias in the political system. For the government, the optimal taxation is a saddle point where the volume of taxation is maximized while the political costs of taxation are minimized. Political costs of taxation include the risk of disenfranchising the political and business elite from which the regime draws its support. For the taxpayer, the objective is to minimize the tax burden through lobbying for low taxes or simply by tax evasion. There is a tendency for the tax authority to overlook tax evasion when the guilty party is also a political client. Therefore, both the incentives to administer tax as well as the incentives to pay tax are low in a system based on patronage and clientelism along ethnic lines.

The incentives to tax and the willingness of the public to pay taxes are influenced by state legitimacy, which determines the degree of state-society reciprocity. A disenfranchised population has a higher tendency to evade taxes, as taxes are regarded as a way of funding unaccountable state institutions. An effective state is a legitimate state and legitimacy guarantees sustained efficiency.

The state has also failed in its function of allocating public resources efficiently. The allocation of public resources in Burundi is heavily skewed in favor of military expenditures at the expense of social expenditures, such as education and health care. Military expenditures exploded especially since the outbreak of the civil war in 1993, increasing from an average of 7 percent of government expenditures in the 1980s to about 15 percent in the 1990s. In contrast, in the 1985–1997 period, expenditures on education represented less than 3 percent of GDP, compared to an average of 4.9 percent for sub-Saharan countries. The military-intensive fiscal policy has imposed high opportunity costs on the country in terms of lower social service provision and lower growth.

Inequality in the access to national resources is especially marked in the area of education. The post-independence regimes have perpetuated the colonial legacy, which gave advantage to members of the royal family and the Tutsi ethnic group in the access to education. Under the Bagaza regime (1976–1987), the government established secret screening mechanisms to impose ethnic quotas in the access to secondary school and college. These policies resulted in disproportionately low representation of the Hutu in secondary and higher education. The post-independence regimes increased exclusion in the educational system by reinforcing the domination of the south, through monopolization of the educational system infrastructure. Ngaruko and Nkurunziza provide quantitative evidence that supports the "widespread belief that Burundians from the south of the country have generally been privileged relative to those from the rest of the country."[7]

The Process of State Collapse

Broadly defined, state collapse means that the state has ceased to be a repository of its citizens' political loyalties and no longer exercises supreme authority within the country. In recent years, the state has collapsed in a number of countries, including Lebanon, Liberia, Somalia, and Yugoslavia. State collapse often follows episodes of protracted conflict that undermines the foundations of state institutions. In this respect, the topic is highly relevant for the case of Burundi because the current protracted conflict threatens the foundations of the state and may lead to state collapse, if it is not quickly resolved.

There are many ways of operationalizing the process of state collapse. This chapter uses the analysis proposed by Badredine Arfi in a study of the collapse of the Yugoslavian state. Arfi describes state collapse as a process that evolves through three stages (see figure 4.1): Stage 1 corresponds to the factionalization drive and communal mobilization; stage 2 consists of an erosion of the notion of the state and a crisis of legitimation; stage 3 corresponds to institutional paralysis of the state and assault on state authority. These three stages are demarcated by three consecutive thresholds: (1) widespread negation of political loyalty to the state; (2) complete erosion of state legitimacy; and (3) total disintegration of state authority.

In stage 1, alienated elites mobilize existing communal tensions within the society to pursue a specific political agenda, undermining loyalty to the state.

Process of State Collapse: Generic Case		**Case of Burundi: Dampening Factors**
Stage I: Factionalization, drive, and mobilization ↓	*Threshold A:* Widespread negation of political loyalty to the state	1. Opportunism by leaders (in government and in the opposition) results in fragile alliances (intraethnic, interethnic, or regional alliances). 2. Oppression by government makes it difficult to mobilize against the state.
Stage II: Erosion of state-binding idea and a legitimation crisis ↓	*Threshold B:* Complete erosion of state legitimacy	Absence of credible alternatives to existing idea and structure of the state: 1. Opposition leaders (Hutu and Tutsi) lack "new ideas" of state. Predominance of short-termism, sectarianism, opportunism, and greed. 2. No indigenous material support for alternative state: ethnicity without territoriality. 3. Ethnic leaders lose credibility via internal coups, fratricide, and intraethnic confrontation. 4. No domestic demand, no international support for ethnic balkanization (i.e., formation of Tutsilands and Hutulands).
Stage III: Paralysis of state institutions and assault on state authority ↓	*Threshold C:* Total disintegration of state authority	1. Strong security apparatus and monolithic army allow the state to preserve a minimum level of authority. 2. No natural indigenous substitutes for centralized state authority.
State Collapse		

Figure 4.1. The Process of State Collapse

Source for generic case: Badredine Arfi, "State Collapse in a New Theoretical Framework: The Case of Yugoslavia," *International Journal of Sociology* 28, no. 3 (1998): 15–42.

The elites revive sensitive historical memories and collective identities and exploits evidence or allegations of past and current state bias against particular social groups. At the same time, the alienated elites promise that once in power, they will deliver the material and political benefits that their constituencies have not been able to obtain under past regimes.

In stage 2, each mobilized group promotes an alternative idea of the state that serves its own political agenda. The elite promotes the view that redressing past misgivings by past and current regimes is impossible without reinventing the state. The positions of the mobilized groups become nonnegotiable, and the state becomes unable to meet conflicting demands from rival groups, which erodes state legitimacy.

In stage 3, because opposition leaders see the state as an impediment to the realization of their ambitions, they block all avenues of positive negotiation with the state and start to undercut state institutions. Opposition leaders adopt hard-line positions to promote their credibility vis-à-vis their communal constituencies. This process paralyzes state institutions and undermines the ability of the state to issue commands, make decisions, and enforce obedience. At this point the state collapses.

The Case of Burundi: Why the State Has Not Yet Collapsed

The Burundian state has not yet collapsed despite the damages of the protracted conflict. The state has kept the generic structures and operations of a state, including a security force, a legal system, a central bank, international cooperation, and so on, although state institutions have ironically performed poorly. The Burundian state has survived due to "dampening factors" or constraints operating at each stage of the generic process of state collapse described and illustrated in figure 4.1.

Constraints to Mobilization

Corresponding to stage 1, there is a history of mobilization of the population against the state by Hutu opposition movements, especially after the 1972 massacres. More recently, opposition movements have multiplied, including Tutsi-dominated parties, civilian groups, and armed groups.[8] With the institutionalization of multipartyism in 1992, opposition has been legitimized, although the increase in the number of opposition groups has not resulted in effective mobilization against the state. Two important factors have dampened the effects of popular mobilization and factionalization on state legitimacy. First, repression by the government against domestic demand for power sharing has made it difficult for a coherent opposition movement to develop and take root. In principle, oppression can incite mobilization by alienating the targeted segments of the population, but it can also hinder mobilization by undermining the leadership of the opposition through obstruction, intimidation, and explicit persecution. In the case of Burundi, the government has invested heavily in anti-dissent intelligence since independence. Conscious of the ethnically biased nature of state institutions and the potential for dissent among the Hutu elite and the non-southern Tutsi elite,* the government has effectively managed to keep the opposition under control through dissuasion and persecution. As a result, the state has been able to prevent attacks against its authority despite pervasive abuses of political and human rights.

Second, the leadership of the opposition repeatedly succumbs to opportunism. As a result, intraethnic, interethnic, and regional alliances have proven highly fragile. A few examples can illustrate this opportunism among the Burundian leadership:

- The Buyoya government has formed alliances with leaders of political parties to position his government favorably in the negotiations, while giving the appearance of a nonpartisan and trans-ethnic vision. One example is the "partnership for peace" signed in 1998 by the Buyoya government, the National Assembly, and FRODEBU. The ultimate outcome of the partnership and similar alliances—intended or not—was to weaken the opposition.
- Both the government's party, UPRONA, and leading opposition parties and armed groups have suffered destabilizing internal coups.
- Opposition party leaders have failed to agree on vital issues, including the transition process. For example, while FRODEBU leaders favor the transitional process headed by Buyoya, CNDD leader Nyangoma finds that no progress can be made before the army and the security system are reformed. He suggests that without such a reform, a civilian government cannot function, citing the evidence of the 1993 coup d'état against the democratically elected president Ndadaye and the subsequent paralysis of the FRODEBU government. Nyangoma and his supporters argue that no genuine cease-fire can be enforced without the reform of the military. These differences in opinions among opposition leaders are motivated both by ideological differences and by individualistic political ambitions. Regionalism (the South vs. the rest of the country) also has contributed to the disintegration of cohesion among Hutu-dominated parties.

*The antagonism between the Tutsi elite from the south and that from the rest of the country (especially from Muramvya) dates back from 1966. By the early 1970s, the southern Tutsi elite had largely seized control of power and marginalized the Tutsi from the rest of the country. The Hutu were systematically marginalized in politics and the military following the 1965 crisis, but it is after the 1972 massacres that the Hutu were completely eclipsed from the power circles (the government, the military, and the judiciary).

- Opposition movements have countered the government's attempts to mobilize support by forming alternative alliances (see appendix B). But these alliances are usually short-lived as parties shift their allegiance from one alliance to another as soon as the stakes appear to be changing.

What Prevented a Legitimating Crisis?

The main factor that has prevented a complete erosion of state legitimacy in Burundi is the absence of credible alternatives to the existing idea and structure of the state. Three interrelated factors are especially relevant in explaining this outcome. First, opposition leaders, both Hutu and Tutsi, do not appear to have any "new ideas" of state. Their actions and strategies are characterized by entrenched sectarianism, opportunism, and greed. Therefore, they are unable to formulate consistent ideologies that they can sell to the people of Burundi and the international community to build the foundation of an alternative idea of state.

Second, the history of Burundi does not present material support for a natural alternative idea of state. In the history of Burundi, ethnicity has no territorial foundation. Most importantly there is no widespread domestic demand for separation, as in other cases like Czechoslovakia.

Third, there is no international support for ethnic balkanization, that is, the split of the country into a Tutsiland, a Hutuland, and a Twaland. On the one hand, it is clear that the international community will not preside over the collapse of the existing Burundian state by ethnic balkanization. On the other hand, the prospects for "somalization," whereby the state would collapse despite the attempts of the international community to hold it together are weak due to the lack of sufficient cultural, political, and territorial demarcation among ethnic groups.

What Prevented the Disintegration of the State Authority?

Although state institutions in Burundi have severely malfunctioned, they have not been completely paralyzed. The state has preserved a minimum of authority that allows it to function to preserve itself. A critical factor that has allowed the preservation of state authority is control of the army, secret services, education, and the justice system by the Tutsi elite from the south.

Throughout the post-independence era, the power structure in Burundi has been conceived and maintained with the aim of isolating the central authority from pressure for political opening. Figure 4.2 illustrates this phenomenon. At the center (or the top) of the power structure, there is the president, in whose hands all the authority is centralized. The president maintains

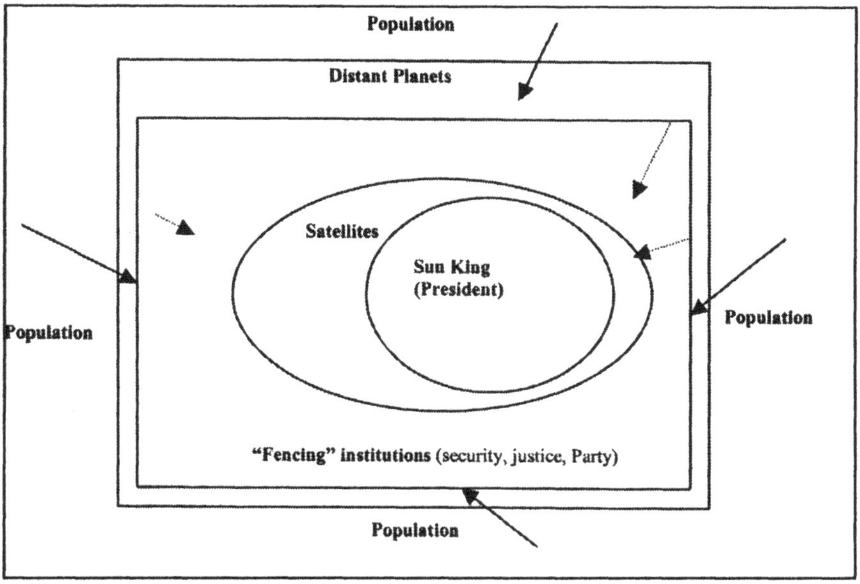

Figure 4.2. The Constellation of Power Relations in Burundi under Monolithic Regimes

Source: Inspired by discussions, in these two sources, of power structure and institutionalized corruption in Zaire under the Mobutu regime:

1. Kisangani Emizet, "Congo (Zaire): Corruption, Disintegration, and State Failure," in *War, Hunger, and Displacement: The Origins of Humanitarian Emergencies*, ed. Wayne Nafziger et al., vol. 2 (Oxford, UK: Oxford University Press, 2000), 261–94; and
2. Richard Sandbrook, *The Politics of Africa's Economic Stagnation* (New York: Cambridge University Press, 1985).

Note: The plain arrows indicate pressure from the population (and distant satellites, to some extent) for political opening. The dashed arrows indicate opportunistic attempts (especially by distant satellites) to penetrate the power circles.

around him a selected group of collaborators, the "satellites," who also enjoy immense power. State institutions, especially the judiciary, the security forces, and the party serve the purpose of perpetuating the status quo by shielding the central authority from political pressure. These institutions are under the complete control of the central authority. The president and his "satellites" are above state institutions. Among the working class, there are collaborators of the regime, the "distant planets," who are nevertheless too distant to influence policy and are not above state institutions. This power structure guarantees that political dissent is suffocated and does not trickle through the layers of institutional fences to disturb the central authority. At the same time, the population remains alienated and *muselées* (silenced).

The second factor that contributed to the preservation of state authority is the absence of indigenous substitutes for centralized state authority. Unlike most other African societies, Burundi has no history of tribal authority. In the case of Somalia for example, tribal authority replaced the central state authority in the creation of tribal states. This is impossible in Burundi.

Despite the factors identified above, state collapse remains a threat. Currently, it is impossible to predict when the conflict will be resolved. The proliferation of armed factions, the growing size of the armies, and the militarization of the civilian population increase the risk for a large-scale massacre. Moreover, due to conflicts in the neighboring countries, Burundi runs the risk of becoming an outlet for the "negative forces" that control the militia industry. This will continue to destabilize the country in the near future.

How to Make the State Relevant and Empower Civil Society

The post-independence state in Burundi has functioned as a *philanthropic ogre.*[9] It has engineered modernization by suffocating civil society. The state's main motives have been to gain power and extend it with the aim of reproducing itself. As a result, all civil society activity was defined by the state, within the state, and for the state. In difficult times—like during civil strife—the objective of the state has not been to protect the people, but to preserve itself, even when it meant sacrificing the lives of the very same people it was meant to protect (as evidenced by the killings of civilians by government troops).

The post-independence Burundian state has suffocated civil society through three main mechanisms. First, by instituting a one-party system under the Union pour le Progrès National (Union for National Progress, UPRONA) the state made it difficult to challenge its ideology. The party served as a symbol of the omnipresence of the state and promoted the notion that nothing exists outside of the state's ideology.

Second, the state penetrated civil society by creating youth and worker organizations that were branches of the unique party. The youth organization, Jeunesse Révolutionaire Rwagasore (Rwagasore Revolutionary Youth, JRR) was used to brainwash the youth and cultivate the belief that there was no alternative to the existing idea of state. The workers union, Union des Travailleurs du Burundi (UTB), served as a network for penetrating the civil service. As a result, the state was able to create civil society in its own image: centralized and ethnicized.

Third, because of patronage and corruption, the private sector that evolved in Burundi has always been highly connected to the political regime. As a result, it is unable to serve as a basis for lobbying for positive change.

For the state to be accountable to the people of the Burundi, the new state will have to give the civil society more breathing space. The institution of the multiparty system has moved the country an important step in the right direction. However, the next step is to make the parties a true forum for debate over social, political, and economic ideologies. As emphasized earlier, the leadership of the existing parties is plagued by opportunism and sectarianism. Moreover, the government has repeatedly obstructed the functioning of parties, once again proving the precarious nature of the legal system.

Civil society must be energized from the local community level. In the past, civil society organizations have been largely elitist, ignoring the interests of the people, just like the state. Current political activism is reminiscent of the past as leaders advance their own political ambitions while ignoring the basic needs of the people.

The Need for New Leadership

A Chinese scholar, Laotzu, said "a leader is best when people barely know that he exists."[10] In the case of Burundi, leadership has been omnipresent in people's lives through excessive interventionism, oppression, and intimidation. At the same time, the leadership remained too distant to understand and care about the needs of the people, yet shielded from any form of protest (see figure 4.2). Over time the political structure has been self-perpetuating, with bad leadership overthrowing and succeeding bad leadership, further alienating the people. As a tribute to Franklin Roosevelt, Walter Lippman stated the following: "the final test of a leader is that he leaves behind him in other men the conviction and the will to carry on. . . . The genius of a good leader is to leave behind him a situation which common sense, without the grace of genius, can deal with successfully."[11] In Africa, there is a very short list of elite leaders who have passed this important test: Léopold Senghor in Senegal, Mwalimu Julius Nyerere in Tanzania, Quett Ketumile Masire in Botswana, and Nelson Mandela in South Africa. In Burundi, there is no such legacy in the post-independence era; leadership has to be reinvented.

Reinventing Leadership

In its attempt to get out of the current deadlock, Burundi must reinvent its leadership. Going back to the past is not an option, as past leadership is part of the causes of the current chaotic situation. The precolonial situation is almost mythical. No one really knows exactly what it was, and even if we knew, we would not know how to replicate it. The postcolonial era, which we know better, can only be an inspiration as far as features of leadership that the country must avoid: exclusion, state-sponsored crime and impunity, alienation, and marginalization. The critical task of a new leadership is to convince the Burundian people that it is indeed new, forward looking, and promoting a new vision of nationalism.

The Burundian state faces a serious danger of crisis of legitimacy. When the European colonizers occupied the country, they faced a problem of imposing a state structure on a population that protested the violation of the sovereignty of its territory. The colonial administration, however, was able to build state legitimacy by colluding with the monarchy to control the population. Today, the country is facing a similar problem. For the disenfranchised population, the state operates very much like an exogenous creation of the elite, just like the colonial state. One important difference is that the national elite is unable to find a natural structure that can play the role that the monarchy played in facilitating state legitimacy for the colonial administration. For the state to be meaningful for the people of Burundi, it must move away from the tradition of centralization. Key state officials, including leaders at the community level (communes and zones), should be elected or at least confirmed by elected local bodies.

Demilitarizing Leadership

Since independence, the monolithic regimes have been created and maintained by military force. In the current conflict, both the government and the opposition have adopted the same logic, that is, seeking political leverage through military power. It is fair to say, as Mamdani points out in the case of the DRC, "the militarization of politics has reduced all credible politics to armed politics."[12] Militarization of politics has marginalized civil society and has suffocated constructive political dialogue. To demilitarize leadership, it is critical to restructure the military to change its monolithic nature.

A Genuinely Home-Grown Leadership

The disintegration of leadership in the country poses the threat of an "imported revolution." The first scenario is an invasion by some "Burundian Patriotic Front," duplicating the experience of Rwanda in 1994. The second scenario is the imposition of some *parachute leader*, duplicating the crowning of Laurent Kabila in the Democratic Republic of Congo in 1996/1997 by Rwanda and Uganda. For Burundi, both scenarios are highly unlikely, but they can serve to emphasize the importance of a leadership that has national legitimacy. In the first scenario, two important factors are hard to replicate in the case of Burundi. The first factor is time. It took more than three decades for the Rwandan exiled Tutsi to produce the victorious Rwandan Patriotic Front. The Burundian diaspora has neither the cohesion nor the patience to mount a credible resistance movement. The second factor was the external support to the RPF, mainly from the Ugandan army. Discrimination by the Obote regime against Rwandan refugees forced them to join Museveni's rebellion. Once in power, Museveni compensated Rwandan refugees with influential positions in his government and the army. However, the increasing presence of Rwandans in Ugandan politics created social malaise in Uganda, which forced the RPF to accelerate its plans to cross the border. There are no such conducive external circumstances for building a credible military force by the diaspora in the case of Burundi.

Similarly, the probability of a leader imposed from outside is very slim in the case of Burundi. Only Rwanda (and the DRC to a lesser extent) has a stake in the nature of the power structure in Burundi. As long as the regime in Rwanda is dominated by the Tutsi ethnic group, the eventuality of a Hutu-dominated regime in Burundi will make Rwandan leaders nervous. The Rwandan government would be even more nervous if the Hutu in Burundi controlled both the government and the military. However, even if the Rwandan government sought to export to Burundi a leader of its own making, it is not clear where it would find such a leader. The fact that an "imported revolution" seems unlikely in Burundi is good news for the Burundian people. As the case of the DRC has shown, a leader promoted from outside will find it difficult to gain national legitimacy. The low likelihood of an imported revolution also implies that the new leadership has to evolve indigenously. Unfortunately, today the country is witnessing gradual disintegration of leadership. The current political discourse is largely centrifugal as the center continuously hollows out, while the extremist wings gain increasing control over the political system.

For an Honest State: The Arithmetic of Corruption

One of the most difficult issues that the post-conflict state in Burundi will have to deal with is the tradition of high corruption, which has worsened recently during the crisis. Corruption can be summed up by the following simple expression:

$$\textit{Corruption} = \textit{Discretion} + \textit{Monopoly} - \textit{Accountability} + (\textit{Hysteresis})$$

The last term of the expression (hysteresis)[13] is from Collier (2000) while the other terms are from Klitgaard (1988). Drawing from Collier (2000), the case of Burundi is analyzed to examine the ways in which corruption could be overcome to build a more honest state.

Discretion and Corruption

The high level of discretion enjoyed by the state arises from two important features of the economic system: pervasive regulation and expanded public procurement. Regulation of the economic activity creates opportunities for "commercialization" of the law through bribery and obstruction of trade through extortion. A typical example is the regulation of external trade and domestic commerce. State officials can exploit the rigidity and complexity of the regulations to extract rent from entrepreneurs. For example, a complex tariff system allows customs officers to manipulate tariff rates and extract rent.

The use of public procurement allows government officials to extract rent through kickbacks and "signing bonuses." This system is highly costly for the economy by creating inefficiencies in the allocation of public resources. Public managers have the incentives to give priority to projects that have high opportunities for kickbacks, especially large projects involving foreign exchange transactions (imports of inputs or hiring of foreign contractors).

State Monopoly and Corruption

Like in other African countries, development policy in Burundi has promoted the expansion of the public sector. However, in the case of Burundi, monopolization of economic activity by the state, coupled with monopolization of political power by ethno-regional entities, has increased the discretionary power of leaders, created an "economy of solidarity," and promoted the "politics of the belly."[14] In Burundi, monolithic power and corruption create the foundation for monopoly in the economic domain (both in the public sector and in the private sector), which expanded opportunities for corruption.

Accountability and Corruption

Lack of accountability in the Burundian political system is attributable primarily to the high centralization of public management and the high concentration of political power and economic power in the hands of ethno-regional entities. Lack of accountability becomes a self-perpetuating process when there are no obvious benefits from honesty in public management while the risks for dishonesty are significantly low. This follows from the monopolization of state institutions by ethno-regional entities. When large parts of the public sector and public service are private domains, patronage and connivance erode the foundation for accountability and expand corruption opportunities.

Hysteresis and Corruption

As Collier indicates, "once a society becomes corrupt there are powerful forces tending to keep it corrupt."[15] Hysteresis contributes to explaining why corruption was perpetuated over time and is also useful in examining how to "cure" corruption. The factors that perpetuated corruption in Burundi can be summarized as follows: because of monopolization of state institutions by ethno-regional entities (the Tutsi from the south), prevention and prosecution of corruption became politically costly; corruption became the norm in public management; then corruption became "expected"; and in the end corruption became a self-perpetuating process. For example, honest behavior (and assiduity at work) by a new public manager is regarded as evidence of "inexperience."[16] Moreover, corruption is vertically and downward contagious. It is a disease that subaltern officials catch from their supervisors, which takes away not only administrative accountability, but also moral guilt.[17]

How to "Cure" Corruption

It is not possible to completely eradicate corruption. Indeed no single society in the world is immune from corruption. The goal is to achieve levels of corruption that are sufficiently low and predictable to minimize transactions and costs.

The first strategy to reduce corruption is decentralization of public management. Decentralization of public decisions accomplishes three things. First, it reduces the rent-seeking base and thus reduces the incentives for corruption. Second, it allows better monitoring as decisions are taken and implemented closer to the final users of public services. Third, decentralization results in "ownership" of public programs by the local community, which increases the incentives for both monitoring and productivity on the part of those involved in public projects. Decentralization can overcome the legacy of colonialism, which has been perpetuated by the military regimes, where the public regards public service as a *corvée* (forced labor), and thus is not interested in productivity and monitoring. Decentralization can also help in overcoming complaisance with regard to corruption and embezzlement of public resources.

The second strategy is to design institutional mechanisms to overcome what has been a chronic disease in Burundian society, which is the culture of impunity. This *mal Burundais* is enormous and will have to be tackled with enormous energy. It poses the most challenging test to the credibility of any post-conflict regime. In the past, the regimes have perpetuated impunity, even as the official discourse condemned corruption (and crime) and pledged to punish it in an exemplary manner. Even when punishment was inflicted, it never was on the key decision-makers. Indeed, subaltern agents often serve as scapegoats in a masquerade of prosecution of economic (and political) crime. Special institutions such as the "Cour des Comptes" (a special court responsible for the investigation and prosecution of corruption and embezzlement of public resources) were instituted, but only to be paralyzed by intimidation and obstruction of justice by politically connected suspects. To overcome the culture of impunity, for both economic crime and crime against humanity, the new state will have to go for the "big push" by targeting the "big fish." New institutions will establish credibility only by proving to the public that they are able to prosecute even influential politicians and politically connected private entrepreneurs. Because the country is already trapped in a *high-corruption local equilibrium*, it cannot move out of this situation by cosmetic changes to the system. For instance, it would be meaningless to set up new special courts for prosecuting economic crime when the legal system is still dominated by ethno-regional entities. Following such changes, the country inexorably regresses back to the original high-corruption local equilibrium.

The third strategy is to establish an incentive structure in the public domain that induces a change in behavior. The assumption is that in Burundi as in any other societies, individuals respond to changes in incentives by changing behavior. Given similar incentives, we can expect similar outcomes across communities, *ceteris paribus*. In areas of public service that are most subject to bribery and extortion, the strategy is to provide high incentives for productivity and honesty while setting high penalties for corruption. These areas include tax collection and inspection services, customs services, procurement services (e.g., Service des Marchés Publics), and anti-corruption courts. Incentives could include salary schemes that are higher than the average remuneration in civil service, including performance bonuses.

Dissuasion also can be achieved by designing institutional mechanisms that increase the risk of being caught in corruption deals. Because corruption involves two parties, the law could include dispositions for rewarding with "amnesty" the party to a deal that decides to break the deal and report to the appropriate government agency (customs services, tax inspection, anti-corruption courts, etc.). If the penalties against corruption and the rewards for reporting are indeed high, the outcome is the classic "prisoner's dilemma" where each party's best strategy is to break the corruption deal. Eventually the temptation to enter into corruption deals will decline when such incentive mechanisms are established and enforced.

The fourth strategy is to develop and strengthen institutional agencies of restraint that control government policy. The objective is to limit the degree of counterproductive discretionary power of the state.[18] This will amount to establishing mechanisms that guarantee the independence of institutions that oversee economic sectors that are prone to abuse of power and corruption by public officials. These include tax and customs audit/inspection agencies, procurement offices, courts and tribunals, and the central bank. The independence of the central bank also is essential to limiting the ability of the government to use seignorage to finance political ventures or channel embezzled resources. Economically, when there are no limits to government borrowing from the central bank, monetary policy is severely constrained by pressure from fiscal indiscipline. Politically, unlimited access to seignorage tilts the political scale in favor of the government in the sense that it relaxes the budget constraint in financing political activities.[19]

In the case of Burundi as in other countries, overcoming corruption will necessitate more than just setting up new institutions and declaring them "independent" from the government. The ability to enforce the rules of the game will depend critically on the balance of power within and outside of the government among various ethnic, regional, and political tendencies.

Development Policy: Back to the Basics—Developing the Country Rather than Preserving the State

To be relevant, the state must satisfy the basic needs of its people. The primary goal of the Burundian state has been to preserve itself rather than to develop the country. Outside of the public sector, economic activity has languished due to lack of both the enabling government policies and negative interventionist policies that have suffocated private initiative. For the state to be meaningful, it must behave as a facilitator, not a hindrance to private initiative.

The causes of conflict in Burundi are political and economic.[20] Therefore, efforts aimed at overcoming the legacy of political upheaval must emphasize strategies for raising the living standards of the population, allowing equal access to national resources, and redistributing wealth equitably. Democratization or institutional building and economic development must go hand in hand in preventing conflict and in post-conflict reconstruction.

Monitoring Social Development Outcomes

To be relevant, the state must pursue development objectives that go beyond macroeconomic performance. The development agenda must give high priority to social outcomes, such as literacy, access to health services, empowerment of local communities in economic decision making, ownership of the development agenda by local communities, gender equity, and other nonconventional but important aspects of economic development. This will involve setting specific targets for each of these objectives and making those targets an integral part of the planning and budgeting process. From one budget and plan to another, funds should be allocated in such a way to correct observed imbalances or shortcoming of previous budgets and plans with respect to particular social development targets. The budgeting and planning process must become transparent enough to allow monitoring of the distribution of public resources between social and military expenditures, the balance between directly productive public investment and social infrastructure, and the allocation of public investment across regions. The objective is to overcome the tradition of pro-military fiscal policy and the legacy of monopolization of public resources by the south and the accompanying marginalization of politically disconnected segments of the population. To achieve effective monitoring of social development, it is necessary to create independent specialized agencies whose mission is to collect quantitative and qualitative information on social development targets and the level of realization of these targets. These agencies should be equipped with adequate human and technological resources and endowed with political autonomy to enable them to produce a credible assessment of social development with a maximum degree of desegregation.

The Need for a "Big Push": Development Assistance

To achieve sustained economic growth, Burundi, like most sub-Saharan African countries, needs a sizeable influx of development assistance. Given its low natural-resource endowment, deep poverty, and long periods of destructive conflict, the country is likely to remain trapped in a low-income, low-growth steady state, unless it benefits from large inflows of new external resources (aid and private capital). In a recent study, the United Nations Conference on Trade and Development (UNCTAD) demonstrated that for the majority of African countries to overcome poverty and aid dependence, the continent needs a sizeable injection of new foreign aid in order to jump-start the economies. Massive infusion of foreign assistance is especially indispensable for countries like Burundi that are in conflict or evolving from conflict given that their infrastructures have been destroyed by the war. The adverse effects of war on the country's productive capacity may persist in the post-conflict period, which retards economic recovery. A sizeable and steady influx of new aid can allow the country to overcome this "war overhang effect" and facilitate economic reconstruction. In addition to new aid, debt relief also can ameliorate the government's budget constraint in the post-conflict construction effort.

However, one issue that remains is the institutional prerequisites for effectiveness of new foreign aid in promoting economic growth in Burundi. Aid will promote development provided that the country has the right institutions that can manage aid efficiently. Aid is most effective if it is supported by fiscally responsible behavior, especially efforts to increase fiscal revenue and allocation of public funds into socially productive and poverty-reducing investments. Under a corrosive institutional environment, there is a risk that aid will be squandered. Aid may even encourage higher public spending (partly due to fungibility of aid) and irresponsible borrowing.

Another issue that arises in the case of Burundi as in other countries in conflict is the possible interaction between aid and conflict. As Addison points out, "aid in conflict situations is both complex and controversial."[21] While aid can be used to diffuse conflict, aid can also fuel conflict if it is administered inadequately. As Boyce puts it, "aid is not like water, which sprayed on the flames or embers of conflict invariably helps to extinguish them. Indeed, it can be more like oil. Appropriate aid can diminish risks of conflict, but inappropriate aid can fuel it."[22] Foreign aid can fuel and/or perpetuate conflict if it tilts the balance of power in favor of one group or the other. This can happen even when donors do not have the explicit intention of supporting one group against others. In general, aid cannot be neutral in a country like Burundi where there is already a substantial imbalance of power. Consequently, the aid community must exercise great caution and take into account the existing configuration of power in administering assistance. Moreover, the donor community should promote mechanisms of decentralized administration of aid, which will enhance aid effectiveness while empowering local communities.

Conclusion

It is evident now that the current state in Burundi will not bring lasting peace in the country and lead the country to economic prosperity. Yet both peace and development are sorely needed by the Burundian people. So the debate must move beyond the causes and consequences of the failure of the state to tackle the much harder question of how to make the state relevant for the Burundian people.

The debate on making the state relevant in Burundi revolves around the issue of power sharing. The country must overcome the legacy of exclusion, marginalization, and oppression along ethnic and regional lines as well as the tradition of centralization that has alienated the people at the periphery of the power circles. Ethnicity has played a key role in the erosion of state stability and it must be taken into account seriously in the debate over power sharing and the design of new state institutions. Three points are worth emphasizing in this regard. First, the political elite must come to terms with the realization that power sharing and the shift from military to civilian rule are the only reliable means of preserving security for all. Second, the political elite must accept the fact that power sharing cannot be reduced to dogmatic application of majoritarian processes that result in winner-take-all outcomes where the minorities (ethnic and regional) are *de facto* excluded from political participation. Democracy must be tailored to the specific features of the social construct of the country and, in the end, it may very much differ from Western democracy. Third, the military must detach itself from the political scene. Only then can the country move to a new era where political office is won through merit rather than by military might. A relevant state in Burundi will be a civilian-led state. Furthermore, the new state structure must be based on the trilogy of commitment, accountability, and credibility. This can be accomplished only with a vastly decentralized state.

The donor community can play an important role in establishing a relevant state in Burundi. The country will need generous infusions of new development funds to finance reconstruction programs. However, it is imperative for the donor community to overcome its statutory aversion to domestic political concerns and pay systematic attention to issues of ethnic discrimination, regionalism, exclusion, and discrimination. Economic development cannot be dissociated from social justice. Therefore, in addition to conventional goals of economic rationality, allocative efficiency, macroeconomic performance, and long-run economic growth, development assistance must promote institutional reform aimed at rebuilding and consolidating peace. Obviously, the peace project has a longer maturity than the conventional economic project, but the long-run returns to the former are as high, if not higher.

Appendix A: Annotated Chronology of Main Political Events in Burundi since the Early 1960s[1]

July 1962: Burundi (with Rwanda) becomes independent from Belgian colonial rule.

October 1965: An attempted coup d'état by Hutu officers against King Mwambutsa IV is followed by massive military repression, especially targeting the Hutu civilian and military elite.

November 1966: A military coup d'état by Army Captain Michel Micombero overthrows the monarchy and establishes the first Republic.

April 1972: King Ntare V is assassinated in Gitega shortly after his return from exile.

April 1972: Massacres of Tutsi civilians by Hutu rebels are followed by large-scale repression by the government army against the Hutu population. Selective killings of Hutu elite extend to 1973.

November 1976: Colonel Jean-Baptiste Bagaza deposes Micombero in a bloodless coup d'état. Micombero is forced to exile where he will eventually die under yet-unknown circumstances.

September 1987: In another bloodless coup d'état, Major Pierre Buyoya deposes Bagaza while the former was attending a Francophony Summit in Canada.

August 1988: Killings of Tutsi civilians by Hutu in Ntega-Marangara in the northern Kirundo Province are followed by military repression against the Hutu population. The army and security services also carry out arrests and extra-judicial exterminations of members of the Hutu elite from the region. A group of twenty-seven Hutu intellectuals sign an open letter to the president calling for an end of selective killings, a national debate on the question of ethnic exclusion, and equitable representation of the Hutu in the political system.

October 1988: Buyoya forms a "government of unity" headed by a Hutu prime minister and comprising an equal number of Hutu and Tutsi.

February 1991: The Charter of National Unity is adopted following a series of public debates on national unity and a referendum.

November 1991: PALIPEHUTU carries attacks against military positions in the province of Cibitoke and around Bujumbura.

March 1992: A new constitution is adopted, establishing a multiparty system.

June 1993: The first democratic presidential elections by direct vote are organized. FRODEBU wins the elections under the leadership of Melchior Ndadaye. FRODEBU also wins the majority of seats in the National Assembly.

July 1993: The military attacks President-elect Ndadaye's palace in an attempt to short-circuit the democratic changes.

October 1993: The military assassinates President Ndadaye along with a number of high-ranking members of the government and the assembly. The assassinations are followed spontaneously by massacres of Tutsi civilians by the Hutu in several provinces. The government's military intervenes by indiscriminately killing Hutu civilians.

February 1994: Cyprien Ntaryamira is nominated by FRODEBU as the new president.

April 1994: President Ntaryamira dies in the same plane crash that killed Rwandan President Juvenal Habyarimana, igniting genocide against the Tutsi in Rwanda. Sylvestre Ntibantunganya succeeds Ntaryamira as president.

September 1994: Twelve political parties sign a "Convention of Government" under the leadership of Sylvestre Ntibantunganya.

March 1996: Former Tanzanian President Julius Nyerere is appointed as mediator in the Burundi crisis at a regional conference on Burundi in Tunis, Tunisia.

July 25, 1996: Major Pierre Buyoya stages his second coup d'état.

July 31, 1996: Neighboring states impose economic sanctions on Buyoya's regime to force him to restore democratic institutions and negotiate with the opposition.

June 1998: The Buyoya government and the National Assembly sign a "Partnership for Peace." A Constitutional Act of Transition is promulgated.

June 1998: Peace talks start in Arusha, Tanzania, under the mediation of Julius Nyerere.

January 1999: The regional economic sanctions are suspended.

October 1999: Former Tanzanian President Julius Nyerere dies.

December 1999: Former South African President Nelson Mandela is appointed as the new mediator in the Burundian crisis.

August 2000: Nineteen parties (including the government and the National Assembly) sign the "Arusha Accord for Peace and Reconciliation in Burundi" under the leadership of former South African President Nelson Mandela.[2]

Appendix B: Political Parties and Negotiation Coalitions (in 2002)

Political Parties

ABASA: Alliance Burundo-Africaine pour le Salut (Burundian-African Alliance for Salvation), created in 1993.

ANADDE: Alliance Nationale pour le Droit et le Dévelopement Economique (National Alliance for Law and Economic Development), created in 1992.

AV–INTWARI: Alliance des Vaillants (Alliance of the Valiant), created in 1993.

CNDD: Conseil National pour la Défense de la Démocratie (National Council for the Defense of Democracy). Founded in 1994 by Léonard Nyangoma, one of the founders of FRODEBU and Minister of Interior in 1993–1994.

FDD: Forces pour la Défense de la Démocratie (Forces for the Defense of Democracy), armed branch of the CNDD.

FNL: Forces Nationales pour la Libération (National Liberation Forces), armed branch of PALIPEHLITU. The FNL has been split since 1992 between the wings led by Etienne Karatasi and Cossan Kabura.

FRODEBU: Front pour la Démocratie au Burundi (Front for Democracy in Burundi). It has existed officially since 1992. The party won the first presidential elections organized in Burundi in June 1993.

FROLINA: Front pour la Liberation Nationale (Front for National Liberation) created in mid-1980s.

INKINZO: "Le Bouclier" (The Shield), created in 1993.

PALIPEHUTU: Parti pour la Libération du Peuple Hutu (Party for the Liberation of the Hutu People) presided over by Etienne Karatasi. The party was created in the 1970s by Burundian Hutu refugees in Rwanda.

PARENA: Parti pour le Redressement National (Party for National Recovery), created in 1995, presided over by Jean-Baptiste Bagaza, former president of Burundi (in 1976–1987).

PIT: Parti Indépendant pour les Travailleurs (Independent Workers' Party), created in 1993.

PL: Parti Libéral (Liberal Party), created in 1992.

PP: Parti du Peuple (People's Party), created in 1992.

PRP: Parti pour la Réconciliation du Peuple (Party for the Reconciliation of the People) advocating the return of the monarchy and created in 1992.

PSD: Parti pour la Socio-Démocratie (Party for Social Democracy), created in 1993.

RADDES: Rassemblement pour la Démocratie, le Développement Economique et Social (Rally for Democracy and Economic and Social Development), created in 1993.

RPB: Rassemblement pour le Peuple du Burundi (Rally for the People of Burundi), created in 1992.

ULINA: Union de Libération Nationale (Union of National Liberation), created in 1996.

UPRONA: Union pour le Progrès National (National Union for Progress). Nationalist party created on the eve of independence in 1961 and led by Prince Louis Rwagasore, hero of the fight for independence who was assassinated in October 1961. UPRONA was the state party in Burundi between 1966 and 1993. The party was split in October 1998 over the issue of participation in the Arusha peace talks.

Negotiation Coalitions

L'Alliance Nationale pour le Changement (A.N.A.C.–National Alliance for Change): FRODEBU, PP, PARENA, SOJEDEM, Former Prime Minister Anatole Kanyenkiko, MP André Biha, and MP Térence Nahimana.

La Convergence Nationale pour la Paix et la Réconciliation (CNPR) (National Convergence for Peace and Reconciliation): UPRONA, FRODEBU (internal wing), PSD, RADDES, INKINZO, PIT, ANADDE, ABASA (internal wing), and PL (internal wing).

G3: Composed of UPRONA, the Government, and the National Assembly.

G7: Comprises the "Forces du Changement Démocratique" (Forces for Democratic Change), a group composed of the parties with a large Hutu component or exclusively Hutu: FRODEBU (external wing), CNDD, PALIPEHUTU, FROLINA, PP, RPB, and PL.

G8: Comprises all of the so-called small, predominantly Tutsi parties: PARENA, PRP, AV-INTWARI, ABASA, PSD, INKINZO, ANADDE, and PIT.

Other Groups

AC-GENOCIDE CIRIMOSO: Action Contre le Génocide—Plus Jamais Ça (Action Against the Genocide—Never Again): Organizes meetings on the twenty-first of every month in memory of the massacres of October 1993 following the assassination of President Ndadaye.

JRR: Jeunesse Révolutionnaire Rwagasore (Rwagasore Revolutionary Youth), a branch of UPRONA.

UTB: Union des Travailleurs du Burundi (Workers Union), a branch of UPRONA.

PA: Puissance d'Autodéfense—Amasekanya: a self-defense organization for youth created in 1995.

SOJEDEM: Solidarité de la Jeunesse pour la Défense des Minorités (Youth Solidarity for the Defence of Minorities), created in 1993.

Notes

1. Witter Bynner, The *Way of Life According to Laotzu*, cited in John Bartlett, *Familiar Quotations*, 13th ed. (Boston: Little, Brown and Company, 1955), 912.

2. Walter Lippman, *Roosevelt Has Gone* (April 14, 1945), Bartlett, *Familiar Quotations*, 952.

3. A September 1999 inquiry in Bujumbura by the International Crisis Group (ICG) revealed that after a year of negotiations, some delegates were able to purchase houses. After ten two-week negotiation sessions in Arusha, delegates collected up to $20,000 (at a rate of $150 per day, covering lodging and other expenses). By comparison, the salary of a government minister is about 300,000 Burundi francs per month (or about $300 at the 1999 parallel market exchange rate).

4. Although this analysis may be applicable to other countries that have experienced state failure due to social conflicts, the generalization should be done very cautiously.

5. See International Crisis Group, *Burundi: The Issues of the State: Political Parties, Freedom of the Press and Political Prisoners*, ICG Africa Report No. 23, July 2000, for further discussion of this issue.

6. International Crisis Group, *Burundi*, 52.

7. Floribert Ngaruko and Janvier Desire Nkurunzizi, "An Economic Interpretation of Conflict in Burundi," *Journal of African Economics* 9, no. 3 (2000): 382.

8. See appendix B for the list of political parties and other groups that have evolved in the course of the ongoing peace negotiations.

9. I borrowed the expression from Octavio Paz, "The Philanthropic Ogre," *Dissent* 26, no. 1, 1979: 43–52.

10. Bartlett, *Familiar Quotations*, 912.

11. Bartlett, *Familiar Quotations*, 952.

12. Mahmood Mamdani, "Preliminary Thoughts on the Congo Crisis," *Social Text 60* 17, no. 3 (1999): 59.

13. Paul Collier, "How to Reduce Corruption," *African Development Review* 12, no. 2 (2000): 197.

14. I borrowed the concept from Jean-Francois Bayart, *The State in Africa: The Politics of the Belly* (London: Longman, 1993).

15. Collier, "How to Reduce Corruption," 197.

16. The honesty and assiduity of a new public manager are regarded as "amavamuhira" (literally meaning "the energy of someone freshly arriving from home"). The insinuation is that once acclimated, the new public manager will "join the club" and start shirking his or her duties while filling his or her private purse from the public coffers.

17. In Burundi, the code of wisdom in public service is "impene irisha aho iziriste" ("a goat grazes wherever it is tied in the prairie") or "nta mbwa ikugana igufa mu kanwa" ("no dog barks with a piece of bone in its mouth"). The message is that it is acceptable (expected) to be corrupt under the blessing of a corrupt leader.

18. The book edited by Paul Collier and Catherine Pattilo, *Investment and Risk in Africa* (New York: St. Martin's Press, 2000), especially pp. 3–30, contains studies with

extensive discussions of various mechanisms for reducing investment risk by emphasizing institutions of restraint on government policy.

19. Evidence from African countries shows that monetary creation tends to rise before and during presidential campaigns in regimes where the central bank has no independence from the government. A recent example is Kenya during its recent presidential elections.

20. Quantitative cross-country analysis has established a significant link between conflict (and humanitarian emergencies in general) and a range of economic factors including (low) levels of income. For examples, see Wayne Nafziger and Juha Auvinen, "The Economic Causes of Humanitarian Emergencies," in Wayne Nafziger et al., eds., *War, Hunger and Displacement: The Origins of Humanitarian Emergencies*, vols. 1 and 2 (Oxford, UK: Oxford University Press, 2000), 91–145.

21. Tony Addison, "Aid and Conflict," in Finn Tarp, ed., *Foreign Aid and Development: Lessons Learnt and Directions for the Future* (London: Routledge, 2000), 392.

22. James Boyce, "Beyond Good Intentions: External Assistance and Peace Building," in Shepard Forman and Stewart Patrick, eds., *Good Intentions: Pledges of Aid for Post-Conflict Recovery* (Boulder, CO: Lynne Rienner Publishers, 2000), 367.

NOTES IN APPENDIX

1. For details, see, among others, Rene Lemarchand, *Rwanda and Burundi*, (London: Paul Mall Press, 1970); Rene Lemarchand, *Burundi: Ethnocide as Discourse and Practice* (New York: Cambridge University Press, 1994): and Thomas Melady, *Burundi: The Tragic Years* (New York: Orbis Books, 1974. For more references on the history of Burundi, see Morna Daniels, "Burundi," in Robert Neville et al (eds.), *World Bibliographical Series* (Oxford, UK: Oxford University Press, 1992).

2. The participating parties are (see Appendix B for the meaning of the acronyms): the Government, the Assembly, ABASA, ANADDE, AV-INTWARI, CNDD, FRODEBU, FROLINA, INKINZO, PARENA, PALIPEHUTU, PIT, PL, PP, PRP, PSD, RADDES, RPB, UPRONA.

5

Making the State Relevant in the Democratic Republic of the Congo

Musifiky Mwanasali

MUCH HAS BEEN WRITTEN ABOUT THE STATE (and the "crisis") in Africa[1] and in the former Zaire, in particular.[2] Although researchers agree that a deep, multifaceted crisis has long affected most African economic and political systems, consensus is still to be reached among scholars and policymakers regarding the nature of this crisis, the reasons for its intractability and its relationship to the state. Some have even wondered loudly whether the continent is really in "crisis" and whether what is seen as a crisis is not actually Africa's normalcy, a sort of the continent's "way of being."[3] And assuming there is a real crisis in Africa, how similar or different is it from crises in other parts of the so-called developing world? What theories can be used to explain this difference?

While researchers have been striving to clarify these and several other conceptual and policy issues, a new discourse on African conflicts has emerged, mainly among Western-based Africanists, with a new set of sonorous labels on the African state. Headings like the "politics of the belly" of the African state became obsolete, having ceded the center of Africanist stage to colorful epithets and sound bites like "mafia state," "vampire state," "shadow state," "state collapse" or simply "failed state." Some scholars have gone so far as to repudiate altogether the term "state" in the African context, preferring expressions like "city-state of Luanda," "city-state of Bujumbura" or "city-state of Kinshasa" (Brazzaville, Freetown or Monrovia, depending on the country of focus). These scholars find such expressions realistic and more appropriate to the present African political context than those hitherto used, that is, the Angolan state, the state of Burundi, the Liberian state and others.

The flurry of new epithets on the African state is somewhat related to the rise of increased academic interest in African conflicts, a policy area that was once dominated by inter- and nongovernmental organizations. Interesting parallels can indeed be traced between the new discourse on "the state and conflicts in Africa" and the old literature on the state and the crisis in Africa. In some studies, it is even possible to substitute the term conflict for crisis without affecting much the substance of the argument. The same reasoning applies, *mutatis mutandis*, to the old expression "local community" of the 1970s and 1980s and the conceptually fuzzy "civil society."

This is not the place to conduct a detailed examination of the influence of the old literature on the state and the crisis on the new theories on the state and conflicts in Africa. All I wish is to make the case for the need to revisit the old theories and review some of the rich conceptual apparatus developed more than two decades ago, rather than engaging in a confusing (semantic) debate over the conceptual and empirical relevance of the new epithets on the African state.

The idea is to engage in a reflection over the best policy, practical modalities and theoretical axis along which the state can be made relevant to the majority of its citizens. To this end, it may be useful to start this exercise from where the debate on the state and the crisis was abandoned. Indeed, those crises are yet to be resolved. In large and significant measures, the scourge of violence and civil wars that have afflicted the African continent since the end of the Cold War is the result of the very crises of African economic and political systems that scholars and policymakers had reflected on, or coped with, in the 1970s and 1980s. Even in the event these conflicts find a lasting solution, scholars and policymakers will still be called upon to design conflict-proof political and productive systems, a task that is now variably qualified as peace-building or post-conflict reconstruction.

Like Archie Mafeje, I deplore the "grosso modo mold" of the African state, which is presently dominant in Africanist research and policy circles. I share Mafeje's call to reorient the Africanist discourse by focusing on "more detailed and specific information about what is happening on the ground as against universalistic theoretical suppositions."[4] It is opportune to go beyond the Afro-pessimistic discourse on "state collapse" and "failed state," and develop sound conceptual and policy-oriented inquiries on how the incontrovertible institution that we rightly or wrongly call the state can (re)gain its relevance in the eyes of its citizens.

Most African people are condemned to live within the confines of—and in compliance with the rules and regulations enforced by—state institutions that they are generally unable to avoid or transform. The proposed inquiries should therefore begin at the level where the relevance or irrelevance of the state would make the most sense, that is, at the level of ordinary people.

It is in this context necessary to pay heed to the remarks made by the late Mwalimu Julius Nyerere, the former President of Tanzania, who, in reaction to the "call emanating from the North for the weakening of the state," pointedly stated that in his view:

> Africa should ignore this call. Our states are so weak and anemic already that it would almost amount to a crime to weaken them further. We have a duty to strengthen the African state almost in every respect you can think of—this being one of the objectives of improving the governance of our countries . . . and thus enable it to serve the people of Africa better.[5]

In Nyerere's view, to advocate (renewed) relevance for the African state is "not holding brief for either an overburdened state or a state with a bloated bureaucracy. [It is] to advocate a state which, among other things has the power to act on behalf of the people in accordance with their wishes. And in a market economy, with its law of the jungle, we need a state that has the capacity to intervene on behalf of the weak."[6]

This is the perspective I have chosen to adopt in this chapter. First, I will discuss the dominant academic and policy debate on democracy in the former Zaire. Next I will survey the labor of the democratic movement, that is, the popular struggle for a new pluralist society under the Mobutu regime. Finally, encouraged by the wisdom expressed by Albert Camus that all great deeds and all great thoughts have a ridiculous beginning, I will conclude with a brief assessment of the political and policy lessons that the present government of the DRC ought to learn from the defunct Mobutu regime, as it strives to rebuild political institutions and processes and make the state relevant to the citizens of Africa's third largest country.

The Democratic Republic of the Congo: A Triple Rift

In February 1992, thousands of Zairean civilians organized a peaceful march in the streets of Kinshasa, calling upon the late President Mobutu to annul his government's decision to suspend the National Conference and allow delegates to freely continue their debate on the future of the country. Sponsored by the Roman Catholic clergy, the marchers were met with violent reaction, and hundreds of innocent civilians lost their lives simply because they sought the betterment of their country. Their political courage made them Martyrs of Freedom, and the political and patriotic ideal that they showed publicly fully justify the approach I take in this chapter and my choice of the former Zaire as the focus of my inquiry.

A serious crisis of citizenship ran rampant in this country, especially during the last two decades of the Mobutu regime. Alain Touraine writes that citizenship entails both the consciousness of belonging to a political society and a willingness to participate in choosing its representatives.[7] A citizen, he adds, is a person who sees to it that the political institutions run properly, respect individual rights and enable equal representation to the diversity of social interests. Evidently, this was not the case in Zaire, as manifested by the deep sense of alienation ordinary people felt toward a country that they were told was theirs.

How did such a political alienation come about? From the outset, the political transition that began in 1990 was off to a poor start, mainly because the Mobutu regime chose to implement a pluralist model of politics that, in substance as in its form, was meaningless to the majority of the population. In 1992, for example, various Zairean constitutional experts, acting in the context of the Sovereign National Conference, held a series of live radio and television debates on the meaning of democracy and the difference between unitarism and federalism. Ironically, the discussions were conducted in French and in such esoteric technical language that they were utterly incomprehensible to the targeted audience. Moreover, while the common people expected the political establishment and the opposition to give their vision of the Third Republic,[8] the national debate got bogged down in useless academic debates, partisan infighting and futile quarrels over daily subsistence allowance ("per diem"). In the end, the population developed a corrosive cynicism about politics while a general political ruthlessness was setting in, reminiscent of the first years after independence.

During the 1980s and early 1990s, the name "Zaire" came to evoke the image of a decomposing body in the mind of many people. That image resulted from a fault line that manifested itself in three ways. First, there was the gulf between the central authority in Kinshasa and an increasingly autarkic and secessionist countryside. Second, while that gulf was widening, the mainstream, essentially top-down and export-oriented economic system crashed and was gradually replaced by the horizontal expansion of local networks of trade and social support. The third factor was the confinement of institutionalized party politics to urban areas, with little or no links whatsoever with the countryside.

The consequences of this rift were manifold. In the countryside, the population was regularly subjected to looting and confiscation of property by unruly soldiers and local mobs of the former single-party state. On his own initiative, the commander of the military detachment in the gold-rich village of

Saramabila in eastern Zaire put his troops on alert in early 1994. This was just an excuse for him to search people and houses without warrant and confiscate any gold or valuable assets he deemed to be in wrong hands.

In urban areas, a few military and intelligence officers set themselves the task of terrorizing the civilian population and bullying everyone suspected of sympathy with the opposition. Civilian car owners in Kinshasa bitterly (and vainly) complained about arbitrary seizures of their vehicles by high-ranking military officers. Among the victims were tenured university professors, who had once received a free car from the Mobutu regime, but eventually switched their allegiance and joined the opposition.

In the country as a whole, a general cynicism set in and drove the population toward regional, ethnic and sometimes village-based organizations known as *mutuelles.* Initially conceived as self-help economic and financial groupings, the mutuelles gradually shifted their objectives to focus on political issues. Occasionally, they drifted toward ethnic and regional chauvinism, as was the tragic case of the persecution of the Luba-Kasai peoples in the former Shaba Province in 1993. Like the Luba-Kasai victims, Zaireans caught in the vortex of local ethnic politics were labeled as enemies because of their names, language or physical appearance. Yet many were born, raised and had resided or invested in the places where they were suddenly chased away from as foreigners.

The triple rift that tore the former Zaire at the seams resulted primarily from the lack of political accountability, which Lonsdale calls "public morality [and] the chief end of political freedom."[9] He adds, "Political accountability is part of the moral calculus of power; it concerns the mutual responsibility of inequality [and] raises questions about the control of power and its purposes."[10] In the same vein, Patrick Chabal writes "a principle of political accountability establishes the rules of conduct in a political community. As such, it determines the nature of the relationship between the state and society, and helps understand how power becomes power, how it is exercised, how it is constrained and how it dissipates."[11]

The notion of accountability encapsulates that of legitimacy and representation. Legitimacy and representation concern primarily the political rulers in their relation to the people they rule and what Chabal calls "the mechanics of power." Political accountability, on the other hand, is the central political axis of a community—the way in which that community defines the political rights and obligations of its members and the manner in which its institutions operate.[12]

There is a general agreement that democracy requires the limitation of power by a principle that transcends, regulates and stops it from turning into absolutism. Touraine, for example, equates democracy with political freedom and defines it as "[t]he political regime that allows social actors to educate themselves and act freely."[13] He suggests three conditions for democratic practice to be effective: (1) the recognition of a number of basic rights that must be respected; (2) citizenship, that is, the consciousness of belonging to a polity respectful of the rule of law; and (3) the social representation of the elected officials and their policies. Speaking of the third condition, Touraine wonders quite judiciously how there can be free elections if the electorate has no idea about the political agenda proposed by its representatives or, in the case of the former Zaire, when these representatives are the mere executors of political and economic priorities set outside the country.

For both Chabal and Touraine, therefore, the task of building democratic institutions is secondary because political institutions are created to manage social demands and, in the case of political parties, to compete for office. Their task is not to fix, as is usually stated by some constitutional experts, the conditions whereby the peoples can freely choose their political leaders. This attribute belongs to the citizenry, since citizens are, in the opinion of these authors, the very foundation of a democratic polity.

Academic and Policy Quandary

Little attention has been paid to the issue of political accountability in the sense I use it in this chapter. A survey of the scant literature on political transition in both the former Zaire (and the DRC during the presidency of the late Laurent Kabila) reveals great analytical insights, but few new ideas as to how to address the problems under investigation.

Limiting my search to articles authored by Zairean scholars and/or published in the Kinshasa-based journal *Zaire Afrique*, I noted that, between 1990 and 1996, scholars unanimously advocated the respect for the institutional order defined by the Sovereign National Conference. Yet few noted that the obstruction created by President Mobutu to the implementation of the decisions of the National Sovereign Conference found its justification, in large measure, in the political compromise negotiated by the representatives of the major political forces over the objection of some opposition leaders.[14]

Nzongola-Ntalaja, who has always favored a unitary state, and Wamba-dia-Wamba, at present the virtual leader of a rebellious faction against the central government in Kinshasa, were at the time among the few Zairean scholars who stood out in their appreciation of the ability of the Sovereign National Conference to bring about a new political order.[15] Wamba-dia-Wamba, for example, advocated a type of "emancipative politics" as a people's challenge to the dominant discourse on multipartyism. Stressing the fact that this new politics was to be different from that "which does not start from the notion that 'people think,'" Wamba-dia-Wamba called without further details for the rise of "a [new] leadership, independent of both the Mobutu regime and the opposition party leadership for the pro-democracy movement to start moving again."[16]

It was perhaps the numerous foreign mediations to resolve the political standoff between Mobutu's ruling coalition and the opposition led by Etienne Tshisekedi, that showed clearly the futility of trying to democratize society from the top. In December 1994, the Carter Center in Atlanta, Georgia, organized a one-day meeting on Zaire, whereby the goal was to explore how to put the derailed transition back on the right track. Basically, the majority of the participants in that meeting agreed on a standard package of measures consisting of the adoption of a constitution, the enactment of confidence-building measures to empower the opposition and civil society and the organization of general elections.

These recommendations, like the agreement brokered by the Troika (i.e., the government of France, Belgium and the United States), were neither new nor innovative. Aside from the claimed intention of getting rid of Zaire's autocratic ruler, they actually came close to the position Mobutu had already outlined and defended since his 1990 democracy speech.

A Derailed Transition

Three periods roughly define Zaire's derailed political transition. The first one, which I shall call the period of the triumph of the democratic movement, began on January 14, 1990, when President Mobutu ordered a series of popular consultations to test the popularity of his regime. That period culminated on April 22, 1990, with his decision to dismantle the single-party state and take leave (momentarily, as it turned out) of *Mouvement Populaire de la Révolution* (M.P.R.).

This period was characterized by the travail and ephemeral triumph of the democratic movement, with its rejection of President Mobutu's desire to limit to three the number of political parties and the subsequent massacre of February 1992. That period ended on November 29, 1992, with the official closing of the *Conférence Nationale Souveraine.*[17]

The second period saw the debacle of the opposition, the consolidation of the Mobutu ruling coalition and the unfolding of a new kind of authoritarianism. Starting on December 1, 1992, until the demise of his regime on May 17, 1997, President Mobutu became the chief obstructionist of the democratic movement he had previously been compelled to set in motion. After his dismissal of the prime minister elected by the Sovereign National Conference, President Mobutu tightened his grips over the central bank and state-owned media, and gave free rein to his supporters to terrorize the opposition and the population as a whole.

The third period saw the demise by force of the Mobutu regime by the troops of *Alliance des Forces Démocratiques pour la Libération du Congo, AFDL*, an esoteric coalition of armies, political groupings and foreign economic interests led by the late President Laurent-Désiré Kabila. A year after its rise to power, the AFDL broke down and its chairman, the self-proclaimed president of the DRC, was killed on January 16, 2001, after failing to win a war against his former sponsors and allies, organized in three rebel groups. His son, Joseph Kabila, a 29-year-old major general, was designated as his successor in January 2001. Since then, the civil war has been raging. However, over the last two years, the international community led by the United Nations has been making efforts to resolve the civil war, including the intervention of a United Nations' peacekeeping force.

The People's Triumph

Zairean politics took a decisive turn in January 1990, when President Mobutu appointed a small group among his trusted men to gauge the popularity of his regime and nation's assessment of the ruling institutions of the single-party state. Overwhelmed by the widespread criticism against his regime, President Mobutu dismantled the single-party state and allowed a limited experiment with a Western-style multiparty system. He fixed the duration of the transition to twelve months (to April 30, 1991), and to everyone's surprise, took leave of his M.P.R.

That speech sent a shock wave throughout the entire country. Uncertain about the president's true motives, many former apparatchiks remained pinned together by a fear of losing the privileges they were accustomed to and, possibly, their lives. Some, like Seti Eyale, the former national security adviser, fled the country for better pasture and safety abroad. Others, including Kengo wa Dondo, created or scattered in the few parties later grouped under the label of the Sacred Union of the Opposition. A few moguls, however, held onto the ruling party in an attempt to give it a new lease on life. They included faithful subalterns, like Vunduawe, and ambitious younger members like Banza Mukalay who, at 41, had been appointed first vice-president of the former party-state.

The most important feature of this period of Zairean political history was the sacrifice that the Zairean people bore in a bid to promote and sustain the ideals of the democratic movement. Two incidents marked this struggle. One took place on May 3, 1990, after Mobutu gave a speech that widely suggested a turnabout in his previously stated commitment to a free and multiparty system. Around this time, small political parties, whose membership sometimes consisted of a husband, wife and a few relatives, began to sprout. Nicknamed *partis alimentaires* (parties for food), most were created and funded by the ruling coalition with the purpose of subverting and weakening the radical opposition led by the *Union pour la Démocratie et le Progrès Social* (U.D.P.S.) led by Etienne Tshisekedi. A year later, these parties coalesced with the M.P.R. to form President Mobutu's political family, also known as Mouvance Présidentielle.[18]

It was during this period that the Sovereign National Conference began its deliberations. Originally, the Conference was intended to be a mere constitutional gathering (*Conférence Constitutionnelle*), with a mandate exclusively limited to the drafting of the constitution and the setting up of the institutional framework for the Third Republic.[19] Claiming that, as head of the Zairean state, he was the symbol of the nation's unity, President Mobutu sought to stay above the political fray and be seen as part of the solution to, rather than the cause of, Zaire's ills, a position that the opposition contested.

The wrangling between the two parties, which centered mainly on control of the agenda and chairmanship of the Constitutional Conference, paralyzed the country between July and December 1991. In the end, the opposition won and elected Msgr Laurent Monsengwo Pasinya, the Archbishop of Kisangani, as the Conference's chairperson. Vexed by the outcome, the Zairean government decided to suspend the proceedings. It was forced to reopen the Conference only after dozens of innocent civilians were killed during the 1992 peaceful march.[20]

That period was certainly the most electrifying moment in Zairean politics. It reached a blaze of celebration on August 15, 1992, with the triumphal election by the Sovereign National Conference of Tshisekedi as prime minister of the transitional government. On that night and the following days, throngs of exuberant people crowded the streets, convinced that they had been freed from authoritarianism. So when President Mobutu sent his congratulations to the newly elected prime minister, the euphoria became total. Then, just a few weeks later, the hopes began to crumble.

The Political Impasse Unfolds

The political agreement (*Compromis Politique*) reached by the ruling coalition and some opposition parties, in July 1992, was at the origin of the setback of the political transition. By excluding President Mobutu from the deliberations of the Sovereign National Conference, the agreement actually gave him free rein to derail the democratic movement and impose on the Zairean people an illegitimate political system. The agreement also put the Sovereign National Conference in the odd position of trying to promote democracy while taking unilateral decisions to oppose the wishes of the people to indict and convict those accused of corruption, assassinations, ill-acquired assets and the embezzlement of public funds.

It was, therefore, quite mistaken for Msgr Monsengwo to exult, as he did at the closing of the National Conference, about the achievements of the latter. Also erroneous was his expectation that the new institutional framework (i.e., the head of state, the government and the parliament known as *Haut Conseil de la République*) would work in harmony to lead the country to the Third Republic. Although aware of potential conflicts, Monsengwo nonetheless made his audience to understand that such conflicts would raise doubts not about the adequacy of the new institutional order, but about the goodwill of the office holders. Quite predictably, numerous conflicts arose, some over the relevance of the new institutions, others over the personality of the office holders and many more over both.

This was the political landscape in the former Zaire at the end of the National Conference in 1992. As the general living conditions continued to deteriorate, the opposition was completely thwarted by what Nzongola called the "success of Mobutu's counterrevolution."[21] Years after the beginning of its political transition, Zaire remained perhaps "the only country in the world where the head of state [was] the leader of the opposition to the legally established government, chief economic saboteur, and coordinator of acts of terror against ordinary citizens."[22]

The Survival of the Democratic Movement

Yet the democratic movement did not die. Instead, Zaireans began to mobilize outside institutionalized politics, as was the case of the notorious group of citizens known in Kinshasa as *Parlementaires debout*. Horizontal networks expanded under new names like *O.N.G.* (French for NGO, *organisations non-gouvernementales*). These networks combined the legal notion of A.S.B.L. (French acronyms for not-for-profit organizations, *associations sans but lucratif*), the age-old practice of clan/ethnic solidarity and the idea of self-help embedded in the cooperative movement of the 1970s and 1980s. As the August 1994 conference of Zairean NGOs revealed, not every group had as its aim the uplift of its members' socioeconomic status. Yet all claimed a not-for-profit status as a cover for their desire to become a channel of grassroots political activism.

A survey conducted in Ngaba, Kinshasa, in 1993 revealed that 74.3 percent of the population saw the democratic movement as an outrage by the people against Mobutu's political abuses and the destruction of the economy (35.9 percent). The majority of interviewees explained the looting that ravaged the country beginning in September 1991, as an expression of popular revolt against widespread hunger and the mismanagement of the national economy by the Mobutu regime. The majority of the respondents (70 percent) considered the peaceful march of February 1992 as a people's courageous call for genuine democracy. Asked what democracy meant to them, nearly 58 percent stated equal treatment for all before the law and control by the people over their representatives. Asked about their perception and expectations about the outcome of the Sovereign National Conference, 51.8 percent considered it as an opportunity for national reconciliation and to debate a new *projet de société* (32.9 and 18.9 percent respectively).[23]

This survey also showed that the Zairean peoples understood quite clearly that the road to democracy was riddled with several political obstacles. They recognized that transparency in the management of public affairs (29.6 percent), the end of tribalism and regionalism (27.5 percent) and the eradication of corruption (12.5 percent) had to be the highest priorities for the Third Republic. At the same time, 80 percent among them fully realized that long-term successful implementation of democracy hinged on the cooperation of the army and the political elite.

One can extend the conclusions of the authors of the survey to the majority of urban areas in Zaire. Indeed, De Saint Moulin and Umba correctly concluded their study as follows:

> The democratic movement . . . is very alive in Ngaba. It shows the will of the masses to react against the abuses of a political regime that never subjected itself to any kind of institutional control. It seeks to eliminate excessive inequalities that hinder the fulfillment of social justice.[24]

The Roman Catholic Clergy

For many years, the Roman Catholic clergy echoed similar sentiments and its persistent denunciations of political abuses are now legendary. Despite serious internal disagreements within the hierarchy of the clergy, the Zairian

Conference of Roman Catholic Bishops regularly issued pastoral messages and letters denouncing the political standoff which it considered as the consequence of downright criminality organized as state terrorism.

It is important to recall here that the position of the Roman Catholic clergy toward the Mobutu regime was not always unambiguous. In general, parish priests (*jeunes abbés*) usually adopted—and have continued to do so—a more radical stand against political, human rights and humanitarian abuses than the majority of their bishops. Unlike his predecessor, the late Joseph Cardinal Malula, Frédéric Cardinal Etsou was seriously criticized for displaying neutrality toward the Mobutu regime, largely because both were from the same region.[25]

Ever since the onset of the political transition in 1990, the Roman Catholic clergy became the voice that expressed the people's hopes in the democratic movement. The Conference of Bishops expressed its initial support for the new democratic movement on March 1, 1990, in a document entitled *Mémorandum*, which echoed the complaints of ordinary Zaireans and denounced the mismanagement of the common good by the Mobutu's regime. Fearing that the political transition might be mishandled if left to irresponsible politicians, the Bishops made clear that they were determined to be involved in the political transition to prevent the politicians from appropriating the process.

For the clergy, the roots of the country's ills lay in the hybrid political system instituted in 1967 with the creation of the single party. At the time, President Mobutu tailored the constitution to give the MPR political preeminence over all other existing institutions. The Roman Catholic clergy accused the Nouveau Régime, as the Second Republic came to be designated, for adopting a type of market system just to enable the ruling minority to accumulate personal wealth, while instituting a Soviet-style totalitarian regime in order to consolidate its power and ensure political acquiescence. As the Nouveau Régime gradually slid into autocracy and absolutism, it became increasingly dependent on foreign assistance for its survival.

The Bishops' *Mémorandum* called for a national debate to deal with the basic principles that would underlie the new political system. It urged for an end to the preeminence of the single party-state, the termination of the monolithic presidency, the adoption of a new constitution and the implementation of a legal and institutional framework that would set the country onto a prosperous future.

In conformity with its "prophetic vision of giving hope and denouncing all kinds of abuses,"[26] the Conference of Bishops, through its Permanent Committee, issued between April 1990 and February 1992 five statements in support of the democratic movement. Such a fervor put the Roman Catholic clergy in the unique position of being the most consistent advocate of the people's yearning for political freedom.[27]

Fearing that President Mobutu was about to block the course of the political transition, the Bishops issued, in May 1990, a document entitled *Tous Appelés à Bâtir la Nation* (All Called to Serve the Nation), in which they accused the Mobutu regime of delaying institutional reforms. The Bishops also castigated the continuous use of state terror, particularly after the crushing of the student squabble at the campus of Lubumbashi University in May 1990.

The continuous deterioration of the political situation inspired, on September 22, 1990, a third declaration entitled *Libérés de Toute Peur* (Free from All Fear). While saluting the irreversible march towards democracy, the Bishops stigmatized what they called *démocratie à deux vitesses* (that is, two-gear democracy). They claimed that, while a free press was asserting itself in urban areas, very little information was reaching the rural areas about the popular struggle for democracy carried out in the main cities and towns.

Another message was issued on February 23, 1991. Inspired by the success of the political transition in the West African country of Benin, Zairean Bishops, for the first time, explicitly proposed the convening of a "National Conference or a Round Table," which they saw as the most appropriate venue for the national dialogue they had been requesting. They invited Zaireans from all walks of life and all schools of thought to build a new consensus in the search for a cure to the ongoing crisis of society and its institutions.[28] Entitled *Libérer la Démocratie* (Freeing Democracy), the document invited a national debate over a new *projet de société* and its institutional framework. The new social contract would have as its aim to (1) determine the profile of public officials and the mode of their designation; (2) adopt a new constitution; and (3) put in place the institutions of the transition to the Third Republic.

On January 27, 1992, echoing the widespread anger over the suspension of the National Conference, the Bishops issued a document entitled *Pour Un Nouveau Projet de Société Zairoise* (For a New Society in Zaire). In it, they emphasized the need for a national consensus over the nature of the new *projet de société* before the holding of general elections. It was largely in response to (and in conjunction with) this message that parish priests organized the fateful march of February 1992.

Mpati, a Zairean scholar, is thus right to assert that the Catholic clergy had made the process of democratization the cornerstone of its pastoral mission.[29] Following the lead of *jeunes abbés*, some Bishops eventually grew attentive to the sentiments of their flock and, with great courage, took the risk of translating, in their pastoral letters, the frustrations and expectations of a people that had always been at the mercy of its authorities.

In view of all these initiatives, it is, therefore, not possible to discuss the democratic movement (or the relevance of the state) in the former Zaire without paying due consideration to the pronouncements of the Roman Catholic clergy.

Making the State Relevant: Building Endogenous Democracy

It is not possible to build a bottom-up democratic movement without involving traditional authorities. In spite of some of the negative considerations about traditional authority, the latter remains, in most instances, the only credible institution that has continued to provide a modicum of organized political life in the rural areas. Whether they are liked or despised, traditional authorities should be included in the process of rebuilding the relevance of the state in this country.

Building a bottom-up democratic movement entails a significant devolution of power to the local level and the political will to let local communities devise the ways and modalities for taking charge of their own existence. Three major steps are necessary in this respect: a new definition of political accountability at the national and local levels; the promotion of horizontal economic and financial networks; and a reevaluation of local traditions.

Making the state relevant is, therefore, tantamount to building a democratic system that will make it impossible for anyone to get to power and/or consolidate it against the wishes of the majority of the citizens. It is about creating a political system that puts the people at the center of the country's political life. If the people understand the logic of the new political system and realize that the latter has been set up to address their needs, they will be more willing to take an active role in its operations.

These proposals imply that new political roles and expectations will have to be negotiated, not assigned, before being enshrined into the constitution. They also explain the use of the term "endogenous," which is used to indicate where the roots of the new political system ought to grow.

Paulin Hountondji used the term "endogenous" to refer to the task of identifying and "dwell[ing] on the origin of a cultural product or value that comes from, or at least is perceived by people as com[ing] from, inside their own society, as opposed to imported or 'exogenous' products or values."[30] The concept of "endogenous" democracy suggests that, instead of dismissing the "age-old heritage of local knowledge" and political practices, this heritage should be revitalized and used in a new way.[31]

One such way concerns the generation of political interests among rural masses in selecting traditional chiefs and determining the nature and scope of their authority, as well as the new spectrum of civil and political rights of men and women, whether native or nonnative residents, to manage their own existence. Since their forced integration into the Congo Free State from 1891 to 1990, traditional authorities were used as either vectors or agents of political domination. Under the guise of modernization, the state—whether Leopoldian, colonial or postcolonial—had only been concerned with territorial control and the consolidation of its hegemonic power. In subordinating traditional chiefs to central authority, it showed no concern over the fact that it was creating institutions and putting in office rulers who not only lacked legitimacy but, in many instances, showed little regard for their subjects.

In due course, the Second Republic took a series of administrative reforms aimed at curbing the autonomy of traditional authorities. In 1968, the Political Bureau of the M.P.R. banned the distinction between the state and the party, and made local authorities *de jure* and *de facto* members of the single party. The administrative reform of 1973 abrogated local traditions over the national territory. It ended the judicial autonomy of chiefs and turned them into civil servants liable to be transferred out of their traditional areas.[32] In 1978, the government issued yet another administrative reform abrogating the 1973 law in favor of the election of local chiefs. But that decision was still awaiting its implementation when, in 1987, another reform instituted local elections of village representatives while reserving to the party-state the right to appoint local party bosses.

The political and institutional dualism created by various administrative reforms led to gross abuse of authority at the local level by representatives of the single party, who were thus made accountable to nobody in the area where they operated but instead to their superiors residing in the provincial capital. It was therefore not surprising that, in the early 1990s, many such local party bosses began to flee their areas of responsibility for fear of reprisals by the local population. However, there were also instances where local communities took upon themselves, with some success, the decision to manage their own affairs, sometimes against the interests of the local single-party establishment. In one such instance, the chairman of a single party's village council kept his position by popular insistence against the decision of the provincial hierarchy to remove him, because during his tenure, he took a personal and political risk of distancing himself from the Mobutu regime. Among his major political "mistakes," his superiors accused him of launching a campaign to convince the population to build bridges and maintain roads, instead of requesting the government's subsidies through the provincial governor.

In another instance, local communities decided to regulate game hunting and agreed to entrust to local smiths the task of making hunting guns and bullets, and to assign to expert hunters the task of leading hunting expeditions.

When they heard of this arrangement, the local party establishment and the military commander decided to ban it and to strictly enforce Zairean anti-gun legislation. Ironically, the local military commander and the single-party boss were themselves the area's chief traders of game.

Finally, there was also the case of one traditional chief who decided to negotiate a judicial power-sharing arrangement with the local military commander, according to which the officer would request the chief's advice on all matters presented before him. The arrangement aimed to curb arbitrary judicial decisions by the military and, though it did not last long, it nonetheless ushered in some security for the villagers and their property.

The examples above are meant to illustrate the central argument of this chapter on the need to root democracy in the revitalized age-old heritage of local liberating practices in order to make the state relevant in Africa. Evidently, the chapter did not address in detail the structural problems inherent in the peripheral character of a "proto-capitalist" state like Zaire, whose economy and security needs were defined and managed from abroad. Hence, I am mindful of what Georg Sørensen has called "unsubstantial states."[33] According to Sørensen, such states are characterized by a lack of coherent national economy capable of sustaining a basic level of welfare for the population; by political-institutional deficiencies and a lack of legitimacy, capacity and resources; and, as such, they can by no means guarantee security, law and order, and justice for their citizens.[34] Clearly, Sørensen's observation is correct: In order for the Congolese state to become relevant to the lives of ordinary citizens, the economy needs to be restructured; the political institutions need to be transformed; and basic human needs need to be met. My central point is that while it is true that state relevance covers myriad issues, including those proposed by Sørensen, the transformation of the political system and its power relationships must be at the center of the exercise in the case of the Democratic Republic of the Congo. This would include looking within and identifying the internal dynamics that will enable the rooting of a new democratic practice at the local level. Only then can we talk genuinely about citizenship, that is, the control by the common people of the agenda of their representatives and, above all, their participation in the management of local affairs. This is the path that, as scholars and policymakers, we ought to continue investigating if we want to make ordinary citizens feel that the state is truly theirs!

Conclusion

The foci of this chapter were on several issues. First, the poor performance of the Congolese state during the Mobutu era was examined. Second, the chapter discussed the efforts made by various internal groups—including the Catholic Church and the Sovereign National Conference—to reconstitute the Congolese state. Third, the chapter deciphered the obstacles to the state reconstitution process, including the civil war that deposed the Mobutu regime.

Finally, the basic finding of the chapter is that political transformation, including the devolution of power and the empowerment of ordinary people at the local level, must build the foundation of making the state relevant to the lives of the majority of the Congolese people. Using this foundation, the other dimensions—economic, social, etc.—of making the state relevant can be pursued. In short, the building of a new political system must be the fulcrum of making the state relevant in the Democratic Republic of the Congo.

Notes

1. Ann Seidman and Frederick Anang, eds., *Twenty-First Century Africa: Towards a New Vision of Self-Sustainable Development* (Trenton, NJ: Africa World Press, 1992), 24–43.

2. Research on the state and the crisis in the former Zaire may be grouped into four broad categories, depending on which framework they closely identified with. The first category comprised works inspired by a pluralist approach to politics adopted by Crawford Young and Thomas Turner, as well as the late David Gould. The second category encompassed studies of personal rulership and included works by Thomas Callaghy, Jean-Claude Willame and, to a certain extent, the pamphlets written by President Mobutu's opposition leaders in exile like Nguz-a-Karl I Bond and Cleophas Kamitatu. The third category was dominated by studies using radical or class analysis approaches, represented by Georges Nzongola-Ntalaja, Ilunga Kabongo, Sang Mpam and Michael Schatzberg. The fourth approach, which is mainly concerned with "capital accumulation," evolved independently from, but sometimes in conjunction with, the three categories just listed. This literature focused on the hopes and frustrations of capitalist expansion in the former Zaire, and was represented by the collective work edited by Bézy and also by Jacques Depelchin, Janet MacGaffey, and Vwakyanakazi. With the exception of Vwakyanakazi, who did not then explicitly include an analysis of the Zairean state in the process of accumulation, all the other studies in the above categories regarded it as the most important agent in explaining the general degradation of living conditions in the country.

3. On the relevance or irrelevance of the term "crisis" in what was known as Zairean studies, see Ilunga Kabongo in *The Crisis in Zaire: Myths and Realities*, ed. Nzongola-Ntalaja (Trenton, NJ: Africa World Press, 1986)

4. Archie Mafeje, "Households and Prospects for Agricultural Revival in Africa," *CODESRIA Bulletin* (1991): 9.

5. Julius Nyerere. "Governance in Africa," *Newsletter of the African Association of Political Science (AAPS)* 4, no. 2, new series, Harare, Zimbabwe (May–August 1999).

6. Nyerere, "Governance in Africa."

7. Alain Touraine, *Critique de la Modernité* (Paris: Fayard, 1992), 421–22. The translation is mine.

8. The term "First Republic" refers to the Kasavubu regime that ruled the country—known then as the Democratic Republic of the Congo—from independence in June 1960 to 1965. "Second Republic" or "Nouveau Régime" is also the name for the Mobutu regime. From April 1990, Zaire entered in principle in a transition to the "Third Republic."

9. John Lonsdale, "Political Accountability in African History," in *Political Domination in Africa Reflections on the Limits of Power*, ed. Patrick Chabal (New York: Cambridge University Press, 1986), 128.

10. Lonsdale, "Political Accountability in African History."

11. Patrick Chabal, *Power in Africa: An Essay in Politics Interpretation* (New York: St. Martin's Press, 1992), 54.

12. Chabal, *Power in Africa.*

13. Touraine, *Critique de la Modernité*, 418.

14. The ten-point *Compromis Politique Global* was signed on July 31, 1992. Basically, it put President Mobutu above the law, and forced the opposition to tone down its attacks against the Mobutu regime.

15. Nzongola criticized not the National Conference but the July power-sharing arrangement, which he publicly opposed before the National Conference. See Nzongola-Ntalaja, "Zaire I: Moving Beyond Mobutu," *Current History* (1994): 221. Wamba-dia-Wamba attacked the political impasse this gathering led into. See his "National Reconciliation in Zaire: reasons for the impasse," *CODESRIA Bulletin* 2 and 3 (1993): 10–13.

16. E. Wamba-dia-Wamba, "Democracy, Multipartyism and Emancipative Politics in Africa: The Case of Zaire," *Africa Development* 18, no. 1 (1993): 95–118.

17. Actually it was closed *manu militari* on December 5, 1992.

18. The M.P.R. and its affiliates (the ruling coalition) used different names throughout the transition: *Mouvance présidentielle, Forces démocratiques unies*, i.e., United democratic forces, or even *Forces politiques du Conclave*, a label referring to the common front the president's political family presented during the July 1992 negotiations for a government of national unity. In Zairean politics, a stigma was usually attached to the label "mouvance," as its members were widely seen and referred to as *taupes mobutistes* (i.e., Mobutu's moles), "dinosaurs" or simply political opportunists.

19. The National Conference started in July 1991, under the name of Constitutional Conference. Later, it changed its name to *Conférence nationale souveraine*, i.e. sovereign national conference. The ruling coalition continuously disputed this claim of sovereignty.

20. See also Nzongola, "Zaire I," 220–21.

21. The *cohabitation* scheme succeeded in splitting the opposition into two irreconcilable (i.e., moderate and radical) wings. The moderates, or reformers, were members of the political parties that opposed some aspects of the Mobutu regime but were willing to collaborate in the hope of moving the country toward democracy. This group was headed by Kengo wa Dondo, a long-time prime minister. The radical opposition, on the other hand, advocated the demise of the Mobutu regime and the strict

implementation of the National Conference's institutional order. Tshisekedi is still considered its leader and, in certain political circles, was the country's "true" prime minister until the collapse of the Mobutu regime.

22. Nzongola, "Zaire I," 219.

23. L. de Saint-Moulin and Umba di Mambuku, "Le Mouvement de Démocratisation dans la Zone de Ngaba à Kinshasa," *Zaire Afrique* 274 (1993): 233.

24. Saint-Moulin and Mambuku, "Le Mouvement de Démocratisation dans la Zone de Ngaba à Kinshasa," 233. Ngaba is a largely poor, populous residential neighborhood in Kinshasa.

25. The pastoral documents discussed in the following sections were drafted for the Conference of Catholic Bishops and disseminated by parish priests during Sunday Mass.

26. Monsengwo Pasinya, *L'Eglise Catholique au Zaire: ses tâches, ses défis, ses options* (Kinshasa: Editions Saint Paul, 1991), 470–71. See also Eglise du Christ au Zaire, "Message de l'Eglise du Christ au Zaire au Peuple Zairois en Détresse," *Zaire Afrique* (1991): 259.

27. Protestant churches, grouped in the *Eglise du Christ au Zaire*, joined the debate on democratization very late and almost reluctantly.

28. These messages can be found in the following issues of *Zaire Afrique*: 242–43 (1990); 255 (1991); 262 and 266 (1992); and 275 (1993).

29. N. Mpati ne Nzita, "L'Episcopat Zairois Face à la Démocratie Naissante au Zaire," *Zaire Afrique* 265 (1992): 268–274.

30. Paulin Hountondji, "Producing Knowledge in Africa," *African Studies Review* 38, no. 3 (1995): 6–7. Hountondji quickly adds that since "there is no absolute origin at all . . . the concept of endogeneity itself should be revitalized."

31. Hountondji, "Producing Knowledge in Africa Today." Numerous monographs have been produced on this subject at the Faculty of the Social Sciences at the University of Lubumbashi in Zaire.

32. Mpinga Kasenda and David Gould, *Les Réformes Administratives au Zaire, 1972–1975* (Kinshasa: Presses Universitaires du Zaire, 1973); Isango Idi Wanzila, "La Présence des Chefs Coutumiers dans l'Administration Territoriale du Zaire: quelle opportunité," *Zaire Afrique* 262 (1992).

33. Georg Sørensen, "A State Is Not a State: Types of Statehood and Patterns of Conflict after the Cold War," in *International Security Management and the United Nations*, ed. Muthiah Alagappaa and Takashi Inoguchi (Tokyo: United Nations University Press, 1999), 28–30.

34. Sørensen, "A State Is Not a State."

6

State-building in Ethiopia

Kidane Mengisteab

ETHIOPIA IS ONE OF THE COUNTRIES that appeared to have initiated a promising process of state-building after the fall of the brutal regime of Mengistu Hailemariam and the end of the country's thirty-year-old conflict with Eritrea in 1991. Some observers even regarded Ethiopia as representing a successful transformation to democracy.[1] Despite the promise of the early 1990s, ethnic tensions in the country are once again simmering. The country's lingering crisis of state-building has created the need to carefully assess the country's strategy of state-building, which is largely anchored on ethnic-based federalism.

Historically, the initial stages of state-building were generally accomplished by coercive means through conquests or in the process of resisting conquests. Referring to nationalism in nineteenth-century Europe, for example, Lewis Namier notes that, "states are not created or destroyed, and frontiers redrawn or obliterated, by arguments and majority votes; nations are freed, united, or broken by blood and iron, and not by a generous application of liberty."[2] State-building in the older European states was then consolidated through various mechanisms such as economic integration, socialization, standardized educational systems, and gradual democratization. In Africa, the colonial state curved out African countries without promoting mechanisms that consolidate state-building. Unlike in the rest of Africa, in Ethiopia the modern state was created through internal expansion. However, the expansionist Ethiopian state, not unlike the European colonial state, did not develop the mechanisms that promote state-building. Both the post-independence African state and the post-expansion Ethiopian state have also not been able to develop conditions that facilitate consolidation of state-building.

Given the continent's general conditions of extreme uneven development and extroverted economic structures, which prevent internal interdependence, the process of state-building is highly complex in Africa. Moreover, considering their limited capabilities to control conflict and the increasing concern over human rights violations in the present global system, African countries are unlikely to contain centrifugal forces merely by coercive means. The more promising option is an approach that relies on peaceful negotiations among the different entities to reach some acceptable consensus in the manner of African traditional conflict resolution mechanisms. Such an approach to state-building is likely to result in a relatively ethnically more neutral polity, which can serve as a catalyst for successful state-building. For a state-building approach that relies on coercion, however, even if it succeeds in suppressing subnationalist forces, the success is likely to be short-lived as such forces are likely to reemerge.

This chapter attempts to explain why Ethiopia has continued to face a crisis of state-building even after it instituted a new constitution and a federal arrangement, which renounce force as a device for state-building. The rest of the chapter is divided into three parts. The first examines Ethiopia's state-building problems during the *ancien regime* roughly between 1890 and 1974. The second part examines the failure of the military government (1974–1991) to promote state-building. The third part examines the achievements and failures of the current regime in promoting state-building. The conclusion proposes some ways in which state-building could help make the state relevant in Ethiopia.

Ethiopia's State-building Crisis during the *Ancien Regime*

Although its roots can be traced to the Abyssinian Empire (c. 1270–1750), the Zagwe Empire (c. 1100 to 1270), and the Axumite Empire (c. first millennium B.C.E. to tenth century, C.E.), the modern Ethiopian state was essentially created in the second half of the nineteenth century. By the middle of the nineteenth century the Abyssinian Empire, which had splintered into many small principalities ruled by largely autonomous feudal lords for about a century, was unified. The new empire expanded southward during the era of scramble for Africa establishing Ethiopia's present-day boundaries.

With the expansion of the empire, the inhabitants of the newly incorporated areas were largely treated as subjects. The Oromo, Gurage, Wollamo, Sidama, Kefa, and the Shanqella were subjected to slave raids and large-scale looting. As late as 1907, between six thousand and eight thousand slaves were exported yearly from Keffa, for example.[3] With the exception of those who submitted with little resistance, the local elite were also replaced by administrators from the northern nucleus (Abyssinian) nations of Amhara and Tigray. Moreover, the nations that were incorporated by Emperor Menelik II had large portions of their lands expropriated.[4] Menelik allowed his troops and administrators in the newly occupied territories to occupy land in lieu of payment for their services. The masses in the incorporated territories were largely reduced to a class of sharecropping tenants by their conquerors. For the most part, the cultures, languages, and identities of the southern peoples were also suppressed. It was not, for example, permissible "to publish, preach, teach or broadcast in any Oromo dialect" until the end of Haile Selassie's reign.[5]

Despite the stark difference of its origins from those of most African states, which were created by Western colonialism, Ethiopia during the *ancien regime* shared a number of state-building problems with the rest of African states. These problems were manifested by a number of violent uprisings and revolts in different parts of the country. Eritrea's thirty-year old struggle for independence following the abrogation of its UN-instituted federation with Ethiopia and its annexation in 1962, is one such rebellion. The Raya-Azebo Revolt in 1928, the Woyane Rebellion of Tigrai in 1943, the Bale Revolt in 1964, and the uprising in Gojjam in 1968 are other cases.[6]

At least three reasons can be identified for the failure of state-building during the *ancien regime.* One major obstacle to state-building was the failure of the political elite to craft an ethnically neutral state. The state during the *ancien regime* in Ethiopia was culturally, linguistically, and religiously identified with the Amhara ethnic group, which spearheaded the creation of the modern Ethiopian state and the incorporation of the southern and southwestern parts of the country. Moreover, the colonialist attitude, which was epitomized by the Amharic saying "*Amhara yazzal inji aytazzezim*" (the Amhara is to rule, not to be ruled), was arrogantly maintained.[7] Senior government offices were also dominated by the Amhara. As late as the mid-1960s, more than 80 percent of all senior government offices were occupied by people from the Amhara areas of Shewa, Gojjam, and Begemdir.[8] The land tenure system that subjected a large segment of the peasantry to landlessness, especially in the newly incorporated territories, was also preserved by the ruling elite until 1975. In a multiethnic country, such as Ethiopia, it is perhaps not possible to create a completely neutral state. It is, for example, not feasible to use all the languages in the country as official languages or as media of instruction in schools. It is, however, essential that the state does not advance the interests of some ethnic groups at the expense of others, and that it creates an inclusive polity instead of preserving ethnic hierarchy.

A second major obstacle to state-building is the failure to develop integrating economic systems supported by homogenizing educational and socialization mechanisms. While Ethiopia managed to avoid direct colonialism, it did not escape the neocolonial distortions of its economic system. As the modern Ethiopian state was consolidating into its present form, the country was being simultaneously incorporated into the international capitalist system. Initially, incorporation took the form of trade. Ethiopia imported firearms and other products from Europe in exchange for gold, ivory, and coffee. Beginning in the second half of the twentieth century, however, there emerged in Ethiopia a small commercial sector dominated by foreign investment. The emergence of this sector led to an emphasis on the production of cash crops for export to the metropolitan countries. As in many other developing countries, this sector was viewed as the engine of growth and transformation of the economy. Both government policy and market forces collaborated closely to direct resources to the new sector. The three successive Five-Year Development Plans of the Imperial Government (1958–1973) clearly concentrated resources in the commercial sector. Landlords also pressured their sharecropping tenants to produce cash crops instead of food crops.[9]

Under the extroverted economic structures, a peripheral center, which linked the rest of the country with the international economic system, evolved around Addis Ababa. Such economic structures, however, did not succeed in transforming the country's economy. Much of the rest of the country and close to 80 percent of the population remained in the traditional subsistence sector, which is internally fragmented and has minimal linkages with the modern sector. The educational system and other public services such as health care and transportation facilities also remained concentrated in the urban areas and largely inaccessible to the peasantry. This concentration of public services, especially educational facilities, also led to severe underrepresentation of some ethnic groups among the educated elite. Uneven development associated with the extroversion and compartmentalization of the economy, in combination with the hierarchical ethnic relations resulting from internal colonialism, did not allow a healthy integration of the different ethnic identities in the country.

A third factor that contributed to the problem of state-building was the absence of an appropriate vision of state-building. Following decolonization, state-building in Africa was widely perceived as forging a nation-state with a common culture and identity. Nations and ethnic groups were expected to give up their identities and to adopt some common national culture, which essentially meant the culture of the dominant nation (or ethnic group). In the process, they were expected to transfer their loyalty from the nation to the state. With few exceptions, African leaders of the era of decolonization viewed federalism and other forms of decentralization as divisive arrangements that would reinforce ethno-nationalism and lead to secessions. As a result, a centralized unitary strategy of state-building was widely adopted.

Ethiopia's state-building strategy following its expansion was no exception. It was characterized by a high level of centralization. The different national entities, especially those newly incorporated by conquest, were allowed little space for autonomous cultural development, much less for self-rule. They were instead expected to assimilate into the culture of the dominant nation—mainly the Amhara nation. Despite creating a parliament to disguise the nature of his rule, the last monarch, Emperor Haile Selassie, remained absolute with little regard for cultural diversity and the rights of nations to some form of self-governance. When faced with ethnic-based rebellions, the concern of the leadership was primarily of how to suppress them rather than of how to address the legitimate concerns of the rebelling entities.

Under conditions of competent and visionary leaders, a centralized system has some advantages. It is possible, for instance, that centralization allows faster implementation of policies and thereby expedite development. Since such leadership is not always available, however, decentralization becomes a mechanism of reducing risks. It also allows different groups to participate through self-governance mechanisms.

Ethiopia's centralized unitary and ethnically hierarchical strategy of state-building clearly allowed assimilation of individuals and groups into the dominant culture. The patronage extended to the assimilated elite, in fact, served to mask the ethnic character of the state, since some of them were successful in rising to join the top echelons of the military and the ranks of the ruling elite. Yet, as Mohammed Hassen notes, "the cost for those who assimilated or Amharized was that they ceased to be themselves.'"[10] For the large majority of non-Amhara citizens, who viewed themselves as subjects of an empire, loyalty to the Ethiopian state and loyalty to their ethnic group remained largely at odds.

The Failure of Ethiopia's First Revolution

The collapse of the imperial regime of Haile Selassie provided a good opportunity to establish new foundations for the process of state-building in Ethiopia. However, the military government (the *Derg*) that overthrew the monarchy in 1974 had neither the vision nor the commitment to address the factors that impeded state-building during the *ancien regime.* In an attempt to gain political support and to reduce social unrest, the military government implemented a radical land redistribution program. This largely freed the southern tenants from the bondage of the landlords, who were mostly descendants of the occupation troops and administrators. Land redistribution reduced the discontent of formerly dispossessed ethnic groups. However, the land redistribution proved to be insufficient to promote state-building. The program was undermined by a number of factors. Failure to create access to essential resources other than land for the peasantry prevented revitalization of the country's agriculture and the transformation of the subsistence sector. The government's dogmatic socialist policies and its attempts to collectivize peasant agriculture made the situation worse. The *Derg* thus brought little improvement to the country's fragmented economic structures. It also failed to narrow the gap among the different ethnic groups in terms of access to public resources and services.

The absence of serious political reform to decentralize decision-making was another factor, which contributed to the continued discontent among ethnic groups. By the time the *Derg* came to power, a number of ethnic-based liberation movements were fighting against the government in different parts of the country. In addition to those in Eritrea (The Eritrean Liberation Front and the Eritrean People's Liberation Front), the Tigray People's Liberation Front (TPLF), the Oromo Liberation Front (OLF), the Afar Liberation Front (ALF), and the Western Somali Liberation Front (WSLF) were operating in different parts of the country. Instead of addressing the problems of nationalities peacefully, the *Derg*, like its predecessor, resorted to military buildup in order to suppress the different liberation movements. The *Derg*, for example, failed to accept a proposal by its first chairman, Aman Andom, to grant Eritrea some autonomy, until well after the intensification of the conflict.

Although the domination of the Amhara in senior government positions was somewhat reduced under the military government, the continued excessive centralization did not advance the ethnic neutrality of the state. More importantly, the military solution to the ethnic and regional problems proved unsuccessful. Instead, it alienated ethnic groups even more and brought the country to the brink of total disintegration. It also wrecked the country economically. Military expenditures rose from about 18 percent of total current expenditures in 1974 to about 50 percent in 1988. The government's program of resettlement of large numbers of peasants from the northern parts of the country into the south also exacerbated ethnic animosities.

Pressed by the advancing troops of the EPLF and the TPLF, the military government in its final days resorted to unmasked use of the ethnic card. It attempted to incite public anger against what it called the "Tigray-Tigrignie" (Tigrigna-speaking ethnic group) threat to Ethiopian unity.[11] In the end, the military government left Ethiopia more divided than it found it.

Ethiopia's Novel Policy of Ethnic-based Federalism

In May 1991, the forces of the Ethiopian People's Revolutionary Democratic Front (EPRDF) overthrew the military government and its violent centralized authoritarian system, which suppressed ethnic and regional expressions. This regime change created another opportunity for a new beginning of state-building in the country. However, indications are that this new opportunity has also slipped away. Actual outcomes in ethnic relations and structural and institutional changes that facilitate the process of state-building are the gauges for assessing progress or lack thereof in state-building. Actual outcomes can be measured by looking at the decline or continued occurrence of ethnic-based rebellions. The structural and institutional conditions can be assessed by looking at the three criteria identified at the outset, namely, vision of state-building, ethnic neutrality of the state (a critical component of democratization), and internal economic integration. Unlike the two previous regimes, the EPRDF came to power with the lessons learned from the two previous regimes—that coercion, assimilation, and a centralized unitary strategy have failed in promoting state-building in Ethiopia and that a different solution to the country's ethnic and regional problems was needed. Unfortunately, instead of implementing genuine decentralization and devolution of power, it too designed a strategy of masked centralization, which has come to rely increasingly on coercion.

In July of 1991, the EPRDF, which was made up of the TPLF and two other small fronts, the Ethiopian People's Democratic Movement (EPDM), which in 1994 changed its name to the Amhara National Democratic Movement (ANDM), and the Oromo People's Democratic Organization (OPDO), called for a National Conference in which twelve assorted political groups with four hundred delegates participated. The conference adopted a provisional charter and a transitional coalition government, led by the EPRDF with a number of other movements and political groups, was formed.

The transitional government of Ethiopia (TGE), in line with the charter, quickly recognized the unconditional right of every nation in the country to self-determination, including the rights of self-governance and cultural autonomy, as well as secession. A constitution that endorses these changes was ratified in December 1994. The new constitution provides for the election of a 550-member Council of People's Representatives from all electoral districts on the basis of the size of the population and special representation of minority nations. At least twenty seats are identified for small minorities.[12] The highly centralized system of governance has also been replaced by a federal arrangement among the newly demarcated and largely ethnic-based ten states, including Addis Ababa, the capital city, which constitutes a separate administrative unit. The other nine states are: Tigrai, Afar, Amhara, Oromia, Somali, Benishangul/Gumaz, Southern Nations, Gambela Peoples, and Harari People. It is possible that new states can be formed since the constitution grants small nations within the newly created states the right to form their own states at any time.

The new constitution also provides for the creation of a Federal Council that is composed of representatives of nations. Each nation is represented in the Federal Council by one member and by one additional member for each one million of its population.[13] Among the tasks of this council are: (1) to decide on claims by nations for self-determination, including secession; (2) to settle disputes and misunderstandings between states; and (3) to determine the division of revenues derived from joint federal and state tax sources and subsidies by the federal government to states. The creation of the Federal Council to manage ethnic and regional relations also frees up the Council of People's Representatives to deal with other pressing national issues.

The Ethiopian experiment has generated a great deal of concern from two sides. On the one side, many charge that the new ethnic-based federalism is a prelude to the disintegration of the country along ethnic lines. Marina Ottoway, for example, argues, "[B]y following the Soviet lead, the Ethiopian government had embarked on a path bound to lead either to increased repression or to mounting ethnic conflict and the eventual disintegration of the country."[14] Walle Engedayehu also argues, "[D]ividing them (the Ethiopian people) on linguistic, religious, or regional differences will not only lead to social disharmony but will also arouse the desire by groups to press for secession in the future."[15] Tegegne Teka also claims "[I]t is wrong for the state to allow itself to become a testing ground for social experimentation."[16] Another observer also views ethnic democracy as oxymoron.[17] Many newly formed political parties such as the All Amhara People's Organization (AAPO) and the Council of Alternative Forces for Peace and Democracy in Ethiopia (CAFPDE) also oppose the ethnic-based federal arrangement as well as the inclusion of the right of nations to secede in the constitution.

On the other side, the groups that viewed the federal arrangement as a positive step in the right direction accused the EPRDF government of failing, in sharp contrast to its bold policy declarations, to allow ethnic groups to organize freely. This group of critics argues that the EPRDF manufactures ethnic organizations that march to its own orders and suppresses independent organizations.[18]

As noted already, when the EPRDF assumed power, relations between the state and various ethnic groups were already poisoned by the previous two regimes and the country was clearly on the verge of disintegration along ethnic lines. The multiplication of ethnic-based liberation movements is indicative that ethnic relations within the state had reached an impasse. Even if liberal democracy, which safeguards the rights and freedoms of the individual, would be a solution to Ethiopia's ethnic problems, as Donald Crummey suggests,[19] this would not be attained quickly and the country's ethnic problems would need immediate attention.

Despite the risks involved, bold policy measures toward a federal arrangement was essential to stop the perpetual bloodshed, to avert the country's total disintegration, and to initiate a process of state-building. The TGE's ethnic policies initially paid notable dividends. Eritrea's bitter conflict ended with a peaceful settlement; and the two countries had embarked on economic integration and cooperation in a wide range of issues before a border conflict, which erupted in 1998, ended all of this. The bloodshed in the rest of the country, however, largely subsided. Armed liberation and independence movements in the country were largely replaced by political parties. The OLF, for example, entered into a coalition with TGE.

The second charge, which essentially questions the government's commitment to democratization and genuine federal arrangement, is more convincing. Ethiopia under the EPRDF undertook some encouraging steps toward state-building as well as democratization. The freedoms of the press and organization are, for example, now more respected in the country than ever before. The constitutional recognition of the rights of ethnic groups and the establishment of a federal arrangement are also essential prerequisites for democratization although they do not, by themselves, signify a democratic system or real devolution of power. Nevertheless, state-building through assimilation has ended. The country's constitution also establishes that state-building by means of force is no longer feasible. In principle, thus, a novel state-building strategy through peaceful means has been initiated. Implemented properly, the new strategy would seem to have the potential to empower all ethnic groups by allowing and respecting their self-governance and cultural autonomy. It would also potentially enable ethnic minorities to reduce the power of the majority by controlling their local affairs and by building coalitions across ethnic lines at the national level. The freedom to secede can be used by all ethnic groups as a safeguard from domination. Moreover, such rights may serve as therapeutic treatment to the nations that suffered generations of oppression.

There is, however, a notable discrepancy between the constitutional pronouncements and reality on the ground. The initial promise of the new strategy has also begun to unravel. Ethnic-based liberation fronts have resurfaced in the country. The OLF, which initially joined the government in a coalition, has resumed armed struggle. The Ogaden National Liberation Front (ONLF) and the Islamic Front for the Liberation of Oromia are other active fronts. Polarization among the major ethnic groups in the country—the Oromo, the Amhara, and the Tigray—has also escalated. Far from depoliticizing ethnicity, the new strategy appears to have made ethnic groups more militant.

The strategy of ethnic-based federalism is rather risky and difficult to manage. When implemented improperly it can be dangerous. In this case, there are a number of problems with its implementation.

As noted already, in a multiethnic country, especially where relations between the state and some ethnic groups are antagonistic, any strategy of state-building requires the ethnic neutrality of the state both in essence and in appearance. The EPRDF government has faired poorly in projecting an ethnically neutral state. Among the characteristics of an ethnically neutral state are: wide representation of ethnic identities in the government, drafting the rules of the game (at least the constitution) in a consensual manner, and a democratic system of governance that respects individual as well as group rights.

When these criteria are used as a litmus test, it becomes apparent that the EPRDF government has largely failed in implementing its own strategy of state-building. To begin with, the coalition that forms the EPRDF is dominated by the TPLF, which is an exclusive organization of Tigray. Despite the efforts to broaden the coalition by inviting or forming other ethnic-based parties, the TPLF has largely monopolized power. Key decision-making positions are held by TPLF officials. This has not made the EPRDF a truly neutral representative body of all ethnic identities in the country. As the previous two regimes were identified with a single ethnic group, the Amhara, the present government is also identified with one ethnic group, this time the Tigray.

Ethnic or nationalist groups are rarely unitary actors. However, Oromo nationalists, by and large, view the EPRDF takeover of power as a mere transfer of power from the Amhara ethnic group to the Tigray ethnic group. In their view, the Oromo continue to be denied self-determination and remain dominated by northern ethnic groups.[20] In their view, there is little genuine decentralization in the country's political system, despite the federal arrangement. The EPRDF through the ethnic parties it manufactured largely controls policy-making at all levels. Ethiopia has, thus, essentially remained a centralized empire state.

Among the Amhara the EPRDF government has also faced serious opposition. The All Amhara People's Organization is among the most vocal and bitter opposition parties. Various exiles, whom Paul Henze refers to as "Amhara-centrists, bitter at losing the dominant position they enjoyed in Ethiopia for a century,"[21] also fiercely oppose the EPRDF.

The TPLF is also widely accused of favoring Tigray in its allocation of resources.[22] The validity of this claim is debatable. However, there is little doubt that the EPRDF government is not viewed as ethnically neutral. For purposes of state-building the image the state projects is critical. While creating the ethnic-based federal arrangement (*kilil*), the TPLF reclaimed from the Amhara region two districts which Emperor Haile Selassie took away from Tigray after he suppressed its Woyane Rebellion in 1943, in order to weaken the rebellious province. The TPLF reclaimed Hummera from the former province of Begemdir and Raya District from the former province of Wollo. These measures, while perhaps justifiable, contributed to the image that the EPRDF government is partial to Tigray.

There are also notable complaints that the rules of the game—including the ethnic-based federal arrangement and the constitution that grants nations the right to secede—were not crafted in a consensual manner. With the exception of the EPRP and MEISON, most political organizations were invited to the July 1991 National Conference. Considerable consultations were also held during the constitution drafting process. Yet, there remains widespread opposition to some critical aspects of the constitution. More importantly, different ethnic groups have taken different stands on some of these contested issues. While Oromo and Tigray nationalists, by and large, are favorable to the rights the constitution grants to nations, Amhara nationalists, by and large, are in favor of centralization.

The 1998–2000 border conflict with Eritrea has brought about a rapprochement between the EPRDF government and some opposition groups, particularly among the centrist groups that are bitter about Eritrea's independence. This, however, is unlikely to be sustained. The nationalist elements within the TPLF—those that played a key role in the outbreak of the conflict with Eritrea by unilaterally issuing a new and enlarged map of Tigray, which incorporates areas that Eritrea claims as its own—have little in common with the centrist elements other than the shared hostility against Eritrea. Moreover, an alliance between Tigray's nationalists and Amhara centrists is likely to increasingly alienate the Oromo, who are opposed to centralization.

Democratic governance is another mechanism that helps foster neutrality of the state. As noted, the EPRDF government initially undertook some promising steps in this regard. One observer even characterizes Ethiopia's democratization process as "a success story."[23] There is little doubt that Ethiopian citizens now enjoy greater freedom of expression and organization than ever before. It also needs to be pointed out that democracy in which the general population controls decision-making is a long process and not a finished product that is made available in a short period of time. Yet Paul Henze's assessment is preposterous. As sober analyses by John Young, Richard Joseph, and John Harbeson[24] demonstrate, it is far from certain that Ethiopia under the EPRDF is on a clear path to democracy. Democratization is an arduous process. The development of democracy when the state is rightly or wrongly viewed to be ethnically biased is an almost impossible task.

Despite extending freedom to organize, the government has not been able to conduct elections that opposition parties and observers would consider free and fair. Several opposition parties boycotted both the 1994 constituent assembly elections and the 1995 parliamentary and regional council elections alleging a number of unlawful activities by the ruling party. A number of election observers corroborated some of the allegations by noting some election irregularities.[25] The May 2000 elections were also marred by claims of irregularities by opposition parties.

The election irregularities were, at least in part, due to inexperience and lack of capacity in handling national elections, as many of the international observers noted.[26] However, part of the explanation lies in the nature of the TPLF and the rest of the political organizations in the country. As a liberation front, the TPLF has dual objectives. One was to liberate Ethiopia from the repressive military regime of Mengistu Hailemariam and to democratize it. An alternative objective was to liberate and create an independent and "Greater Tigray" state.[27] After overthrowing Mengistu, the TPLF clearly wants to keep the country together and to promote state-building. At the same time, like all political parties, it also wants to keep itself in power. The fact that Tigray is the minority among the three dominant ethnic groups in Ethiopia's ethnic landscape is likely to have contributed to the TPLF's determination to control power even through some ingenuous methods. In any case, its failure to share power has sparked ethnic tensions in a country where most political parties are organized along ethnic lines.[28]

Intensification of opposition and especially armed struggle such as that waged by the OLF have also made the realization of democracy more difficult. The threat of violence has already created a situation that has made the government increasingly less tolerant to democratic rights and even more repressive. Suppression of Oromo nationalists and sympathizers and the mass deportations of Ethiopian citizens of Eritrean origin along with Eritrean citizens following the conflict with Eritrea are among the indications.

A third criterion for gauging the process of state-building is the level of internal economic integration. In this regard also the EPRDF government initially made some progress. There is little doubt that it paid more attention to the agricultural sector than the previous two regimes. Expenditures on agriculture, for example, rose from about 2.9 percent in the late 1980s to 5.9 percent in 1994.[29] The government's agricultural extension program and fertilizer subsidies are claimed to have led to a seven-fold increase in consumption of fertilizers between 1993 and 1995. In conjunction with good weather, this has led to very good harvests in the country over the 1993–1997 period. The performance of the overall economy has also been encouraging. Until drought and war with Eritrea changed the situation in the late 1990s, Ethiopia was regarded among the better performers in Africa.

However, even without the war with Eritrea and the 1998–1999 drought, it was unlikely that the progress could be maintained since there was no fundamental change in the extroverted structure of the economy. The government has increasingly liberalized the economy and has begun to reduce its support of peasants through subsidized fertilizers, which is critical for the transformation of the subsistence sector. The ideology of globalization and the pressure of the international financial institutions have begun to reduce the ability of the government to pursue policies that would promote internal integration. Moreover, the rising ethnic tensions have made Ethiopia too unstable for serious economic progress to take place.

Making the State Relevant

In order for state-building to succeed so that the state can become relevant to the majority of Ethiopians, several major issues must be addressed. There is a need to revisit the constitution-making process and some of the provisions. Specifically, there is an urgent need to re-engage in the crafting of a new constitution through a people's-led process of discussions and dialogue. Also, the process must involve addressing some of the concerns that various groups have with some of the provisions of the constitution. This is important because various stakeholders have legitimate concerns about both the constitution-making process and some of its substantive provisions. Thus, by revisiting the constitution-making process and addressing some of the provisions, the process of national reconciliation would be enhanced concurrently.

Central to making the Ethiopian state relevant to the lives of the majority of Ethiopians is the need for the state to be ethnically neutral. In other words, the state must be the embodiment of the hopes and aspirations of all Ethiopians. Moreover, in the performance of its functions, the Ethiopian state must serve all of its citizens irrespective of their ethnic backgrounds.

Although the Ethiopian state has made some progress in the area of political liberalization, much work has to be done in the broad area of democratic governance. The Ethiopian state needs to build on the progress it has made thus far not just by expanding the ambit of political rights and freedoms, but by institutionalizing accountability and transparency in the state's operations, and including Ethiopians from diverse ethnic, regional, and political backgrounds in the decision-making process. Moreover, as part of the democratic governance enterprise, steps need to be taken to address the plethora of issues that underlie the authoritarian political culture that has dominated the Ethiopian state.

Linked to democratic governance is the exigency of the development of a culture of regular, free, and fair elections. The Ethiopian government must develop an electoral system that is respected and trusted by the various political parties and the citizenry at large. This is quite critical to the establishment of a system of accountability and the orderly change of leadership.

The demon of the centralization of power needs to be exorcised, if broad political participation is to be promoted. Whether within the context of a federal or other type of state arrangement, power and authority need to devolve to the local levels. This is not only important for the promotion of political participation, but for empowering people at the local level to help shape the policies that direct affectly their lives.

Also, various economic challenges need to be addressed. For example, steps need to be taken to address class inequalities. This could be done by designing and implementing policies that would help narrow the gaps in wealth and income. Also, employment opportunities need to be created as a collaborative effort between the state and the private sector. The general living standards need to be improved.

Similarly, at the social level, measures need to be undertaken for the purpose of improving public education and public healthcare and addressing the related issues of housing, transportation, sanitation, and access to safe drinking water. These social issues are at the heart of the "bread and butter issues" that modulate state-society relations: Good state performance accentuates the relevance of the state to the citizenry. Conversely, poor state performance distances the state from the people by making the latter irrelevant.

Conclusion

The Ethiopian experience suggests that African countries are caught up in a seemingly impossible vicious circle. State-building in this era requires democratization and internal economic integration. Democratization and internal economic integration, in turn, depend on progress in the process of state-building. The task of breaking this vicious circle is indeed daunting. As evident from the experiences of collapsed states, the outcome of widespread failure, which is a real possibility, is frightening.

Breaking the vicious cycle requires a formula of state-building that is based on a broad consensus among the different ethnic and political groupings. Unfortunately, for Ethiopia, the present regime has failed in this regard. The regime is now clearly viewed as sectarian and the regime is not likely to shed this image. The federal arrangement was a formula that had potential to work. Its misapplication is likely to have discredited the arrangement in the eyes of the population. There is thus the danger that in a post-TPLF regime, Ethiopia may throw the "baby with the bath water" and revert to centralization instead of properly implementing a federal arrangement.

Hence, in order to halt the rising tide of state irrelevance, several major issues must be addressed: the constitution-making process and some of the substantive provisions; the establishment of an ethnically neutral state; the need for democratic governance; the devolution of power; addressing various economic issues; and providing for the social needs of the citizenry. Addressing one or two of these issues in isolation would not be enough. Instead, the Ethiopian state must address all of these issues as integral parts of a common process of state-building. The performance of the state in addressing these issues would continue to be the major determinant of state relevance.

Notes

1. B. Paul Henze, "Ethiopia: A Political Success Story," *Journal of Democracy* 9, no. 4 (1998): 55–61.

2. Quoted in Benjamin Schwarz, "The Diversity Myth: America's Leading Export," *The Atlantic Monthly* 275, no. 5 (May 1995): 60.

3. Richard Pankhurst, *Economic History of Ethiopia: 1800–1935* (Addis Ababa: Haile Selassie I University Press, 1968), 82–83.

4. Pankhurst, *Economic History of Ethiopia.*

5. P. T. W. Baxter, "Ethiopia's Unacknowledged Problem: The Oromo," *African Affairs* 27, no. 308 (July 1978): 228.

6. Gebru Tareke, *Ethiopia: Power and Protest* (Cambridge, UK: Cambridge University Press, 1991); Worku G. Lakew, "Behind the News: Revolution in Ethiopia," *Capital and Class*, no. 46 (Spring 1992): 16.

7. Donald Levine, *Greater Ethiopia* (Chicago: University of Chicago Press, 1974), 149.

8. Christopher Clapham, *Haile Selassie's Government* (London: Longman, 1968), 77.

9. Kidane Mengisteab, *Ethiopia: Failure of Land Reform and Agricultural Crisis* (New York: Greenwood Press, 1990).

10. Mohammed Hassen, "Ethiopia: Missed Opportunities for Peaceful Democratic Process," in *State-building and Democratization in Africa: Faith, Hope, and Realities*, ed. Kidane Mengisteab and Cyril Daddieh (Westport, CT: Greenwood Press, 1999).

11. Alemseged Abbay, *Identity Jilted or Re-Imagined Identity?* (Lawrenceville, NJ: The Red Sea Press, 1998), 200.

12. Article 54 of The Constitution of the Federal Democratic Republic of Ethiopia (unofficial English translation), Addis Ababa, December 8, 1994.

13. Article 61 of the 1994 Constitution.

14. Marina Ottaway, *Democratization and Ethnic Nationalism: African and Eastern European Experiences* (Washington, DC: Overseas Development Council, 1994), 47.

15. Walle Engedayehu, "Ethiopia: Democracy and the Politics of Ethnicity," *Africa Today* 40, no. 2 (1993): 39.

16. Tegegne Teka, "Amhara Ethnicity in Making," in *Ethnicity and the State in Eastern Africa*, ed. M. A. Mohamed Salih and John Markakis (Uppsala: Nordiska Afrikainstitutet, 1998), 124.

17. Donald Crummey, "Ethnic Democracy? The Ethiopian Case," paper presented at the thirty-seventh annual meeting of the African Studies Association, Toronto, 1994.

18. Hassen, "Ethiopia: Missed Opportunities for Peaceful Democratic Process"; Leenco Lata, "The Making and Unmaking of Ethiopia's Transitional Charter," in *Oromo Nationalism and the Ethiopian Discourse*, ed. Asefa Jalata (Lawrenceville, NJ: The Red Sea Press, 1998), 51–77.

19. Crummey, "Ethnic Democracy? The Ethiopian Case."

20. Lata, "The Making and Unmaking of Ethiopia's Transitional Charter."

21. Henze, "Ethiopia: A Political Success Story."

22. Kiflu Tadesse, "Border of Economy," *Tobia* (Amharic monthly) 5, no. 12 (July 1998); Lata, "The Making and Unmaking of Ethiopia's Transitional Charter"; and *Addis Tribune* (English weekly newspaper) (September 4–9, 1998).

23. Henze, "Ethiopia: A Political Success Story," 55–61.

24. John Young, "Ethnicity and Power in Ethiopia," *Review of African Political Economy* 23, no. 70 (December 1996): 531–42; Richard Joseph, "Oldspeak vs. Newspeak," *Journal of Democracy* 9, no. 4 (1998): 55–61; John Harbeson, "A Bureaucratic Authoritarian Regime," *Journal of Democracy* 9, no. 4 (1998): 62–69.

25. D. Gilbert Kulick, "Ethiopia's Hollow Election: Observing the Forms," *Foreign Service Journal* 69, no. 4 (1992): 41–45; National Democratic Institute for International Affairs and the African American Institute, *An Evaluation of the June 21, 1992 Elections in Ethiopia*, 1992.

26. Steve McDonald, "Learning a Lesson," *Africa Report* 37, no. 5, (September/October 1992): 29.

27. Tareke, *Ethiopia: Power and Protest.*

28. Kidane Mengisteab, "New Approaches to State-building in Africa: The Case of Ethiopia's Ethnic-based Federalism," *African Studies Review* 40, no. 3 (December 1997): 111–32.

29. Federal Democratic Republic of Ethiopia, Central Statistical Authority, *Ethiopia: Statistical Abstract* (Addis Ababa: Government Publications, 1993).

7

The State, Its Reform, and the Question of Legitimacy in Kenya

Godwin Murunga

> Politics has to be much more than an elite affair and the people must become true objects of participation rather than objects of manipulation in the socio-economic and political process. Democratization must be our watchword. By this I mean a steady and systematic empowerment of the people, their communities and constituencies in a direction that empowers them to dictate and determine the content and context of politics with emphasis on pro-people issues.[1]

THE STUDY OF STATE FAILURE AND COLLAPSE IN AFRICA has grown over the last decade. A significant aspect of this literature is the typology it draws on the process of collapse in Africa. State collapse, the literature argues, "is not a short-term phenomenon; not a crisis with a few early warnings; not simply a matter of a coup or a riot. State collapse is a long-term degenerative disease. However, it is also one whose outcome is not inevitable: cure and remission are possible" outcomes.[2]

An entry point on Kenya is contained in the argument that loss of political legitimacy is a crucial indicator of potential state failure and collapse. State legitimacy is established when the functions of its existence are satisfactorily met and when the balance between the state's coercive and rewarding functions are maintained. "When the state overplays its control functions, it loses the willing allegiance and legitimizing support of its population."[3] This, in turn, may create alternative centers of power within the territorial space of the nation-state—and in viewing the breakdown of good governance, law and order and unsatisfied economic expectations, diverse categories of the population rise to challenge the political center. This may occasion state collapse especially in cases where the branches of the central government including the executive, legislature, and judiciary bureacracy are destroyed. "Collapse occurs when centralized institutions of penetration are unable to 'tame' the contiguous periphery."[4]

This partial typology of state collapse is relevant to our discussion of Kenya insofar as the issue of state legitimacy is probed as an avenue to collapse. The exigencies of governance have often led citizens to question and challenge the state and lead it, on the one hand, into extreme illegitimacy and, on the other hand, to tolerate when objective conditions indicate that the state is responding to their requirements. Strictly, Kenya has never been a collapsed state in the sense of maximum breakdown of institutional service and decay. While the Kenyan state has occasionally reached dangerous levels of illegitimacy, it is the swing between legitimacy and illegitimacy that will form the concern of this chapter. This will be examined in historical perspective with a view of explaining how the Kenyan state has survived and what is needed to reestablish greater state relevance.

The African expectation out of the transition to pluralist politics in the late 1980s and early 1990s was best articulated by Wamba-dia-Wamba. He argued that multiparty politics ought to usher in emancipative politics that could make the destructive transformation of the state from what it was constituted in colonial and independent Africa possible. The nature of this destructive transformation would entail enabling the mass of Africans to develop not only a capacity for self-control but also a control of their leaders. In this way, leaders would be made responsive to the needs and aspirations of the masses, a fact that is indispensable if independent African political structures are to be developed and democracy as imperialist policy is to be avoided.[5]

Indeed, the hope that Africa was set to make a radical departure from the state as it was colonially constituted and adopted at independence was made possible by a number of factors. Among these was the resilience of democratic forces on the continent even at a time when authoritarianism was at its crudest. The active opposition to the oppressive state structures was so sustained that some extremely conservative regimes like the Zairian, Kenyan and Cameroonian ones were literally forced to accept multiparty politics, long after many other African countries like Zambia had gone to pluralist polls.

In Kenya, one would hasten to add that a second factor played a crucial role in ensuring that the Moi regime acceded to multipartyism. The role of external donors and other agencies was instrumental in forcing Moi to accept multiparty politics as the new reality. This reform movement had numerous rationales, the most significant among them being the donor driven concern for the opening up of the economic and political space. These came to combine political conditionalities that went with economic reform. The livid expression of these conditionalities was articulated at the Carter Center of Emory

University during its inaugural seminar for the African Governance Program in 1989. During the seminar, faith in market reform was articulated and the need to add political conditionalities to economic reform emphasized. The thrust of the Carter Center's argument found easy adoption by the major donor agencies especially the Bretton Woods Institutions (BWI). While we cannot tell for sure that some of the scholars gathered at the Carter Center were working for or in close contact with donor institutions, the mere fact of the broad similarities of the arguments adopted by the latter would seem to indicate that dangerous liaisons had been formed.

In Kenya, Smith Hempstone, the U.S. ambassador, among other people and groups forcefully fronted such economic and political reforms. Hempstone arrived in Kenya in 1989 with clear intentions about his political mission. He had little time for diplomatic etiquette. He pushed the government of President Moi, harassed the ministers and, in this, apparently enjoyed eager support from a section of the educated Kenyan elite and opposition politicians. He patronized some of these opposition leaders and elite, funded others and protected them through the advantages of diplomatic immunity. His stated mission to Kenya was "to get rid of Moi."[6]

This chapter argues that the reform movement arose in response to critical levels of state illegitimacy generated by misuse of its coercive functions and intermittent economic slumps. But the reform movement missed the objective target when it narrowed its agenda to the personality of President Moi rather than to the destructive transformation of the state, as it had been historically constituted. Consequently, concern for the legitimacy of the state to the mass of Kenyans was not the priority of the reform movement led by local elite with eager support of external forces. Rather, the reform movement went full blown into instituting measures to enhance the capitalist plunder of the country, this time with the support of the group of elite politicians aligned with the opposition parties and nongovernmental civil society groups. The chapter redirects our attention to the fact that for the state to gain in legitimacy and greater relevance—after the decade of superficial reform, donor generated "irrelevant" democratic renewal and presidential and parliamentary elections—the total reform of the state is necessary. Basic questions related to the role of leaders in relation to those they lead; the development of working and efficient institutions; the empowerment of hitherto marginalized categories and the state itself; the review of the constitution and new global thinking about Africa need to be put at the center once again. This way, a new social contract between the state and citizens will be initiated, in which case, it is hoped, issues related to what the state should stand for in a plural setting will be put into closer focus, discussed and acted upon in a participatory manner.

The Independent State in Kenya

In this section, I postulate that the state as it was constituted after independence moved from its nationalist legitimacy to new levels of illegitimacy—occasioned, first, by the concessions "state nationalism" made to the colonial forces and, secondly, by the failure of the independent leaders to effectively respond to the needs of the majority of Kenyans during *uhuru* (independence). These failures were the backdrop against which the need for reform was predicated. It needs to be explained why, even in their harsh nature, reforms were enthusiastically received. The feasibility and impact of reform can then be assessed.

The notion of "state nationalism" provides a theoretical entry point into the discussion of the independent state in Kenya. This notion can be traced back to Mamdani who argued that in most of Africa, "state nationalism of the 1960s cannot be considered as the flowering of the popular nationalism of the 1940s; rather, the former arose from the ashes of the latter."[7] This argument implies that by 1960, the popular nationalism of the 1940s was dead and in its place was a form of nationalism that lacked popular voice and support. To Mamdani, state nationalism was in fact an ideology of colonial counterattack designed to stabilize the control the colonial state was quickly loosing to the popular struggles waged in Africa for independence.

Nationalism as state ideology emanated from a stark reality within the colonial state that force alone was not an effective way of dealing with African political struggles. It was an ideology forced by African struggles to democratize colonial state structures so that the reactionary African nationalists could be accommodated into the leadership structures in the construction of the independent state. Nationalism as state ideology began to delegitimize popular struggles by questioning the genuineness of its leaders; their maturity and the morality of their methods of struggle; and the morality of violent resistances like Mau Mau. State nationalism was therefore a last-minute attempt when the popularity of nationalist resistance was overwhelming colonial forces. The colonial state sought to reconstitute itself, first by "detaching [nationalism] from any moorings in the popular struggles of the 1940s"[8] and criminalizing all other struggles anchored in civil society as immoral, immature and divisive.

The need to guide African nationalism was best evident in British decolonization policy. For one, they maintained the belief that Africans were basically immature to handle the requirements of independence. As Furedi argues:

> The policy of decolonization did not imply a revision of the British view of African nationalism. The consensus was that African nationalism was still an im-

> mature movement, but a dangerous one that had to be met with guile and not just with force. The policy was to guide it not just to fight it. . . . The idea was to manage African nationalism by staying ahead, encouraging collaborators and retaining the initiative.[9]

As if to reinforce this position, Lord Hailey had argued in 1937 on the need to interact with the aspiration of Africans in order to neutralize the danger posed by nationalism. "Thwarted it can be dangerous; met in the right spirit; it can be guided into fruitful and constructive channels."[10] But this process was only poised to succeed, if concessions to the demand for self-government were granted. It is for this reason that alongside the management of African nationalism was a process of negotiation for political reform toward independence.

The Creation of Illegitimacy under the Kenyatta State

In Kenya, delinking from popular nationalism was most evident in the manner in which Mau Mau was demonized first by the colonial state and latter by Jomo Kenyatta, Kenya's first president. Kenyatta had been the foremost nationalist in Kenya who was seen as the leading threat to the colonial state. He was described as a leader unto darkness and death. This was because he was assumed to be the leader of Mau Mau, a leading violent movement for the attainment of *uhuru* in Kenya. The colonial state responded to Mau Mau through excess repressive force and psychological labeling. The violence of Mau Mau was dismissed as a savage and primitive reversion to traditional barbarism. It was argued that the African populations involved had failed to cope with the reality of modernization introduced through colonialism. In pushing this argument, Jomo Kenyatta was targeted as its leader and was for this reason incarcerated in 1956. Phillip Mitchell described him as "dangerous and corrupt."[11]

In the long run however, attempts to stabilize the colonial state in Kenya were successfully played out in conferences pitting the elite negotiators of independence (reformists) and the radical Mau Mau adherents and supporters in the city of Nairobi against the settlers and colonial state. In the city, there was a large section in neglected African quarters that had gone beyond feasible conditions of human habitation. In these quarters were located demoralized and dehumanized African populations. Their conditions predisposed them to embrace any movement whose goal was to ameliorate their woes. In these quarters, control was completely absent and crime thrived in broad daylight. This became the best location for the sprouting of anti-colonial struggles. Indeed, in these quarters existed African crowds that not only hated the colonial state but also all those highly placed Africans who worked or identified with it; the *asomi* as they were referred to. It was therefore easy to notice resentment among African urban populations pitting the deprived African crowd in the city against the *asomi*. Like the colonial state, even the *asomi* became targets of harassment by these crowds.

While the *asomi* had been target of hate throughout the colonial period because they were the loyalists who made up part of the colonial administrative structures, a group of young educated Africans arose that "sought reform within the colonial administration."[12] This group later came under the political influence of Jomo Kenyatta, the future leader of the independent state. As the radicals tried to force radical reform of the colonial state, the educated Africans came to oppose them. This was clearly indicated in 1947, when the African Workers Federation called a strike and Jomo Kenyatta, in retaliation, called a mass meeting and disassociated his Kenyan African Union (KAU) party from it. From then onward, the educated leaders keenly struggled for incorporation into the structures of leadership but failed to address the faulty rules of the game that inhibited popular African participation in the colonial state. This delinking of political parties from the other popular avenues for independence struggle marked the start of the serious decline of the popular nationalist struggle culminating in the defeat of Mau Mau and its demonization by Kenyatta.

The surprise turn came when Kenyatta condemned Mau Mau. For most part of the colonial days, Kenyatta was an absentee hero of African nationalism. "Absence from Kenya's political scene had been the most outstanding feature of Kenyatta's political career until 1961. From 1931 to 1946, he lived in England, and from 1952 he was in detention."[13] This reality cushioned him from close interaction with the nationalists in Kenya and enhanced his heroism without any real scrutiny of his predisposition and capabilities. All through the colonial era, other nationalists sacrificed for his sake, stepped down to let him take leadership and even postponed crucial political developments awaiting his release or using it as leverage to fight for his release.

Consequently, an exaggerated version of Kenyatta's popularity in Kenya grew, which at independence became the "object of an official campaign of adulation."[14] A form of emperor-worship engulfed the personality of Kenyatta such that even when in 1952 he denounced and condemned Mau Mau as having "spoiled the country," this did not have any lasting negative effect on him and his political career. At Kiambu in August 1952, he asked those who were against Mau Mau to raise their hands and the "response was immediate and unanimous."[15] But evidence seems to point to the fact that Kenyatta may not have been the radical or Pan-Africanist he was made out to be.

For example, reports of Kenyatta's Moscow years indicated that he shunned revolutionary talk and was never convinced of the correctness of revolutionary struggle.[16] He seemed to have more respect for bourgeois habits and looked at the Soviet Union with cynicism. His comrades in London also had negative comments on him, especially insofar as the ideals of Pan-African brotherhood go. As such, Kenyatta of the colonial era was a mythical creation and his true self began to emerge late into the colonial period. His undemocratic and dictatorial tendencies, for instance, were first seriously hinted at by W. W. Awori, the Vice President of KAU, who resigned his position in August 1947 "claiming that Kenyatta had become a dictatorial leader of the party."[17]

On becoming the first head of independent Kenya, he instituted a personalized regime that rotated around him and an inner cabinet popularly referred to as "the family." By 1978, when he died, the Kenyan state had been transformed and formed in his dictatorial and illegitimate image. It was by and large a Kenyatta state. Indeed, "a lot of the politics in the country [came to] revolve around [Kenyatta's] political style."[18] The stability of Kenya during the Kenyatta era lay not in the respect people accorded him, but because of the regime he built. The cornerstones of the state he established laid in the balance within the military, the centralization of power within state structures and neutralization of potential foci of organized opposition.[19] Compared to Moi, Kenyatta would appear more organized and less authoritarian, but this misses out the essential continuity between these two regimes. That is, the systematic imprint of his personality that Kenyatta left to the institution of the presidency at the expense of other arms of government. It was this personality that Moi replaced, but he used the structure Kenyatta inhered to the institution to further plunder the country and render it largely illegitimate.

Thus, the problem with the state in Kenya is not one of either Kenyatta, Moi or Kibaki, but rather, it is a systemic problem of how the presidency has come to construct the state. It is the overall system that has laid out structures that allowed both Kenyatta and Moi and their cronies to plunder, exploit and repress Kenyans into silence and muted submission between 1969 and 1991. The seemingly imminent systemic breakdown of the late 1980s, which would have heralded state collapse, backlashed into allowing concerted resistance to presidential authoritarianism and economic mismanagement. It achieved some victories in the early 1990s with the re-introduction of multiparty politics. But, as we shall argue, this was not enough to reestablish the state as the legitimate structure of power in Kenya.

The colonial state was never radically transformed to accommodate Africans of all social standing before the law. Rather the rules and structures of the colonial state were largely retained in the Kenyatta era, and often proved very useful in the Moi era. Even some of the gains made with decolonization were reversed in the interest of one-person rule that Kenyatta created in Kenya. Some of these gains included the opening of democratic space for popular expression and competitive electioneering. This space was steadily constricted as Kenyatta transformed himself from prime minister into executive president. This involved coercing the Kenyan African Democratic Union (KADU) party into joining the Kenyan African Nationalist Union (KANU) and instituting a one-party rule. It is from the one-party rule that one-man dictatorship emerged and Kenya was turned into a de facto one-party state. Attempts to form other parties were defeated through the executive powers of the president until 1991.

Political competition in independent Kenya was construed to imply challenge to the person of Kenyatta. This bordered on treason, because the president was above the law. Kenyatta was not to be challenged by anyone given the official myth that lauded him as *Mzee* (the old man), whose wisdom was all encompassing, and as a father figure as the founder of the nation. Indeed, given the power of the presidency, Kenyatta became increasingly intolerant to criticism, a fact that made his leadership actions not only unaccountable but also binding. As Throup and Hornsby posit, "Jomo Kenyatta was a symbol of Kenya's independence and nationhood, a leader whom no one could criticize, the founding father of both nationalist politics and the nation."[20] In his office were powers not only to appoint his vice-president, ministers, parastatal heads, chief military and police officers and the electoral commission but also the powers to fire them without recourse to anybody or any advice.

The president was accountable to no one in particular. That is why on some occasions, as if to demonstrate the extent of his power, Kenyatta publicly told ministers and members of parliament (MPs) to keep quiet and toe the line. In March 1974, he reminded ministers that he had nominated them and instructed them "should any of them become disobedient, I will kick them out."[21] Later in 1975, it was MPs who were on the firing line following their outbursts concerning the murder of J. M. Kariuki. Kenyatta warned those who did not toe the line that he would crush them "like a hawk among the chickens."[22] As if to make good his promise, within two years of Kariuki's death, Martin Shikuku, J. M. Seroney and George Anyona were arrested, some even within the precepts of parliament in complete contravention of the Parliamentary Powers and Privileges Act. This action indicated that the legislature tumbled in the presence of the executive.

What made the legislature less powerful in the presence of the executive was the fact that many of the parliamentarians also owed much to the president for their positions than to elective mandate. To underline the irrelevance of the voters to the tenure of some MPs, Mbiyu Koinange, Kenyatta's brother-in-law and Minister of State in charge of security, used to tell the electorate in Kiambaa Constituency that, after all, he did not need their votes to go to parliament. He needed only two voters: those of Kenyatta and his wife, Mama Ngina.[23] Thus, while it was true that a level of free competition for parliamentary office was maintained in Kenyatta's days, this was only so if the said aspirant was in good books with Kenyatta and his inner circle of which Koinange and Dr. Njoronge Mungai were members. The plight of Oginga Odinga is enough to indicate that freedom was circumscribed within the acceptable limits set by Kenyatta and "the family." The parliamentarians would not dare challenge Kenyatta on crucial issues for fear of losing their seats and the economic resources that access to parliament assured. Indeed, the president also had powers to dissolve, summon and prorogue parliament just like he had in relation to the cabinet.

But perhaps one of the main pillars of the state built by Kenyatta was the provincial administration and the bureaucracy. This administration and bureaucracy were colonial both in design and, to some degree, in content. Until 1975, the Africanization policy had been done cautiously without seriously altering the basis on which the colonial state was built and maintained. For instance, the chief's act remained and was only seriously reviewed in 1997. The provincial administration became a state agent in the provinces with devolution of their powers following very closely on the British colonial style. The province was headed by the provincial commissioner (PC), the district commissioner in the district, the district officer in the division, the chief in the location, the sub-chief in the sub-location and the *Liguru* in the village.

The above structure of state power was as colonial as it could be, getting worse in independent Kenya because the lower-ranked officers were mainly poor old men (they were mostly men) with little traditional customary authority. They also existed in a period when gerontocratic authority was becoming less recognized. As such, they invoked the force of state power to enforce and maintain compliance. The *Liguru* was, for instance, not a government officer with recognized remuneration. To fend for himself, he relied on crude, corrupt and illegal means to earn a living. Some of these crude means included confiscating valuables from poor and ignorant villagers when they failed to heed the call to pay tax, to contribute to *harambee* or when they were caught with traditional liquor, a product that ironically is illegal in Kenya. At other times, he extracted rewards from both willing and unwilling villagers using the threat of force. The *Liguru* was the overt sign of Kenyatta's or Moi's presence and power in the village while the sub-chiefs and chiefs assumed similar powers in their respective jurisdictions. Coupled with the fact that many of them rose to those positions through corrupt means and that there was no legitimating contract with the villagers over whom they ruled, they abused their positions with impunity. Consequently, "the chief signifie[d] power that is total and absolute, unchecked and unrestrained."[24] Just as the powers of the president were abused at the national level, that of the chief or sub-chief or *Liguru* was equally abused at the local level. Indeed, at the lower location, sub-location and village levels, the state was consequently translated into an illegitimate structure of power that had to be dodged because of its oppressive, coercive, extractive and exploitative nature.

Kenyatta asserted, "civil servants are not impartial. They are KANU civil servants."[25] He demanded their loyalty and in turn constituted them into a party organ. Both civil servants and provincial administrators translated state policy into action at their respective levels. To these officials were attached state security agents who ensured not only compliance through threat or use of force, but also that what happened at this lower level was keenly reported to the center of the state. For their duties, they were heavily rewarded through allocation of state land and related economic rewards. Some held multiple state appointments, a fact that made their dedication to duty and service to citizens unsatisfactory. Public malfeasance emerged and developed partly as a result of this.

What further complicated this picture was that the provincial administration and strategic positions in the bureaucracy were heavily ethnically partial to the favor of the Kikuyu, Kenyatta's community. By the time of Kenyatta's death, four out of the eight PCs were Kikuyu.[26] In 1974, seven out of the twenty cabinet ministers were Kikuyu and five of these seven were from Kiambu, Kenyatta's home district. At the University of Nairobi, for example, then Kenya's only public university, "all the top ten administrative positions . . . were held by members of the Kikuyu community."[27] While in colonial times the army was composed mainly of the Kamba and Kalenjin, by 1967, 22.7 percent of the officers were Kikuyu.[28] So ethnicized was the provincial administration and strategic positions in the civil service that even the permanent secretary in charge of provincial administration was a Kikuyu. In 1970, there were nine Kikuyu permanent secretaries out of the total of twenty-two. The worst part was that their selection and posting were so irregular that even illiterate ones were posted to crucial positions.

There were also some presumed gains for the Kikuyu community when Kenyatta was the Head of State, which led to non-Kikuyu resentment of the Kikuyu. This resentment has been nurtured and allowed to develop to the extent that it keeps popping up regularly. The state, in this ethnicized politics, was construed to be helping those from whose community the president hailed. Other communities have to wait for their turn to occupy the state and "eat." The truth of the matter is that some people from the said community benefited. This can hardly be gainsaid. But the generalization that all people of that community benefited is inaccurate at best. The irony is that even in the context of this reality—that not all the people from the Kikuyu community benefited from the Kenyatta state—however, a feeling of attachment to a Kikuyu-controlled state developed to unprecedented levels and that "most

Kikuyus . . . still regarded the presidency as their legitimate inheritance and guarantee to their privileged position."[29]

Ethnicity consequently developed into a crucial resource that defined the state in Kenya both in the Kenyatta and Moi eras. The politicization of ethnicity developed to dangerous levels in which stakes over historical incidents of injustice especially on land issues were squared in the Moi era. Ethnicity also became a basis of social exclusion, since access to job opportunities, property, state contracts, and so on, was determined in many instances on this basis. It is important to point out, for example, that as part of the state construction of patronage networks in the Kenyatta era, favored people were pampered and rose through the ranks basically because of ethnic affiliations. The example of Waruhiu and Muite Advocates, a firm owned jointly by Paul Muite and George Waruhiu, is apt for two reasons. First, it illustrated the ethnic posture of patronage in Kenya, since these two lawyers are Kikuyu. Second, it demonstrated the extent to which the political opposition in Kenya, like elsewhere in Africa, was constituted by people guilty of installing the dictatorship and corruption they claimed to fight.

Waruhiu and Muite Advocates monopolized lucrative government and parastatal briefs in the Kenyatta era and enjoyed close association with the Kikuyu political establishment, a fact that made Muite, an opposition parliamentarian during the Moi era, extremely unpopular in the Law Society of Kenya.[30] It is in this illustrative example that one can locate the difficulty the opposition has had in effecting change to make the Kenyan state relevant, because many of the opposition legislators were part of the system that installed the illegitimate regime.[31]

An important component of the state structure in the Kenyatta era was the external context of the Cold War, a factor that made the international constituency uncritically supportive of and less stringent with the Kenyatta regime. The international constituency was guided by American Cold War diplomacy that led them "to embrace any dictator who joined [them] in [their] fears [of] communism."[32] In Kenya, American diplomacy aided Kenyatta in his fight against Oginga Odinga and the latter's eventual suspension from KANU. U.S. Ambassador William Attwood was directly involved in ensuring that Kenyatta followed American directions. He did not bother with the state's record on human rights, justice, freedom, accountability, transparency, corruption and related issues. These have now become the superficial catch phrases in the new world economic dispensation. Rather, democracy at the moment was seen in terms of making sure that communism did not find its way into East Africa through Kenya. It is this international context that cushioned Kenyatta, but played the opposite role during the Moi era, at least in the late 1980s and 1990s.

The Moi State and Further Slippage into Illegitimacy

If the strong imprint of the personality of the president characterized the state in the Kenyatta era, then presidential powers were not reduced following the ascension to power of Moi. Rather, the person of Moi took over that of Kenyatta in defining state operations in Kenya. Initially, Moi consolidated his rule trying in every instance to legitimize his leadership and reconcile the numerous forces jostling for the presidency prior to Kenyatta's death. Between 1978 and 1982, Moi was very successful and made enormous gains in cementing unity and prosperity. He preached continuity, captured in his slogan of *Nyayo*, which simply meant following in the footsteps of Kenyatta. *Nyayo* came to be elevated in daily political talk to a philosophy whose basic ingredients were peace, love and unity. For some time, Moi achieved a feat that few thought he would, and in this convinced many analysts that he was set to improve on the path laid down by Kenyatta—that of "one-party democracy."

But inherent in Moi's slogan of *Nyayo* was an element of change that few perceived early enough. As Morton has demonstrated, "while the country's new leader promised to follow in the footsteps of the late President, he implied that there would be change within that continuity."[33] It must be stressed that Moi was Kenyatta's vice president for eleven years. He saw and learned Kenyatta's leadership tactics. Again, Morton seems to have perceived this correctly when he posited "his [Moi's] eleven-year apprenticeship as Vice-President was sufficient training, giving an unparalleled insight into the *realpolitik* and personalities of Kenyatta's ruling elite."[34] The few years between 1978 and 1982, when he was popular both within and without, could be said to have been his years to consolidate his personality within the Kenyan state and eliminate potential foci of opposition like Kenyatta before him.

During these years (1978 and 1982), Moi emphasized the need to curb corruption, reallocate grabbed land, clean up the cabinet, serve *wananchi* (citizens) to their satisfaction, deal with tribalism and enhance the image of KANU being the party that fought and won independence. In many of these endeavors, he enjoyed the goodwill of the Kenyan masses and indeed became very popular for lifting the harsh, criminal rule Kenyatta had installed. The state created in the image of Moi became popular and people identified with it even more than when populist moves were made to win Kenyans. In those early years of his rule, Moi pronounced free education at the primary school level and, to encourage those from disadvantaged backgrounds, he provided free milk for primary school children. This has been construed to imply that he was in fact targeting his Rift Valley communities whose participation in education was low at the time.

The Moi regime started facing problems when evidence of failing economic management of state resources and their allocation became very clear. This was as much governance as it was a political issue. While Kenyatta comparatively left professionals to handle such issues, so long as they did not pose any challenge to him, Moi did not seem to have paid specific attention to people's specialties and qualifications before appointing them to such technical and crucial areas. In the long run, the legislature, executive, judiciary and, most importantly, the bureaucracy were led by ignorant, inept and at times illiterate officers. Many of them presided over high levels of public malfeasance and corruption. They constituted one reason for state failure, since poor economic performance and questionable delivery of public services were traced to such inept officers. However, one cannot overlook Lonsdale's plausible argument that "Kenyatta was a lucky President in terms of the world economy, Moi unlucky."[35]

The international economy in the Kenyatta days favored a state that was intrusive in the daily running of public affairs and allocation of resources. This arose from a form of Keynesian economic thinking that came with the end of World War II and helped install Fordism. Such a form of government existed until the 1970s, when the oil shocks and rising rates of inflation introduced conservative regimes in Britain, Germany, the United States and Canada. These were under Margaret Thatcher, Helmut Kohl, Ronald Reagan and Joe Clark respectively. This configuration of forces dovetailed neatly with the rising importance of the notion of efficiency and market reform that gained ground as a result of the evident slumps in the world economies and growing illegitimacy of many local African states.[36]

Trends toward economic crises were inherent in the world economy prior to Moi's ascension to power in 1978. According to Holmquist et. al., the economy slowed down in the late 1970s. The oil shocks of 1973 and the growing inflation witnessed significant growth rates though these were at lower rates than in the 1960s. Further, being in the nick of the Cold War, "foreign aid was generous from Western donors who saw Kenya as an anti-communist bulwark in the uncertain political and strategic arenas of East and Central Africa." As late as 1972, British support for the regime was still a crucial component of foreign policy and this cushioned the Kenyatta regime from harsh economic realities that were gathering storm toward his death in 1978. "The oil shocks of 1973 and 1978, soft foreign markets for exports, inflation in the West raising the cost of imports, declining inflows of foreign private capital, growing foreign debt, and high interest rates, all made it increasingly difficult to maintain a large state sector and juggle political tensions generated by the economic sectors and ethnic calculations as a strategy of rule."[37]

By 1982, the fragility of the state in Kenya was increasingly becoming apparent as the attempted coup revealed. Political tensions were contained in the rising direct and indirect opposition to the Moi regime. Direct opposition came from sustained challenges to its policies of reform from the Kenyatta ones. Rich Kikuyu bourgeoisie who felt orphaned by the absence of Kenyatta largely engineered this opposition. It crystallized in movements like Mwakenya and in the university where leftist arguments were fronted in support of democracy. Indirect opposition came through tactics aimed at undermining the regime through heightened levels of corruption in the bureaucracy, further land grabbing in strategic areas, subversion of popular policies and a general inefficiency that illustrated that the state was losing control. Moi confessed in his biography that his trusted technocrats and politicians let him down on numerous occasions. But rather than get better and well-meaning officers and leaders, Moi embarked on greater personalization of power in his own hands after 1982.

After the 1982 coup attempt, Moi felt that "his magnanimity had not been reciprocated by his colleagues."[38] Following the coup attempt, "the conflicting advice he had received from experts taught him to trust such counsel less and listen harder to the mood of the country. Moi came to admit that he had allowed others, notably Charles Njonjo, G. G. Kariuki and other State House insiders, to establish a cordon sanitaire around him, which left many influential voices, particularly from Luoland, out in the cold. Politically, the days of easy-going camaraderie and collective decision-making . . . abruptly ended."[39] Unfortunately, trust seems to have been replaced by loyalty to the person of the president and collective decision-making replaced by individual decision-making. These have certainly not acted for the better of Kenyans.

To begin with, one-person rule intensified to levels previously unknown in Kenya. These began with the introduction of a bill in parliament that made Kenya a de jure one-party state in 1982. The manner in which the bill was drafted and passed in parliament was extremely unprocedural. Furthermore, those who were responsible for this bill spoke volumes about the role and potential of the Kenyan opposition at that time in effecting radical state reform if elected. They included Paul Muite and Mwai Kibaki. Muite, then Njonjo's lawyer, drafted the bill, while Kibaki, then leader of government business in the National Assembly (now the new President of Kenya), ran through the process in a record forty-five minutes; and the bill was passed.

Both Oginga Odinga and George Anyona, who attempted to form a rival party to KANU at the time, were detained. The Preventive Detention Act was invoked, having been introduced in 1966. From then onward, numerous persons were either detained without trial or were forced into exile. The space for free expression, speech and association was further constricted since then. Challenge to the government was viewed as challenge to Moi and was heavily punished. The mechanisms for punishment were many, but the KANU Disciplinary Committee formed in January 1986 became the notorious one. Since

KANU was the only legally acceptable party, aspiring politicians were denied nomination once they were perceived to be anti-government (read: anti-Moi). In a very big way, Moi became the government and the government Moi.

Between 1982 and 1988, fear and self-censorship became the norm. The network of the state's special police spying branch was spread wide and far as each market and village was full of government spies. Fear became synonymous with the Moi state at the time. KANU further surpassed parliament in importance, as it screened and determined who was eligible for election on KANU's ticket, the only ticket. Moreover, statements made in parliament could be used by the KANU Disciplinary Committee to punish so-called errant MPs. As a result, new heights were reached in terms of parliamentary subordination to the ruling party, KANU. By 1989, expulsions from KANU were the norm, curtailing many people from seeking elective mandate and competition because there was only one mandated party, KANU, on whose ticket parliamentary vote could be sought.

The Moi regime also went a step further in centralizing state power in the presidency: In 1987, Moi moved in on the judiciary with a constitutional amendment that sought to remove the security of tenure of High Court Judges, the Attorney General and the Auditor General. All these put the judiciary at the mercy of the president because in the event of disobedience to state (read: presidential) orders, the judge would be sacked. The judiciary was extensively affected because, then and onward, it has never been impartial in politically sensitive cases. At some point, foreign judges were employed and, given the contractual basis of their terms, they became outrightly partial. These issues were documented fully in the initially critical *Nairobi Law Monthly* magazine. To be sure, this magazine later on ceased to be critical of the KANU government, a further comment on how temporary and inconsistent the opposition to Moi was. The abuse of the judicial system seemed to have peaked in the era of Chief Justice Allan Hancox, which started in 1989. Hancox was evidently partisan and on occasions condemned lawyers especially the Law Society of Kenya (LSK) for being anti-government. He asked them to be loyal to the president; the position of the LSK was that they only needed to be loyal to the Constitution of Kenya.[40]

By compromising the judiciary, the overt expression of authoritarianism of the Kenyan state became more manifest as channels of redress over injustice were sealed. The state and its agents became the creator, dispenser and guarantor of justice. Democracy can be operationalized differently in diverse contexts, but there are cardinal issues that it must embody at any time. These are the "basic principles of inclusion, participation, freedom, justice and equity for all who find themselves in any of our African countries at any given time."[41] Justice is put in operation by allowing aggrieved parties to seek redress on issues over which they feel justice has either been delayed or denied. By closing down avenues of impartial arbitration over political and economic disputes, the Moi government, in a manner akin to the Banda regime in Malawi, sought to constantly monitor, manipulate and mutilate words, to impose silence and to build a nation where, to paraphrase and quote Zeleza, only the monotonous story of *Nyayo's* achievements was told and retold—"a state of dull uniformity that criminalized difference, ambiguity, and creativity, an omniscient regime with a divine right to nationalize time and thought, history and popular will."[42] It is in this context that KANU was deified—when on occasion songs were composed specifically and exclusively for the president and religious tunes were adopted as military marching tunes.[43] In this, state agents like the PCs, DCs, DOs and chiefs accumulated enough extralegal extortionist powers that made the state have questionable relevance at the grassroots level and susceptible to the downward trend of collapse.

In the wake of such constricted political space, the plunder of the economy intensified in earnest. Most of the state corporations were put under unqualified heads as part of the tokens from political patronage. Agriculture was seriously affected, since the National Cereals and Produce Board, the state cooperation dealing with buying and marketing cereals, especially maize and wheat, made significant loses during the years 1978 and 1979. According to one anonymous writer,[44] the board was characterized by poor storage facilities, expensive middlemen and a virtual monopoly over the movement of Kenya's staple cereal maize from the producer to the market. Between February 1978 and July 1979, nearly 200,000 tons of maize was exported at a loss of Kshs. 165 million. This was at the crucial time when drought and economic crisis were looming. Other state marketing boards did not fare well during the same era. They included the Kenya Meat Commission, the Kenya Co-operative Creameries and the Coffee Board of Kenya to name but only these few.

It should be added, however, that all of the economic crises especially in agriculture couldn't be blamed exclusively on the government of President Moi. As indicated earlier, the *Nyayo* era was ushered in amidst "significant economic constraints." Kenya's rate of GDP growth had dropped from 6.5 percent average for the period 1964–1972, to 4.7 percent for the period 1972–1977.[45] Both internal and external factors decelerated the rate of growth in Kenya. The oil shocks of 1973 and 1979 led to a general world recession that had its negative impact on the Kenyan economy. Internally, the 1979–1980 droughts, the growing national population and the inability to convert the large arable land into productive use, plus the poor translation of projected policy initiatives into actual results, all worked to provoke economic crisis. The Kenyan economy was also too extroverted, relying mainly on multinationals and a large-holder export sector of which the state was the creator and protector.[46] In consequence, the Kenyan government came to rely much more on external aid, a fact which opened it further to external manipulation.

All these factors had their toll climaxing in 1988 when, during the elections, undemocratic party election procedures were employed by KANU both in the primaries and in the general elections. These elections were conducted in an atmosphere full of state repression, suspicion, and silence. The party adopted not only the queue voting method but also allowed all those who got over 70 percent of the total votes in the party primaries to go to parliament unopposed. During the primaries, many popular leaders were rigged out through unscrupulous means. The election also witnessed massive rigging in which the provincial administration was used against candidates disliked by the state. The provincial administration was generally a Moi administration, which meant that no impartiality could be expected in the elections. The rigging was blamed on the provincial administration and feigned ignorance of Moi. It is doubtful that Moi was completely ignorant of this widespread rigging.

The consequence of all these developments was that the state became ineffective and illegitimate in a number of ways, especially in its redistribution and allocation of resources roles and its maintenance of a fair and just system of governance. Its major legitimating arms were under the direct control of the president and were used to rubber stamp decisions arbitrarily made elsewhere. The eighth parliament was such an institution that lacked considerable elective mandate. What the 1988 elections did was to push many popular leaders out of the legal political space and install stooges. In terms of competitive politicking, these parliamentarians could not compete since the general mass of Kenyans had popular leaders out of parliament.

As a result, a popular constituency was introduced out of the legal political space that posed grave dangers to the legitimacy of the regime. In particular, the legal profession and the church played such a role. Through the church, for instance, illegal but protected space was created for challenging the legitimacy of state power. The Moi regime's human rights record and failing economic policy were questioned. Such outdated laws like the Preventive Detention Act of 1966 and the Public Order Act (itself a colonial relic) were openly challenged from the safe though politically illegal space of the church. The church, funerals and the *matatu* were for some time popular sites where the state was challenged. These spaces were important because a license had to be obtained in order to hold a rally and this was acquired from respective officers within the provincial administration. Given that politicians considered to be anti-government could not access such a license and that the police was always at hand to unleash terror against rallies that had no such licenses, it became prudent to run away from state terror by holding rallies in safe places, like at funerals or in the church, where no license was required, given the sensitivity of the freedom of worship clause.

By the beginning of the 1990s, support for anti-state forces was overwhelming and the collapse of the Soviet Union and changes in Eastern Europe had ushered in new international thinking that could no longer guarantee support for illegitimate regimes like the Moi one at the time. Such support coalesced in the formation of pressure groups to demand political pluralism and democracy. The government was challenged on many fronts to account for its actions, to be transparent and accountable and to demonstrate strong commitment to inclusive economic and political policies. Its nonparticipatory nature was clearly at odds with the new local and international developments; its intrusive nature in economic processes was quickly questioned as being the reason why economic crises dotted the country. The end result was that the state had to be reformed to avoid further deterioration into collapse.

By the end of the mid-1980s, the need for state reform was apparent in Kenya. This arose from the growing illegitimacy of the occupants of state power who presided over corruption, nepotism, decaying economy, growing impoverishment, authoritarianism and so on. The centralization of state power was the main cushion that bolstered such illegitimate activities within the state. Such power was rarely legitimated through prudent planning and acceptable results. At the political level, no attempts were made to translate the *ability* to command into the *right* to command and demand obedience. In other words, power was not translated into authority. Reform, it ought to be emphasized, needed to be total, encompassing all sectors of the sociopolitical and economic realms of the country.

The criterion for the transformation of the state ought to have been a thorough overhaul of the networks that sustained illegitimacy in the Kenyan state both in the Kenyatta and Moi eras and not a piecemeal concern with individual leaders. The reform movement, controlled by an international system that had little interest in the mass of Kenyans, narrowly focused on piecemeal reform—beginning first with President Moi and his inner cabinet of conservative KANU leaders—and in the process missed the goal of total state reform as a way of making the state relevant. The consequence was to condemn the state by condemning the personality of Moi, and also to nurture a false hope that opposition legislators would have provided a worthy replacement to Moi. This hope had a checkered history, one that did not lend itself to consistency. It was a history that did not offer an alternative because it hoped to do away with Moi without destroying *Moism. Moism* like Mobutuism was encapsulated in the nature of the state in Kenya; hence, if the state during the post-Moi era has to be made relevant, then alternatives to Moism must be sought.

The ideas that have formed the gist of the reform debate rotate around the argument that African states, including Kenya, have failed to translate their enormous resources into gains for their citizens. Ironically, this thinking is touted mostly by Western donor agencies and governments. The Bretton Woods Institutions (BWIs) and dominant Western donor countries have embraced this thinking to the extent that shrinking the state is taken as the only alternative, if Africa has to attain development and assure her population the fruits of development. Isn't it ironic that for over three decades, the concern in international development has been on the relevance of the state to the African masses and all through the policies of development planning in the 1960s, basic needs in the 1970s, structural adjustment in the 1980s and now good governance in the 1990s, we are still concerned about the relevance of the state, even when SAPs in their most recent argument push for rolling back the state? Today, the state in Africa is actually rolled back to levels that it never has been before, yet we are still witnessing rising poverty, decay in economies and infrastructure and unfulfilled promises of democratization. The acute problems facing Africans at the moment are "mainly due to the decomposition of the African state."[47]

In Kenya, state reform was clearly a demand sustained since 1963. It became a real issue toward the end of the Kenyatta regime when, in 1969, Tom Mboya was assassinated, and in 1975 when J. M. Kariuki was murdered with the connivance of the Kenyatta regime. Expressions of discontent were evident in the streets of Kisumu and Nairobi. At that point, on March 21, 1975, Kenyatta was forced to demonstrate to the people of Kenya that military power would be invoked to stop the protest-prone people. In 1990, again as a result of the murder of Dr. Robert Ouko, Kenyans came out in large numbers to protest against the murderous Moi state. But precisely at this time, Kenyans were eagerly joined in their struggles by the international forces. The alliances drawn between the masses and the international community appeared, with the advantage of hindsight, to have been predicated on no common objective as to why the state had to be reformed.

The international community, represented locally by the economic powerhouses of BWIs and multinationals, derived its logic of reform from the recessions occurring in the international economy. This recession had been building for long and it was essentially generated by the economically strong countries of the West. To take care of the crises, a reversal of roles and responsibilities took place where the weight of reform was removed from the shoulders of the economically strong and placed on those of the economically weak. The secrecy with which these (reform) programs were designed and the authoritarianism with which they were implemented reinforced the sense of siege and imperial onslaught the programs were locally conceived to entail.[48] The programs diagnosed the problems in Africa as irresponsible monetary and fiscal policy, indiscriminate allocation of resources and rent-generating resources without any guarantee of reciprocal action by recipients, failure to maintain physical infrastructure, negligence of markets as an effective means of resource allocation, failure to promote agriculture and, lastly, failure to introduce policies to support diversification of exports.[49]

In essence, the donor argument was that the state in Africa has failed and generated economic crises through "misguided policies and pervasive interventions." Its capacity for policy analysis and implementation is captive to anti-development forces within society. Robert Bates talked of the urban-bias thesis and argued that an urban coalition held sway over the state and oriented policy against the rural productive enterprise. Other scholars based in American universities pushed forward similar arguments but clothed them in catchy phrases and derogatory epithets—their analytic value and familiarity with the continent was questionable.[50] Around these faulty arguments came the prescriptions on the new path that African states needed to adopt. A quick prescription was renewed faith in the role of the market in resource allocation. This called for rolling back the state since it had "proved" ineffective and illegitimate. The state in Africa was roundly condemned and, in its place, calls were made to strengthen civil society, at the time conceptualized as the bastion of liberty and democracy.[51] State reform in most of Africa was to follow the directives issued by the BWIs, and Kenya was no exception. In particular, the call for privatization and liberalization predominated.

Governance was the most important reform every African state was forced to undertake in the 1990s (this trend still continues), though mainly as an afterthought. Governance is supposedly designed to reform the process of managing public affairs to allow for greater freedom, competition, ensure human rights and generally democratize in all conceivable ways. Further disbursement of aid has come to rely on these conditions of greater freedom and democracy. In a narrow manner, democracy was consequently measured in terms of political pluralism and thus the constant holding of competitive party elections was used to gauge the growing relevance of the state. Unlike other states, like Liberia, Zaire (DRC), Uganda, Somalia and Sudan, Kenya has had a very stable post-independence history. Except for isolated instances, Kenya is one of the few African countries that has held periodic elections on a relatively competitive basis since independence. Its post-independence economic record had been impressive compared with many African countries. Its delivery of services to the citizens has been comparatively good until recently when the combined effect of reforms, public malfeasance and internal corruption have greatly constrained its ability to deliver. But this record is underpinned by large doses of external non-African input.

The relative illegitimacy of the Kenyan state was therefore exacerbated by the alliance between external forces opposed to the Moi regime with internal opposition dominated mainly by rich and largely ethnically constituted bourgeois. While these forces aimed to fight a regime whose legitimacy was increasingly lost, they seem to have further reinforced this illegitimacy. The opposition was made up of people brought together not by their love for democracy and justice, but rather people who felt threatened by the policies pursued by the state under Moi, policies that excluded them from the center of state power. The struggle shifted from democracy for the people to state power for the excluded elite. The external forces were not happy with internal affairs in Kenya and rallied behind the only available excuse to intervene. The American interest was clearly demonstrated in 1984 through the writings of Robert I. Rosberg of the Massachusetts Institute of Technology. He wrote that outside observers "blame a leadership that is highly centralized, ethnically divisive, and visibly corrupt for Kenya's lack of direction and slump in morale." He insisted that the United States should "rethink the security of its strategic alliance with a Kenya that is as fragile as it was once thought unthinkable."[52]

Clearly, the alliance between external and internal forces had no common objective. While the donor community was undergoing serious ideological transformation necessitating the restructuring of peripheral states to open up economies to international capital and requiring less government obstruction to the flow of hegemonic capital, internal concerns centered on routing Moi from the presidency. This, unfortunately, was soon equated to reform. None other than the North American scholar Larry Diamond, then attached to the Hoover Institute at Stanford University, in fact predicted the end of President Moi. In a conversation with a Kenyan scholar in 1993, Diamond said, "the Moi regime will not last three years." This exuberance was motivated by the fact that on his way to Kenya, Diamond passed through Washington, DC, and in his own words, "the donor countries, I was told, will not give you a penny because your elections were rigged."[53] Certainly, the idea of reform as evidenced in the conjuncture between external and internal opposition was ill defined.

In Kenya, the internal opposition came to coalesce around a fragile alliance that was united by the mere need to remove Moi from the presidency. This opposition lacked a program beyond their commonality of grievances against Moi. Their abnormal fixation on the incumbent president was best expressed in the opposition slogan of "Moi Must Go." At rallies, in conferences, during street demonstrations, at press conferences and even deputations to metropolitan countries, this abnormal fixation on the incumbent president was easily equated to state reform; and Moi's removal seen not only as a precondition for reform but in most cases as reform itself.

The then–U.S. ambassador to Kenya, Smith Hempstone, who was clearly anti-Moi, fronted the external initiative. He clothed his arguments in terms aimed at translating global neoliberal transformations into practical applications locally. This thinking strove to impose ideas of market reform and good governance with the attendant conditionalities for aid disbursement as cardinal ingredients of state reform. In May 1990, while addressing Kenyan businessmen, Hempstone stated, "the United States would give preference in its grants of foreign aid to those countries which nourished democratic institutions, defended human rights and practiced multiparty politics."[54] Indeed, in the same year, the U.S. Congress asked the Bush administration to defer $7 million in economic support and $8 million in military support. In September 1991, Denmark froze all new aid to Kenya, while in November 1991, the Paris Club, which includes most donor countries, deferred for six months the commitment of aid to Kenya for the 1992 calendar year "pending progress on political and economic reforms in the country."[55] There was unrestricted genuflection among sections of the opposition elite in Kenya as further conditions were spelt out to the Moi government.

But despite the concerns on economic issues, the immediate demands of external donor countries centered on competitive elections, which, they hoped, would have translated into a defeat of Moi. They consequently came to insist on pluralistic politics as an important component of democratization. In the words and deeds of foreign stakeholders, the message was "open up the political space for more parties and the economy for private investors." Smith Hempstone pointed this out in the following words:

> What we do care about, and we care about it a great deal, is that the political process should be free and fair because only when the government of the day enjoys the genuine mandate of the people can there be peace, stability and progress. And that, and only that, is what the U.S. government wants for Kenya.[56]

As Throup and Hornsby argue, "Hempstone was merely enunciating opinions that were widely held in Congress."[57]

The donor community position differed slightly in emphasis from the position adopted by the BWIs that was largely on economic reform. Only later did they get concerned with good governance. The BWIs required that corruption should be halted and spending of foreign aid must be in a transparent and accountable manner. Many other requirements by these donors were bizarre to say the least and simply did not conform to the aim of ensuring a stable state. For instance, requirements concerning the downsizing of the civil service, reduction of expenditures on welfare services like education and health and the instituting of cost sharing all were punitive solutions in Africa. Also, concern was raised about conditions demanding provisions of an environment that was consistently supportive of private investment and initiative. In many ways, this appeared more like a euphemism for re-colonization than a way of introducing reform for the benefit of Kenyans. Furthermore, demands requiring the rolling back of the state failed to note that the "state remains, even as it changes its form and confronts new situations, one of the most important features of contemporary political organization."[58]

The consequence for the reform demands were evidenced in the immediate repeal of section 2(a) of the Kenyan Constitution on December 10, 1991, which had made Kenya a de jure one-party state. The pressure to introduce political pluralism in the form of more parties had won the day. Subsequent to this repeal, the assumption set in that, come elections, Moi would be trounced just like Kenneth Kaunda had been trounced by Frederick Chiluba in Zambia. This abnormal fixation on Moi had been the main factor that sustained the fragile unity in the opposition ranks. Once this unifying factor was removed through the repeal of section 2(a), the internal divisions within the opposition were revealed as it split into numerous parties. Ethnic suspicion, greed, personal ambition and the generation gap all acted to fragment the opposition to Moi as elections neared. Further, Moi's advantage of incumbency came in handy as he manipulated the electoral commission and the provincial administration, which, like Kenyatta, he declared was not impartial. He won the 1992 general elections.

Evidence suggests that most of the opposition demands for reform were driven by personal considerations. It is known, for instance, that most of the opposition politicians were in fact part of the team that helped Kenyatta and Moi to install personal dictatorship. Mwai Kibaki, for example, had defended Kenyatta's economic policy saying that Kenya will not pursue a policy of social justice at the expense of individual freedom, that is, the freedom to get rich.[59] Paul Muite was responsible for the drafting of the bill that turned Kenya into a de jure one-party state, a bill that Mwai Kibaki unprocedurally rushed through parliament in record time. Moreover, all through the struggle for reform, Kibaki was a fence-sitter, and he is noted for having castigated the opposition to KANU during the years of struggle. He only decamped from KANU when it was safe to do so.

With the advantage of hindsight, it was increasingly difficult to know exactly which politician was a trusted and consistent reformer in Kenya. Some of the formidable challengers to the Moi state like Paul Muite were accused of extorting money relating to Goldenberg scandal, a scandal that involved an enormous rip-off from Kenyan public coffers. Richard Leakey, Raila Odinga, George Anyona and Gitobu Imanyara (the editor of the then-critical *Nairobi Law Monthly*), on the other hand, were safely working with and defending the Moi regime making it difficult to trust any of them with the task of spearheading initiatives at making the state relevant. For external forces, their faith and consistency on pro-people reform remains questionable. In 1997, the BWIs stopped further aid to Kenya arguing that it needed to restore microeconomic stability and sustain fiscal balance. They also lambasted the Moi regime for being corrupt and demanded, inter alia, that the Goldenberg scandal should quickly be solved. A total of $205 million aid in Enhanced Structural Adjustment Facility was suspended pending clampdown on corruption and speedy reform in the public sector. But in 2000, the BWIs restored aid to Kenya, despite the fact that the requirements for which the aid was stopped in the first place were not met. Why, then, was aid to Kenyan withheld in the first place?

The basic problem in the relationship between the BWIs and the Kenyan opposition was the assumption by the latter and especially the print media that the interests of the donors were consistent with those of Kenyans. Whether this was feigned or real ignorance was not very difficult to establish; but the reality was that Kenya was spending too much time and resources trying to please the World Bank and the IMF to no avail. The World Bank and IMF are global financial watchdog organizations formed largely in the interests of the Western powers. They are watchdog institutions whose baseline interest is to police financial and investment flows in favor of clientele Western governments. Like any police agency, their work is done in great secrecy. That is why the World Bank never states how much profit it makes from Africa. Ultimately, the refusal, by both internal and external opposition to Moi—to concede that "no sustained resolution of the current African crisis is conceivable unless it addresses at the same time the roots of the crisis in the international capitalist order"[60]—made their reform initiatives suspect and dishonest.

The example from Zambia, where multiparty elections were held and the incumbent regime of Kenneth Kaunda was defeated, is an instructive reminder to Kenyans that multiparty elections per se do not guarantee democracy and state reform. Also, it is an instructive indicator that conforming to the BWIs' requirement is no guarantee of the relevance of the state in Africa. The people of Zambia did not experience any serious change from the economic crises and political repression of the Kaunda era even when they popularly elected Frederick Chiluba, and he went ahead to design a blueprint of reform that could as well have been written in Washington, DC. During the Chiluba regime, the levels of dictatorship increased and economic crisis assumed serious proportions. Even when the Movement for Multiparty Democracy declared Zambia a Christian nation, many of the ministers in the cabinet remained corrupt land grabbers and were involved in drug trafficking. Most of them were politicians frustrated out of the Kaunda regime. Some Zambians, frustrated by the post-Kaunda realities even suggested "running the country without a government for a while."[61]

The story of state reform and democracy does not look good from the dimension of BWIs either. As Mkandawire and Soludo argue, the World Bank cannot boast of any "demonstrated experience in structurally adjusting an economy to induce accelerated development."[62] Indeed, the reform policies have been riddled by ambiguity in industrial reform, poor guidance in financial reform and misleading theorizing in the social sector reforms of education and administration. Toward the end of 1999, a team of new technocrats imposed on President Moi by the BWIs was installed to reform the state and jumpstart the economy that was quickly grinding to a halt. But a cardinal fault of this method of state reform was the lack of local ownership of the reform package and process, which implied that the process lacked popular support among local stakeholders. Those who at one time supported the package later on regretted it in the face of unplanned privatization, laid-off workers, collapsed industries, high foreign exchange rates and inconsistent external demands on Moi. These were also the well-to-do Kenyans whose interest in reform was to get Moi out of the way. Implementation of reform also remained difficult because it was the extremely criminalized, demoralized, harangued and impoverished civil servants who had to implement the reform package. Some were even supposed to implement their own downsizing. By reducing the reach of the state, its ability to implement reforms was also limited. What is worse is that neither the donors nor players in Kenyan politics have thought it prudent that reform should be preceded by public debate, even if this would not be reflected in the policy to be adopted.

Elsewhere in Africa,[63] the role of the BWI-appointed bureaucrats has not been of any serious consequence and Kenya should learn its lesson. Some of these bureaucrats are actually handpicked by the World Bank and the IMF and are authoritarianly imposed on the assumption that they are better economic managers than those appointed from within the continent. Indeed, they are not subjected to competitive appointment procedures, a fact that defeats the donor faith in competition. Many of these technocrats have turned out to be real failures just like the Structural Adjustment Programs have failed. Apart from being political rejects by the electorate, some of these technocrats have not made any difference when appointed. Rather, some of them are known to preside over corruption or have been corrupt themselves. The World Bank and the IMF have been at the forefront as patrons imposing people who could never be popularly elected or competitively appointed but continued to preach the doctrine of free and fair elections and competitive appointment.

Faced with both domestic and international pressure, President Moi made the determination not to seek reelection in the 2002 national elections. President Moi's decision precipitated the intense joggling for position within KANU, the ruling party and the opposition. At the heart of the political tug and pull was the issue of a successor to Moi. As for the opposition, various political parties continued their vilification and demonization of the Moi regime as the centerpiece of their respective platforms. This approach was particularly biased and employed selected factors to argue for a democratic agenda in Kenya.[64] Eventually, a coalition of opposition parties coalesced around Mwai Kibaki, a former chieftain of KANU, who served in various cabinet positions and as the Vice President of Kenya under Moi. After several years of supporting authoritarianism in Kenya, Kibaki decamped from KANU and became a "reformer." Kibaki defeated the candidate of KANU and became the new president of Kenya on December 30, 2002.

Toward State Reconstitution in Kenya?

The Kibaki regime has committed itself to making the state relevant in Kenya by, among other things, addressing some of the major ills that have affected Kenya since its independence in 1960. One of the major ills is the culture of corruption. The Kibaki regime has established a new agency for ethics and government integrity as the bulwark against corruption. It is left to be seen how effective this agency would be in dismantling the ancien "culture of corruption."

Another problem the Kibaki regime has promised to address is the lack of the rule of law. Toward this end, a new Ministry of Justice and Constitutional Affairs has been established. This agency is supposed to serve as the regime's principal arm for ensuring the promotion of, and the respect for, the rule of law.

The Kibaki regime has indicated that judicial reforms would be a major preoccupation of the regime. In order to demonstrate its commitment, the Chief Justice Bernard Chunga was forced to resign. Chief Justice Chunga was criticized for been inept, corrupt and susceptible to influence peddling.

In the area of education, the new regime has also committed itself to the provision of free primary school education with the abolition of all school fees at that level. This policy is intended to create educational opportunities for Kenyans and to improve the country's literacy rate.

On the other hand, there are still other challenging issues such as the economy, basic human needs and constitutional reform. Particularly, the issue of constitutional reform was a major source of conflict within the coalition that brought President Kibaki to power. Recently, the coalition collapsed after failing to develop common policies on critical issues such as constitutional reform and other sectors.

Making the State Relevant: Some Prescriptions

The preceding discussion shows that since independence, growing authoritarian leadership and economic deceleration has, on the main, characterized the

Kenyan state. This has unleashed tendencies inimical to democracy and development, tendencies that have spawned human rights abuse, infrastructural and institutional decay, increased social pathologies especially in urban areas, poverty, disease and illiteracy among others. In such circumstances, to suggest means to reform and ensure state relevance, requires, first, that we acknowledge the enormity of the problem and, secondly, the fact that, already, state reform is underway, though deeply flawed. The reform that is underway is engineered by dominant global forces including donor agencies and countries and is essentially controlled by these very forces. These have arrogated unto themselves the prerogative of designing and implementing reform, with or without consultation with local players and have consequently insisted that local public agencies account directly to them. The source of the flaw in their reform package lies in the insistence that a certain kind of reform is the only feasible one—the one they suggest. The challenge therefore lies either in persuading or struggling for an inclusive reform package geared toward making the state relevant to the mass of Kenyans. In its present strategy of reform, such relevance is not assured.

Rights are not given on a silver platter. They are seized in the process of struggle against the dominant forces. The international community is hardly willing to sponsor inclusive reform initiatives that seek to empower local constituencies. African states must therefore be ready to struggle against numerous odds, to clean their internal mess in order to demand international recognition and respect. Thus, in order to reform and ensure relevance, one ought to recognize that the African state is not encumbered merely by local failure, but also regional and international conditions. To win against external forces, African states must be ready to reform internally as a means of creating greater relevance and support that will help them launch the struggle against the exploitative and oppressive international atmosphere. An interactive process needs to be encouraged from which Africa's enormous resources can be used for its autonomous development. The struggle to reform global thinking about Africa, already underway, needs to be enhanced and mechanisms put in place to ensure that homegrown solutions to African problems are hatched, nurtured and used. Reform at the global level needs to go hand in hand with internal reform in Kenya and Africa at large.

A major flaw in current neoliberal thinking that informs current knowledge on state reform in Kenya, as in Africa in general, has been the coupling of the state and the market, the political and the economic processes in the reform project. The consequent insistence that market forces can regulate economies and stabilize the macroeconomic environment has left too much to chance. Poverty, distortions and inequality characterize the Kenyan economic and political environment, and enforced deregulation has adverse consequences on state legitimacy and its ability to institute reform. Thus, the reform process that has insisted on rolling back the state and minimal state intervention in economic affairs fails to note that a strong and democratic, as opposed to an authoritarian, state is necessary for stability and efficiency. State legitimacy is crucial for sustained reform, equity in resource allocation, political efficiency and internal stability. Since the major component of ongoing reform has been to indiscriminately bash and criminalize the African state, the need for strengthening and stabilizing the state should be prioritized and the international community has a lot to contribute.

Internal state relevance cannot be established where no state worth its name exists in the first place. Relevance cannot be established where the external environment is consistently hostile to homegrown and pro-people policies and where disdain characterizes the perception of these very states.[65] African states need a supportive environment geared toward availing critical support for the development of internal self-reliance. Critical support does not mean support for authoritarian, corrupt and inefficient regimes but transparent and participatory regimes that are responsible to their citizenry. These are regimes that are inclusive and that empower the marginalized categories, not those that are responsive to personal whims and external interests. Thus, deregulation of economies must be predicated on the long-term aim of stabilizing the state as an important player in the national economy. It must be predicated on the assertion of control over the leaders by the people.

During the Moi regime, an instantaneous deregulation of the Kenyan economy caused untold suffering to the vulnerable categories. Increases in inflation with no attendant increase in wages, the rise in commodity prices and fall of prices for agricultural products, the rise on cost of import, collapse of local industries and increasing levels of unemployment, among other things, had significant implications on the levels of poverty in Kenya. There is a need, then, to ensure that any future deregulation is gradual and measured against real and perceived implications on the vulnerable. Poverty eradication should not have been the afterthought it was in structural adjustment. Local products and industries need to be protected from unfair competition from foreign and established companies. These should only be gradually opened to competition when they can compete. As it has been done, local industries have been made to compete with multinational companies that have a long-established history, adequate production capacity and whose products in the local Kenyan market are heavily subsidized by the metropolitan countries. Such companies do have a head start and that is not a perfect condition for market forces to regulate. Markets are not innocent arbiters from heaven but social realities subject to human manipulations. Markets are characterized by cutthroat competition and the younger and less established the industry, the less capable it is for competition to exist in a skewed environment. Consequently, the logic of markets as perfect remedies to distortions has been defeated by the unfair terms of trade, which deregulation allowed. This trend must be arrested and some state intervention and gradual deregulation allowed. A reformed state must be differentiated from a failed or incapacitated one and its strength in running daily affairs included as an essential component of making it relevant to Kenyans.

Internally, it is notable that the leadership in Kenya has not consistently pursued pro-people policies. The internal failure of the state in Kenya has arisen first, from uncommitted leadership; second, from anti-people policies: and third, from unrealizable promises and unfulfilled expectations touted during elections. Where design of policies has been pro-people, corruption, malfeasance, half-heartedness and lack of commitment have mired their translation into practical results. The relevance of the state is assured only if we target the hearts and perceptions of those entrusted with public policy and property. The nerve of the Kenyan leadership problem lies in the manner in which a difference has not been struck between the public and private domains. This imprecision has led leaders to willfully exploit public resources for private gain leaving public coffers poor and indebted to external donors. The difference between the public and private domains must be emphasized to the bureaucracy, the executive, judiciary, the legislature and all other sections of the Kenyan society, which seek rents from the leadership. It is the differentiation of the public from the private that holds the key to professionalism and state relevance in Kenya.

The process of disciplining the leadership, especially the executive leadership in Kenya must target three fronts; the executive itself, the wider Kenyan society and the external environment. A serious process of civic education needs to be developed that will make the wider Kenyan society realize that the perks that the political leadership provides fall excessively short of what would accrue from professional and efficient running of the state. Patronage can only be reduced if the wider society realizes that its members can exercise control over their leaders and justifiably demand their rights and dues. This way, shortcuts to provisions of services would be reduced since efficiency would herald quick and immediate availability of basic needs. An emancipated public is crucial to the introduction of professionalism, efficiency, stability and growth. This can be done through serious social engineering in education and related fields.

At the same time, there is a need to institute a new social contract between the governors and the governed in Kenya. This contract is best laid out in a constitution that mediates the diverse interests and struggles within any state. Constitutions are contracts that define the nature, structure and use of political power.[66] If we recognize that the (mis)use of political power has been the main problem in Africa that has corrupted political leadership, then a new contract that defines the use of power and establishes a culture where respect for these rules are enshrined in daily practice of the political communities and their constituencies is needed. This arrangement is cardinal to stabilizing relations within the political class and between it and the citizenry and will be an added advantage to the creation of professionalism in the bureaucracies.

But it must be recognized from the outset that the process of constitutional review and establishment of a culture of constitutionalism in Kenya has had several false starts since it was truly incepted more than four years ago. This process was riddled with suspicion, tensions and even violence. Since being forced to accede to constitutional review in 1997, the Kenyan state did not go into the process with a decisive resolve to develop a new social contract with Kenyans. Ihonvbere has characterized its approach as "tentative but carefully programmed and [includes] very slow concessions to constitutional reforms aimed at making no concrete changes in the constitutional compacts."[67] On the other hand, greed and self-interest drove those who were opposed to KANU. They were unwilling to open-heartedly negotiate through the process. Some of them were so obstinate and obdurate and were so driven by their hate of KANU and suspicion that KANU's track record did not lend itself to any goodwill. Often times, the KANU politicians outsmarted them through trickery and divisive propaganda making sections of the opposition to defect to the KANU side.

As occasions favored, sections of this opposition were unwilling to operate within the existing legal confines to review the constitution. Barkan and Ng'ethe perceived the dangers inherent in the extreme suspicion between the two sides when they warned that "the task will demand from all parties precisely the flexibility and readiness to give and take that are so conspicuously missing in Kenya's fractious political culture."[68] This made the review process less inclusive in the sense of the domination of the constitutional debate by the opposition-aligned urban lawyers. While not acknowledging it, it seems that such lawyers, like KANU, thought that the general Kenyan populace was too ignorant to participate in the debate. Though there were more reasons why KANU was reluctant about the constitutional review process, among them was that opposition-aligned urban lawyers could hardly be trusted to represent all Kenyans. They, like KANU, just did not have that positive history. Implicit in the argument of the protagonists in the constitution-review debate was an assumption that Kenyans "are too unsophisticated or too backward to understand how to articulate their problems, aspirations, and demands and present these for inclusion in national constitutions."[69] These groups hardly accepted this argument though close observation of their activities and utterances, especially during crises, revealed how low they placed the Kenyan masses.

Clearly, then, the process of developing a new social contract for Kenyans is, like all other reforms underway, deeply flawed. Kenyans and the national interest were missing in the struggle for constitution review. Though mass action in the streets ensured that KANU acceded to reform, the masses were simply instrumentalized for self-serving elite objectives. For one, constitutional review needs to proceed within the framework of the existing laws. Secondly, personal and sectarian interests ought to give way to national interests. Third, greater trust and resolve to negotiate must be introduced into the current process. It was because of a lack of trust and dialogue that the review process splintered into the religious leaders–led initiative dubbed Ufungamano review process and the Parliamentary Select Committee initiative. These initiatives needed to be reconciled for the process to have been credible and useful to Kenyans. This was because none of them could go its way and succeed without the mandate of Kenyans. Indeed, none of them had the full mandate of Kenyans because the former merely holds some moral but lacks legal legitimacy, while the latter had full legal but lacked a large dose of moral legitimacy. That is why the process of establishing a new social contract was preceded by suspicion, urban violence and hate rather than abating these social evils. The way ahead lies in dialogue and the promotion of the national interest. It consists in consulting all Kenyans and allowing for open debate. Objective reporting by the media is a crucial aspect of the construction of the new social contract. Such channels of disseminating information contributed to misinformation and partisanship, and these have to change for the better.

Beyond constitutional review lies the challenge of establishing a culture of respect for the contract and observance of the tenets it enunciates. This critical component is at the heart of making sure that the democratic gains made so far are observed and strengthened and respect for the rule of law and justice are maintained. A state that respects its own rules and laws and enforces them meticulously is a recipe for legitimacy and relevance. It requires dedication and responsibility to see through the development and nurturing of such a state. And the challenge rests not only on the leaders but also on the citizenry. Kenya is past the age where rights are demanded and duties and obligations avoided. A reciprocal process of demand of rights and observance of duties and obligations is crucial for state relevance. It is this reciprocity that one must ultimately emphasize as cardinal to state legitimacy and relevance in Kenya.

Conclusion

Using the Kenyatta, Moi and the new Kibaki regimes as the historical timeframes, this chapter has attempted to address three major issues: the roots and dynamics of state irrelevance in Kenya; the prospects for state reconstitution under the new Kibaki regime; and the offering of some prescriptions for making the Kenyan state relevant. In addressing the first issue, the chapter argues that state irrelevance in Kenya evolved from the authoritarian political system and its attendant derivative of the cult of the presidency. Under both Presidents Kenyatta and Moi, Kenya had a repressive political system that was dominated by the whims and caprices of the president. The problems created by authoritarianism were made worse by social and economic mismanagement and malaise.

Although the Kibaki regime has committed itself to the formulation and implementation of a reform agenda that would make the Kenyan state relevant, it is still too early to draw definitive conclusions about the regime's performance vis-à-vis the prosecution of the reform agenda and its consequent impact on the reconstitution of the Kenyan state. Given his past record as a feverent defender of authoritarianism in Kenya, President Kibaki would have to demonstrate over an appreciable amount of time that he is indeed a "reborn democrat," who is committed to the transformation of the Kenyan state.

Finally, the agenda for making the Kenyan state relevant must address several critical issues. The cult of the presidency needs to be dismantled. This is also important because the president needs to operate within the confines of the constitution and the laws. Much work needs to be done in the economic sector in order to address the problems of inequities in wealth, unemployment and the general low standard of living for the majority of Kenyans. In the social realm, basic human needs—like education and health—must be provided. This will help to reduce the high rate of poverty. The constitution must be reviewed with the aim of creating a new social contract between the governors and the governed in Kenya. The emergent new compact must be enforced and respected by all Kenyans—government officials as well as ordinary citizens.

Notes

1. Statement by Julius Ihonvbere at the African Leadership Forum Conference on Democratization of African Parliaments and Political Parties, at the Grand Palm Hotel, Gabarone, Botswana, July 13–15, 1998, www.democracy-africa.org/afrleader.htm.
2. I. W. Zartman, "Introduction: Posing the Problem of State Collapse," in *Collapsed States: The Disintegration and Restoration of Legitimate Authority*, ed. I. W. Zartman (Boulder, CO: Lynne Rienner, 1995), 8.
3. Zartman, "Introduction: Posing the Problem of State Collapse," 7.
4. G. M. Khadiangala, "State Collapse and Reconstruction in Uganda" in *Collapsed States: The Disintegration and Restoration of Legitimate Authority*, ed. I. W. Zartman (Boulder, CO: Lynne Rienner, 1995), 35.

5. See E. Wamba-dia-Wamba, "Democracy, Multipartyism and Emancipative Politics in Africa: The Case of Zaire," *Africa Development* 18, no. 4 (1993); E. Wamba-dia-Wamba, "Zaire: From the National Conference to the Federal Republic of the Congo?" *Development Dialogue: A Journal of International Development Cooperation*, no. 2 (1995), and his "Mobutuism after Mobutu: The Current Situation in the Democratic Republic of Congo," *CODESRIA Bulletin*, nos. 3 and 4 (1998).

6. A. Morton, *Moi: The Making of an African Statesman* (London: Michael O'Mara Books Limited, 1998), 230.

7. M. Mamdani, "State and Civil Society in Contemporary Africa: Reconceptualizing the Birth of State Nationalism and the Defeat of Popular Movements," *Africa Development* 15, nos. 3 and 4 (1990): 51.

8. Mamdani, "State and Civil Society in Contemporary Africa."

9. F. Furedi, *The New Ideology of Imperialism* (London: Pluto Press, 1994), 68.

10. Furedi, *The New Ideology of Imperialism*, 63.

11. Furedi, *The New Ideology of Imperialism*, 61.

12. F. Furedi, "The African Crowd in Nairobi: Popular Movements and Elite Politics," *Journal of African History* 14, no. 2 (1973): 282.

13. M. Tamarkin, "The Roots of Political Stability in Kenya," *African Affairs* 77, no. 308 (1978): 298.

14. Tamarkin, "The Roots of Political Stability in Kenya."

15. J. Kenyatta, *Suffering without Bitterness: The Founding of the Kenya Nation* (Nairobi: East African Publishing House, 1968), 52.

16. A. M. Pegushev, "The Unknown Jomo Kenyatta," *Egerton Journal* 1, no. 2 (1996): 191.

17. A. Assensoh, *African Political Leadership: Jomo Kenyatta, Kwame Nkrumah and Julius Nyerere* (Malabar, FL: Krieger Publishing Company, 1998), 56.

18. W. R. Ochieng', "Structural and Political Changes," in *Decolonization and Independence in Kenya, 1940–1993*, ed. B.A. Ogot and W. R. Ochieng' (Nairobi: East African Educational Publishers, 1995), 93.

19. Tamarkin, "The Roots of Political Stability in Kenya," 300.

20. D. Throup and C. Hornsby, *Multi-Party Politics in Kenya* (London: James Currey, 1998), 11.

21. Tamarkin, "The Roots of Political Stability in Kenya," 302.

22. Throup and Hornsby, *Multi-Party Politics in Kenya*, 20.

23. K. Wa Wamwere, *The People's Representative and the Tyrants of Kenya: Independence without Freedom* (Nairobi: New Concept Typesetters, 1992), 119.

24. M. Mamdani, *Citizen and Subject: Contemporary Africa and the Legacy of Late Colonialism* (Princeton, NJ: Princeton University Press, 1996), 54.

25. Tamarkin, "The Roots of Political Stability in Kenya," 307.

26. J. D. Barkan, "The Rise and Fall of a Governance Realm in Kenya," in *Governance and Politics in Africa*, ed. G. Hyden and M. Bratton (Boulder, CO: Lynne Rienner Publishers, 1992), 184.

27. D. Odipo, "Public Office and the Politics of Tribalism," *Sunday Standard* (January 10, 1999): 8.

28. Tamarkin, "The Roots of Political Stability in Kenya," 300.

29. M. Tamarkin, "From Kenyatta to Moi: The Anatomy of a Peaceful Transition of Power," *Africa Today* 26, no. 3 (1979): 22.

30. Throup and Hornsby, *Multi-Party Politics in Kenya*, 56.

31. See, J. O. Ihonvbere, "Where Is the Third Wave? A Critical Evaluation of Africa's Non-Transition to Democracy," *Africa Today* 43, no. 4 (1997).

32. S. M. Makinda, "Democracy and Multi-Party Politics in Africa," *Journal of Modern African Studies* 30, no. 4 (1996): 563.

33. Morton, *Moi*, 168.

34. Morton, *Moi*, 166.

35. J. Lonsdale, "The Political Culture of Kenya," in *Political Culture, Local Government and Local Institutions*, ed. B. F. Frederiksen and K. Westergaard, Occasional Paper No. 7 (International Development Studies, Roskilde University, Denmark, 1993), 100.

36. T. Mkandawire and C. C. Soludo, *Our Continent, Our Future: African Perspectives on Structural Adjustment* (Dakar: CODESRIA, 1999), 41.

37. Details gleaned from F. W. Holmquist et al., "The Structural Development of Kenya's Political Economy," *African Studies Review* 37, no. 1 (1994): 76, 79–80, 91, and 98.

38. Morton, *Moi*, 195.

39. Morton, *Moi.*

40. See *Nairobi Law Monthly*, no. 36 (September 1991).

41. T. A. Aina, "Reclaiming the Foundations of Democratic Development in Africa," paper presented at a Roundtable on International Policies, African Realities, hosted by Africa Policy Information Center (APIC) in partnership with the Economic Commission for Africa, www.africapolicy.org/rtable, 2000.

42. T. Zeleza, "Banishing Words and Stories: Censorship in Banda's Malawi," *CODESRIA Bulletin*, no. 1 (1996): 10.

43. *Nairobi Law Monthly*, no. 37 (October 1991): 17.

44. Anonymous, "Looters, Bankrupts and the Begging Bowl: Our Plundered Economy," *Race and Class* 24, no. 3 (1983): 280–81.

45. R. Maxon, and P. O. Ndege, "The Economics of Structural Adjustment," in *Decolonization and Independence in Kenya, 1940–1993*, ed. B. A. Ogot and W. R. Ochieng (Nairobi: East African Educational Publishers 1995), 153.

46. Holmquist et al., "The Structural Development of Kenya's Political Economy," 76.

47. R. Fatton Jr., "Civil Society Revisited: Africa in the New Millennium," *West Africa Review* 1, no. 1 (1999): 4, www.icaap.org/iuicode? 101.1.1.5.

48. T. Zeleza, "The Spatial Economy of Structural Adjustment in African Cities," in *Sacred Spaces and Public Quarrels: African Cultural and Economic Landscapes*, ed. E. Kalipeni and P. T. Zeleza (Trenton, NJ: Africa World Press, 1999), 47.

49. Mkandawire and Soludo, *Our Continent, Our Future*, 23.

50. T. A. Aina, "Globalization and Social Policy in Africa: Issues and Research Directions," CODESRIA Working Paper Series No. 6/96, Dakar, Senegal (1997): 51.

51. A. Olukoshi, *The Elusive Prince of Denmark: Structural Adjustment and the Crisis of Governance in Africa*, Research Report No. 104 (Uppsala: Nordiska Afrikainstitutet, 1998), 14–15.

52. Quoted in G. M. Munene, "Cold War Disillusionment and Africa," in M. Munene et al., *The United States and Africa: From Independence to the End of the Cold War* (Nairobi: East African Educational Publishers, 1995), 42.

53. H. Indangasi, "In the Company of Democrats," in *Writers Speak: Essays on Literature and Democracy*, ed. K. King'ei and H. Indangasi (Nairobi: Writers Association of Kenya, 1997), 40.

54. G. Muigai, "Kenya's Opposition and the Crisis of Governance," *Issue: A Journal of Opinion* 21, nos. 1–2 (1993): 26.

55. Muigai, "Kenya's Opposition and the Crisis of Governance," 28.

56. Quoted in S. W. Nasong'o, "Democratization and Human Rights Issues in Kenya: The Role of American Ambassadors William Attwood and Smith Hempstone," revised edition of a paper presented at the sixth regional conference on American Studies in Eastern Africa held July 8–12, 1997, 14.

57. Throup and Hornsby, *Multi-Party Politics in Kenya*, 73.

58. T. A. Aina, "Reclaiming the Foundations of Democratic Development in Africa," 39.

59. Tamarkin, "The Roots of Political Stability in Kenya," 312.

60. A. Sawyerr, *The Political Dimension of Structural Adjustment Programs in Sub-Saharan Africa* (Accra: Ghana Universities Press, 1990), 14.

61. J. O. Ihonvbere, "Political Pluralism and Crisis of Development in Africa: The Case of Zambia," *Hemispheres*, no. 10 (1995): 71.

62. Mkandawire and Soludo, *Our Continent, Our Future*, 37.

63. See Olukoshi, *The Elusive Prince of Denmark*, 34, for details.

64. G. R. Murunga, "Globalization and the Politics of Selective Blame in Kenya, 1963–1990," paper presented at the International Conference on Mainstreaming Democratic Governance in the Social Sciences, Humanities and Universities for the Twenty-First Century, held September 19 to October 1, 1999, organized by the Faculty of Arts and Social Sciences of the University of Dar es Salaam.

65. Such recent works that exhibit disdain for African states include Jean-Francois Bayart et. al, *The Criminalization of the State in Africa*, and Patrick Chabal and Jean-Pascal Daloz, *Africa Works: Disorder as Political Instrument*, both published by The International African Institute in association with James Currey and Indiana University Press, Oxford and Bloomington, 1999.

66. J. O. Ihonvbere, "How to Make an Undemocratic Constitution: The Nigerian Example," *Third World Quarterly*, 21.

67. J. O. Ihonvbere, "Constitutionalism and Democratization in Africa," paper presented at the Consultation on Participatory Constitution-Making organized by the Commonwealth Human Rights Initiative, Burgerspark, Pretoria, South Africa, August 16–17, 1999, 21.

68. J. D. Barkan and N. Ng'ethe, "Kenya Tries Again," *Journal of Democracy* 9, no. 2 (1998): 46.

69. Ihonvbere, African Leadership Forum Conference, 10.

8

Nigeria: Challenges to the State and Ways of Breaking through the Quagmire

Toure Kazah-Toure

IN THE COURSE OF CONTEMPORARY HISTORICAL AND POLITICAL PROCESSES in Nigeria, the state has shifted, both in practice and constitutionally, from a polity with relatively strong federal units to a more centralized system. At the time of the first military intervention on the national political scene, in 1966, the country had four regions that were comparatively autonomous in certain spheres. Regions (making up the federation) were essentially relying on themselves for the mobilization of resources and revenue generation, which were used in the operation of public governance and the execution of projects, rather than heavy dependence on the central government, which later became the case. Undermining federalism cannot be adequately attributed to the subsequent split of the regions into twelve states—in 1967—and neither does it fall in line with the simplistic contention that the present thirty-six states are not viable for a federation. A major thrust in this analysis is that for three decades of postcolonialism, October 1, 1960 to May 29, 1999, Nigeria experienced protracted military rule (for a total of about thirty years) that bred centralization of public governance. This mode of centralization of power at the different levels of governance was akin to the military command structure, by which instructions and orders are enforced only from top to bottom. It contributed to rendering Nigerian federalism in tatters. There is a widespread view across Nigeria that the country has overstretched its luck due to the dangerous manner its leaders have been toying with the country.[1]

As in many countries on the African continent, a major trigger to conflicts in Nigeria has been decades of undemocratic governance and repression by the state. The recent development in the country is a transition from military rule to civilian rule, as the country is yet to transition to democracy. Democracy is a far more penetrating movement than a shift from military authoritarianism to civilian governance. It is so because quite a number of regimes, both civilian and military, have been authoritarian and repressive.[2] Democracy partly deals with the questions of rights within the state and obligations of citizens to it. Institutions and structures have to be put in place (based on national consensus) for the state to bow to the popular dictates of the citizenry. The citizens ought to live under the same law and practices. Coupled with all of this is the genuine opening of the democratic space for genuine pluralism in national politics.

In Africa, conflicts in recent times have threatened the survival of some states. Markakis argues that conflicts and struggles have been increasingly manifesting in terms of ethnic identities.[3] Many civil wars have been expressed in those forms and assumed ethnic dimensions, even though more complex factors such as class were at the base. Violent and bloody conflicts in multiethnic states, such as Nigeria, have more often tended to take inter- and intraethnic or inter- and intraethno/religious proportions. In contrast, in the mainly ethnically and religiously homogenous state of Somalia, the civil war of the 1990s was fought largely "along subethnic, or clan, cleavage."[4] One outcome of most of the violent conflicts has been either the weakening of the state or the near disintegration of the affected countries.

Globally, ethnic conflicts have become serious challenges of the times. Contrary to the dominant propaganda, Africa has no monopoly of this. Elsewhere in the world, contemporary trends show that many states are not free from the deadly virus of ethnic conflict. On attainment of independence from European colonization (mostly from the late 1950s), many African leaders and regimes kept on with the tempo of denouncing the threat posed by ethnicity and regionalism. Somehow the line was also pushed to justify a one-party system and to stifle pluralism in national politics. A paradox of the position was the reality on the ground that many of the proclaimed anti-regionalist and anti-ethnicist African leaders were themselves using ethnicity and regionalism as weapons to exclude, marginalize and repress those in opposition, and those they perceived as enemies. According to Marina Ottaway, "some shift was witnessed towards the end of the twentieth-century, because after many years of being treated as pariahs, ethnic identities and ethnic nationalism have gained strength and even a degree of legitimacy in recent years."[5]

The project of constructing a pan-Nigerian identity, based on equality, common political practice, operating the same law and having a cosmopolitan outlook, largely remains elusive. As Ihonvbere[6] and Lewis[7] advance, the major direction of the tide tends to be the reassertion of ethnic, religious, regionalist and communal identities. Political mobilization principally seems to remain within the use of sectarian and primordial loyalties of ethnicity, religious bigotry, regionalism and statism. Military dictatorship aggravated the situation, by its oppressive and repressive methods while in power. This contributed in the galvanization of centrifugal groupings to the center stage of national politics.[8] Complex conflictual processes, linked to the compounding divisions and sharp contradictions, for example, got to highly violent phases in the Nigerian civil war, from 1967–1970. Another political conflict engulfed the country in the 1990s, especially after the annulment of the June 12, 1993, presidential elections, presumably won by M. K. O Abiola (a Yoruba, Muslim and Southerner), by what some circles perceived as the Northern-dominated military regime.

The Colonial State and Subversion of Nationalistic Efforts

Going into the postcolonial development, it is necessary to observe that the ruling party that emerged—the Northern People's Congress (NPC)—was composed of the most pro-British, conservative and feudalistic forces in the country. In the colonial conditions, the feudal aristocracies, at the head of the Native Authorities (NAs), were the main buffers between the colonizer and the colonized. Key elites of the party were mainly products of the Katsina College. This was an educational citadel, fundamentally established by the British, for the education of scions of the leading Northern Nigeria NAs ruling dynasties of the former Sokoto Caliphate and Borno.[9] The NPC was not part of the anti-colonial movement, but emerged as a counterforce (propped up by the colonialists) principally to thwart the anti-colonial and anti-feudal Northern Elements Progressive Union (NEPU), and to preempt and compromise the outcome of the struggle for independence.

By 1945, the colonial state had put in motion its counteroffensive directed at the pan-Nigerian section in the nationalist movement in Southern Nigeria. This manifested in attempts at destroying the labor movement (that waged a vigorous and successful national strike in 1945). Worth noting is the banning of the militant anti-imperialist Zikist Movement and repression of its leaders. In addition was the exploitation and manipulation of ethnicity to undermine the national spread of the Dr. Nnamdi Azikiwe–led National Council of Nigeria and the Cameroons (NCNC), as the leading nationalist party in the country. Coupled with this was the internal degeneration of some sections in the NCNC itself, by resorting to playing the ethnic card. The colonialists' clampdown on the nationalist press and nationalistic forces had potentials of linking the North and the South to create a solid national front capable of transcending sectarianism and regional barriers.

NEPU emerged as a fiery anti-colonial party of the peasantry and commoners in Northern Nigeria. Its roots were traceable to decades of struggles waged by the oppressed in the Emirates, in the context of colonial domination, and the experience from the activism of militant youth in preceding nationalistic struggles. The anti-British and anti-feudal ideology of NEPU was very strong and popular. It entered into alliance with the NCNC and the militant/activist Zikist Movement. Within the regional geopolitical setting of the North, NEPU established links with political organizations that stated they were championing the cause of ethnic minorities, such as the Middle Belt People's Party (MBPP) and the Borno Youth Movement (BYM).

The advent of NEPU as a militant anti-British and anti-feudal party, with some high degree of acceptability among the commoner classes in the North, frightened the colonialists and the Emirs. Launching an onslaught, both the British and the Emirs (in charge of the NAs) painted NEPU as an enemy that must be checked. Frightening to the colonizer and local collaborators were the linkages the radical party established with political parties, movements and forces sharing some similarities in terms of ideological currents elsewhere in Nigeria. British propaganda machinery and other organs for the same purpose were stirred in portraying NEPU as an agent of Southern nationalists wanting to infiltrate the North and undermine "Northern interest" from within.[10]

NEPU was inaugurated on August 8, 1950 (as the first political party in Northern Nigeria). The rival NPC was formed—as a formal political party—in October 1951. Daily struggles waged by NEPU—later led by Aminu Kano—against exploitative and oppressive policies and practices, made the party very popular among the peasantry and commoner strata. Whitaker emphasizes that this "was typical of NEPU's approach to the peasantry—the direct advocacy and defense of their interests through informal campaign of enlightenment which informed the peasants of their rights and encouraged them to assert their rights."[11]

Delving into this phase of the nationalist struggle is important for two reasons. It sheds light on the origin of scuttling a potentially solid national project of unity between the North and South. Doing so is also necessary in order to clarify an incorrect myth about a monolithic North in Nigerian politics. For the reality has been that in ethnic, cultural and religious terms the North remains the most diverse geopolitical zone in the country. Linked to all this is the need to understand how a powerful power bloc, which later became the dominant tendency in Nigerian politics, emerged. This dominant faction of the Nigerian ruling class was entrenched and wielded much influence in all the postcolonial civilian and military regimes, from 1960s to the 1990s.

It is very important to reconstruct the history as to how unity among the Nigerian peoples has been fought against by the forces controlling state power.

In the process of decolonization, the colonialists launched a fight to crush popular forces capable and committed to the project of forging a united country. The British designed strategies of pushing the aristocracies to the fore (to take over from the colonizer at independence). A major player in the planning and execution of the project was Bryan Sharwood-Smith.[12] A significant turning point was the victory recorded by NEPU at the primary stage of the legislative elections, in September 1951, in some towns, especially the most populous Northern city of Kano. The party, in conditions in which there was a denial of direct universal suffrage, including the exclusion of women in the North from having no suffrage—not having the right to vote—recorded this victory. In addition there was provision for an automatic reservation of 40 percent of the legislative seats for the Native Authority aristocrats. It was also a common unofficial practice to use the NA police, NA courts, thugs in the service of the aristocracies, and other instruments of state coercion to frame and repress those who do not support the status quo. The entire system was marked by the operation of an Electoral College System dominated by the Emirs and their subordinate officials.[13]

In September 1951, a systematic operation was further geared in motion to stifle NEPU and pave the way for the NPC. This was partly based on a submission by Sharwood-Smith to the higher authorities in which the thrust was maintained that:

> It may well not represent the popular opinion . . . if N.E.P.U. is permitted to pursue its way uninterrupted. If in fact this well-organized minority movement . . . gains further impetus, the activities of the N.P.C.[14] will be of purely academic interest. To repeat what I have frequently said before, the executive of N.E.P.U. and its founding members are a worthless lot in terms both of mental calibre and experience. They do however, possess drive, zeal and appreciable measure of organizing ability. This thing can spread unless responsible Africans who have the real interest of the North at heart get down to it at once and organize a counter offensive.[15]

Issues of concern stressed were that despite earlier warnings, leading officials of the various NAs in the North were complacent and underrating the danger of NEPU achieving a sweeping victory in the region. Sharwood-Smith was seriously perturbed "that once this quite worthless movement is permitted to gain adequate momentum, it will effectively penetrate the rural areas after which the fat will be well and truly in the fire."[16]

Immediately as this line of action was advanced, there was an official declaration of the NPC as a political party. The party was much linked to the colonizer and subsequently it became the major beneficiary (among the three emerging dominant ruling regional blocs, located in the East, North and

West) of getting concessions at the different constitutional talks in the decolonization process. A major concession the British gave was that 50 percent of seats or constituencies in the National Parliament (Senate and House of Representatives) were to go to the Northern Region. The Western and Eastern Regions (the Western Cameroons inclusive)[17] were to share the other 50 percent representation. The main criterion was population and the census has ever remained a major controversial question in the country. Census figures have, subsequently, somehow, influenced the number of states created in Nigeria (along the North/South divide) and partly a strong criterion in the distribution of resources to states by the central government.[18]

Ultimately, the NPC inherited power from the colonialists at independence in 1960. The NPC was the ruling party both in the Northern Region and at the center. Significant was the decision of the president of the party, Sir Ahmadu Bello, to hold fort at Kaduna (the capital of the North), as premier of the Northern Region than to become prime minister of Nigeria. The deputy president of the NPC, Sir Abubakar Tafawa Balewa, was sent to the then-capital of Nigeria, Lagos, by the former, to occupy the position of Nigerian prime minister. In the 1959 federal elections, the NPC had enough seats to form the central government in a parliamentary system. However, the reality of it—being absolutely a Northern party—influenced the NPC into the practical politics of looking for an alliance to enable it to run affairs at the center. Perhaps this was partly aimed at giving the Federal Government a desired national outlook. Of course, there were grievous implications for postcolonial Nigeria if the Federal Government was to be run by Northerners only.

The NPC formed the government at the center in alliance with the NCNC, which was increasingly sidelining its militant wings as well as allies, and fast declining into the politics of ethnicity and regionalism. The NCNC did not consult its NEPU allies and the latter never became part of that political arrangement throughout the period of First Republic from 1960 to 1966. However, the NCNC insisted that it had no ideological common ground with the NPC, but justified its deal on the basis of the need for national unity.[19] In this arrangement, the foremost nationalist and leader of the NCNC, Dr. Nnamdi Azikiwe, became the ceremonial president of Nigeria. This was in the context of a parliamentary system where the executive powers where controlled by the prime minister. For the NPC there was no pretense about the fact that it was clearly a regional party, right from its name to its electoral practice and participation. Never, for once, did the NPC contest elections outside the Northern Region. It did not enjoy popular support of the people but used state institutions, resources, coercion, and repression to clinch its hold on power.

Despite the difficulties and the kinds of structures the postcolonial project inherited, regional governments were engaged in a sort of undeclared relatively healthy competition toward development of the three—later four—regions. Constitutionally, and in practice, there was relative autonomy for the regions and less financial reliance on the center. In matters such as health, education, police, agriculture and public works, the regional governments were autonomous—such matters were on the concurrent list—and the Federal Government also partook in them within its domain. Defense (that is, navy, army, and airforce), internal affairs and foreign affairs were within the exclusive jurisdiction of the Federal Government.

A major setback in the First Republic was the resorting to political victimization and repression in dealing with the opposition and rivals. In 1963, the central government created a Mid-Western Region out of the Western Region. There was indeed popular agitation for this region by the non-Yoruba minorities in the Edo and Delta Provinces of the West. However, it was obvious that the NPC-led Federal Government had other ulterior motives and calculations, because equally popular demands for new regions by minorities in the North and in the East were not given any concessions.

The official and major opposition in the federal parliament—the Action Group (AG)—was led by Chief Obafemi Awolowo, who was both the leader of the opposition in the national parliament as well as the national leader of the AG as a party. The AG controlled the Western Regional Government. In 1959, which was the eve of independence for Nigeria in 1960, Awolowo relinquished his position as the Premier of the West and went to be the opposition leader at the central parliament. The deputy leader of the AG, Chief Ladoke Akintola, became the new Premier of the Western Region. Later the AG experienced an internal crisis and split. The West was gripped in what appeared as a bitter political rivalry between the party leader Awolowo and his deputy, Akintola, which eventually exploded and got Western Nigeria engulfed in bitter and violent conflict.

In the process of the conflict in the Western Region, the federal authorities, meaning the center, eventually declared a state of emergency there. After this was the arrest of Chief Obafemi Awolowo and some of his key lieutenants. They were charged with treasonable felony, on the allegation of planning to violently overthrow the Federal Government. A verdict of guilt was passed after the trial. Awolowo and many of the accused were imprisoned. This further ignited a state of anarchy in the West, with a lot of subtle and violent opposition to the Akintola-led regional government.

The NPC-controlled Federal Government was accused of fuelling the conflicts in the West, partly to form an alternative power bloc amiable to it in the region. Chief Ladoke Akintola eventually formed his own party, the Nigerian National Democratic Party (NNDC), which forged close political relationships with the NPC and its leaders. The NPC, NNDC and the Mid-West

Democratic Front (MDF) entered into an alliance called the Nigerian National Alliance (NNA) in 1964.[20]

Except for sharing political offices at the center with the NPC, the NCNC had by 1964 embraced a common front of the United Progressive Grand Alliance (UPGA).[21] This was in opposition to the NNA alliance. The main issues of the times included the controversies toward the December 1964 federal elections, the state of emergency imposed by the central government in the West and the reign of terror against the opposition groups and parties in the North. An obvious picture of both the UPGA and NNA blocs was that dominant parties were not engaging the people and popular organizations on popular issues based on broad national interests. Sectarianism, partisan narrowed interest, primordialism, electoral calculations and political fortunes of the ruling classes were the salient targets of pursuit in the dominant contestations.

Curiously, despite the alliance in UPGA, many key members of the NCNC in the Western Region supported Akintola, who was in the NNA alliance, and served in desirable positions in the government. As at the December 1964 elections, the NCNC was with the AG in the UPGA alliance but at the same time remained in the NPC-led central government. Contradictorily the NCNC did boycott the elections in the Eastern Region. The Eastern Premier, Dr. Michael Okpara, who was also the leader of UPGA, used the regional government machinery to ensure that the elections were totally boycotted. However, Dr. Nnamdi Azikiwe (the national leader of the NCNC and president of Nigeria), who initially did not endorse the elections results and refused to call for the formation of a government at the center, later capitulated and called on Prime Minister Sir Abubakar Tafawa Balewa to form an NPC-led government. Thus, the NCNC, once more, effectively switched over to join forces with the NPC as a coalition partner in controlling power at the center. The AG, NEPU, United Middle Belt Congress (UMBC) and others partners in UPGA were, in a way, politically abandoned in the cold by the NCNC.[22]

By 1964–1965, massive levels of political repression directed at NEPU and the UMBC—the major umbrella party of some of the predominantly non-Muslim Northern ethnic minorities—had reached a climax. A militant revolt broke out in Tivland (the nerve center of the UMBC), against the NPC-led government, and it widened the frontiers of the conflict. Tiv uprising was anchored on a popular perception—in Central Nigeria which some analysts called the Middle Belt—about real and imaginary political exclusion, marginalization, ethno-religious chauvinism, discriminatory practice(s) in all spheres of governance and repression by the ruling NPC. In those areas of Central Nigeria such as Tivland, the regional government and the NAs were virtually seen as being synonymous with the ruling party.[23] This, of course, was not rare because NEPU also held this perception.

That situation remained until the first military coup was carried out on January 15, 1966. Majority of its principal movers were Igbo officers, led by Major Kaduna Chukwuma Nzeogwu.[24] Once the coup was perceived as having an ethno-regional dimension, and as exempting leading politicians and military officers of Igbo extraction from physical elimination, the interpretation of the scenario as sectarian and sectional surfaced. Except for the operations and killings in Kaduna, Lagos and Ibadan, elsewhere the coup had flopped. Among those killed were the Prime Minister of Nigeria, Sir Abubakar Tafawa Balewa; the Premier of the Northern Region, Sir Ahmadu Bello; the Premier of the Western Region, Chief Ladoke Akintola; and the Federal Minister of Finance, Chief Okotie-Eboh (a Mid-Westerner). Okwudiba Nnoli depicts how the apparently sectional killings extended to the military where "four out of the five Northern officers of the ranks of Lt. Colonel and above were killed, two out of five from the West, none out of seven from the East and one out from the four from the Midwest."[25]

Subsequently, the coup leaders were rounded up and thrown in detention without trial. State power and national and regional governance was taken over by the top military officers led by the Chief of Army Staff, Major General Aguiyi Ironsi, who was Igbo. What followed was the formation of a federal military government, the banning of political parties and political activities. One significant development was the move by Ironsi's government to reverse federalism and transform the country into a heavily centralized unitary system of government, based on an earlier colonial twenty-two-province structure.

Before the unified unitary system was implemented, officers of Northern origin executed a bloody counter-coup on July 27, 1966. In Nigerian parlance, some analysts have labelled it as the revenge coup, because it was principally targeted at the Igbo. The military faction that came to power, with the then–Lieutenant Colonel Yakubu Gowon as Head of State, could be described as one nurtured by the NPC and the Northern establishment.[26] There occurred a seemingly organized massacre of Igbo in different parts of Nigeria—especially in the North—with some reprisal killings (of much lesser magnitude) of Northerners in the East. In the process of the violent conflict the Military Governor of the Eastern Region, Lieutenant Colonel Emeka Odemegwu Ojukwu, refused to recognize the federal military government led by Gowon. The East further demanded for a confederacy system. Instead, the central government abolished the four regions and created a twelve-state structure of the federation. What escalated the conflict to a peak was the eventual declaration of secession in the Eastern Region, leading to the birth of the Republic of Biafra that was led by Ojukwu. All this culminated in the Nigerian civil war from 1967–1970, which came to an end with the surrender by Biafra. In the last thirty-five years of the twentieth century the Northernist tendency, with roots in the July 1966 counter-coup, remained dominant in all the different military regimes that ruled Nigeria. This was so in spite of the intrigues, coups, and counter-coups within this unofficial faction. Worth noting is that the reincarnated forces of the NPC—but this time around with a national spread and re-alignments all over Nigeria—became the National Party of Nigeria (NPN), which ruled the country during the Second Republic in the period October 1, 1979 to December 31, 1983.

Military Dictatorship and State Havoc

With all sorts of previous problems that Nigeria faced, some gains were made in the different sectors in the 1960s and 1970s. Established and maintained were institutions that many of the citizenry were, generally, proud of. Socio-economic and political crises deepened in the era of structural reforms. From the early 1980s, the economic crisis had begun to set in, and the military partly exploited this to justify the overthrowing of the civilian regime of Alhaji Shehu Shagari on December 31, 1983. By 1986, the country had sunk into deeper crises, of various dimensions and proportions, with the implementation of Structural Adjustment Programs (SAP) by the General Ibrahim Babangida–led junta. Overwhelmingly, Nigerians (workers, women groups, students, academics, farmers and professionals)—through their organizations —gave a verdict of rejection on SAP during the 1985–1986 national debate, that was organized by Babangida himself on the desirability by—or otherwise of taking loans from the International Monetary Fund (IMF). The country began to witness massive street demonstrations in some of the major towns. Demonstrations were not only by workers and students, as was hitherto the experience, but involved broader strata in society. However, the fast-growing authoritarian military junta went ahead to implement new policies, which had negative consequences for the country and its people.

SAP in reality meant the dominant role of market forces in the economy, liberalization and deregulation, devaluation of Nigeria's currency (the naira), retrenchment, privatization of public property to leading ruling elite, withdrawal of subsidies by government, and government retreat in the area of social provisioning and welfare services. Privatization and commercialization of public companies were basically limited to key actors of the regime, their civilian allies, and foreign partners of the dictatorship as they went about accumulating wealth and plundering the country in the most personalized fashion ever.

The last two decades of the twentieth century marked a period of ruining national institutions and the collapsing of key infrastructure partially due to a "cut in public expenditure."[27] The relatively vibrant educational system became a major victim. The university system, founded on a strong intellectual tradition, which produced the most needed skilled manpower, was in effect undermined by the state. Lack of facilities, such as books in libraries and chemicals and reagents in laboratories, became the order of the day. Meaning, basic things for teaching and research were fast decreasing, vanishing and hardly available in the departments and institutes.[28] For the military in power, the search for knowledge and defending the ideals of the university, and even the intellectual vocation, constituted threats to be stifled. Academic freedom and autonomy were further eroded. In 1995, there were enormous problems and profound crises in one of the country's foremost universities. For the first time in the history of Nigeria, the regime of General Sani Abacha resorted to posting a top retired military officer as Sole Administrator (backed by a personal military decree with full power over all organs of university administration).[29]

The Academic Staff Union of Universities (ASUU) struggled through the storming years with credible reputation and played a leading role in the battle against authoritarianism (both civilian and military). Its efforts and concrete actions were continuously depicted as unreasonable and subversive by the military junta.[30] The union waged strikes on matters of national concern, and fought for the course of democracy in relation to the June 12 elections annulment crisis. All this was done at a time most politicians had fled from the struggle or were collaborating with the military regimes. In the course of repression, the military—at different times—threw some ASUU leaders (such as Festus Iyayi and Attahiru Jega) into detention and sacked some of the leaders and activists from their jobs. Of course, this was carried out with the aid of pro-military academics within the university system. In the desperate economic and repressive circumstances, quite a number of intellectuals left the country. In the 1990s, campuses had been generally militarized and there was increased exodus of some of the best and productive brains the country had produced. What followed in 1996 was the promulgation of a decree—which was backdated—proscribing ASUU and all other unions. The National Association of Nigerian Students (NANS) had been banned years before then.

Organized labor unions were unleashed with repression. The military set out to disorganize the labor movement, a historical bastion of pan-Nigerian ideals and struggle. Co-option of renegade labor leaders was intensified. Some of the leading unionists and activists, who defended the interest of workers, and refused to be amenable or sell out to the government, were thrown into detention. Unions that resisted being compromised were either taken over by the government or banned. This happened to the national umbrella labor organization, the Nigerian Labor Congress (NLC), in 1988. It was proscribed for putting a strong resistance to the government unpopular policies.[31] In 1994, when the NLC was geared up by its militant sections—at a time the leadership was reneging in the struggle in defense of the actualization of June 12 election mandate acclaimed to have been won by Abiola and for a democratic order—the union was proscribed. An officer in the State Security Services (SSS) was appointed as the Sole Administrator of the NLC. Partly, it was the collapse of state institutions and the onslaught on civil society—such as labor and students' movements, and professional bodies—which contributed to people further falling back on ethnic associations and religious organizations. Sectarianism was on the rise.

Nowhere in the country did the Nigerian state cause more havoc and repress and oppress peoples and communities than in the Niger Delta. The military carried out brutal operations and physically militarized the area in a fashion that would be appropriately associated with foreign occupiers. Years of exploitation of oil resources derived from the region—from which Nigeria still earns over 90 percent of its export revenue—coupled with the general neglect of the peoples (notwithstanding the fact that local ruling forces, rooted in the Niger Delta communities, cornered some benefits in the name of the people) led to conflictuality. Neglect relates to the area of social provisioning, employment, lack of industries and infrastructure and the destruction of the environment. The exploitation of oil resources, and state repression in the communities, led to serious agitation and protest.[32] Nigerian rulers tended to side with oil companies that were not observing international environmental standards, resulting to the damage done to the area due to oil explorations, and did not take care of the communities from which the resources were exploited. Instead, the state unleashed violent repression on its citizens and the local communities, including women and children. The military rulers deliberately embarked on blackmailing the local elite championing community rights and struggling for environmental protection, by portraying their struggles as attempts in the direction of secession. Oil money from the Niger Delta was crucial and treated as personal by Nigerian rulers and their foreign partners. Billions of dollars were stolen and stashed away in European banks and indeed North America.[33]

A murderous culminating point was reached on November 10, 1995, when Ken Saro-Wiwa, the leader of the Movement for the Survival of the Ogoni (MOSOP), and eight other Ogoni activists were executed. This heinous crime, by the state itself, attracted global condemnation. Some countries further treated Nigeria as a pariah state. Instantly, the country was suspended from the Commonwealth. It is appropriate that many analysts have called the execution of the "Ogoni nine" a judicial murder by the Nigerian state. Assessment such as this is correct essentially because of the lack of substantiation of the allegations of their role in the murder of some Ogoni chiefs, which the activists were charged with. More so there were violations even by the rules, set standard, and the entire violation of the legal procedures prescribed by the General Sani Abacha junta itself. Specified procedures that included the right to appeal, as provided for by the highest military ruling body in the country—the Provisional Ruling Council (PRC)—was denied. The military made public governance more repressive and authoritarian. Tremendously rapid was the affront on the rights and security of the citizenry.

At another level, the regime unofficially employed some measures bordering on state terrorism. Secret squads were set up, outside the official security services, to physically annihilate opponents of the regime. Pro-democracy activists, journalists, and patriots were hunted and thrown into detention or killed. The very prominent cases were the brutal killings of Kudirat Abiola (wife of M. K. O. Abiola) and Alfred Rewane, a financier of the opposition National Democratic Coalition (NADECO). There was the case of physical elimination of the journalist Bagauda Kalto, through kidnapping and subsequent bombing in a hotel toilet in Kaduna. Soldiers often rolled out on the streets with tanks to mow down citizens out for peaceful pro-democracy protests, especially in the Southwest, which was the main zone of opposition to the regime after the annulled June 12 elections.[34]

The remnants of the symbolic distribution of power based on a federal system of government were virtually done away with during the Abacha years. There were widespread serious allegations that military governors, presiding over the governance of federating states, had to personally kowtow to members of the dictator's family—and in some cases give part of the monetary allocation to key officers in the presidency—in order for the subventions to be released. Institutions of governance, and official positions, were used for repression and primitive accumulation. It was an era in which public governance was transformed into a question of unlimited power without responsibility.

Military governments played a part in the politicization of religion. Largesse was extended to religious leaders by the regimes. The dictators went into all sorts of Christian and Muslim circles looking for legitimacy even at the expense of undermining national unity. Deeper grounds were dug in society for religious hostilities, animosities, and hatred. By its actions, the state was the main culprit. It played a dangerous game with a highly emotive issue with the potentials of setting the country in flames. Beyond this was the increased destruction of the relations between people of different faiths in a multi-religious society in which the country's leaders were using labels and symbols, and mobilizing religious groupings for support and extending state resources to them.[35]

Making the State Relevant: The Persistent Quagmire and the Way Out

After several years of controlling state power, the soldiers did not relinquish it in May 1999 just because they wanted to. For years, Nigerians and their organizations waged struggle against authoritarianism. Another side of the matter was that the military was consuming itself due to internal contradictions, which included coups and framed-up coups. A landmark was the physical elimination of real and imagined opponents of the junta. The sudden death of General Sani Abacha, on June 8, 1998, provided an opportunity for the military to save itself, partially from itself. The whole process of the transfer of power was a guided one and did not involve the people. This can be seen—as an illustration—in the way the 1999 constitution was superimposed on the Nigerian people. However, no matter the limitations, the process of transition to civilian rule was a relative victory for the people and organizations that struggle against authoritarianism and somehow provided and opportunity to make a fresh start.

Far from it, federalism and its principles did not fail in Nigeria. A major factor in the damage done to the system is that the military extended its kind of command structure to the arena of governance, and in different spheres of national life. The argument here is that the state (and not the people) has been central to the destruction of federalism. At the core of this has been the concentration of power at the center; that is, the Federal Government. During the First Republic, when oil was not the main resource, the four regions (now replaced by thirty-six states) did tap the resources of their zones and each had a drive in a healthy competition with the other regions. The present states have kept on relating to the center, as helpless babies do to mothers. In the 1963 constitution, it was provided for, in section 140, that the federation shall pay to each region the sum of 50 percent "of the proceeds of any royalties received by the federation in respect of any mineral extracted in that region."[36] Out of the 50 percent balance, 35 percent was shared between the other regions while 15 percent went to the Federal Government. This principle of derivation was virtually thrown out and political criteria were introduced by the military, in the thirst to control oil resource and money. Babangida reduced derivation to 2 percent and Abacha increased it to a mere 3 percent.

In the 1999 Constitution, the derivation was raised to 13 percent.[37] The executive arm of government, presided over by Chief Olusegun Obasanjo, resisted its implementation. However, this has led to the emergence of new dimension in the agitation for "resource control" in the Niger Delta, as some circles have begun to raise the issue of communities where oil is drilled as different from those non-oil-producing ones in the zone. In reality the country must find a way of getting the federating units to harness the resources in their zones and to contribute to the federation account. There is no part of Nigeria without resources. If people are to mostly depend on the revenue they generate, there is most likely to be healthier competition between the states. The center will concentrate on more key matters. An end will be put to units' dependence on "cheap" oil money without any consequential production. A new arrangement should ensure that the combined strength of the federating states—or groups of state—is more than that of the center. But none of states should be stronger than the center. Whatever arrangement is to be made by the people should hinge on deepening democratic structures and institutions, from the hamlets to the central government. Unless this is done as a basic thing, more exploitative and domineering forces (and possibly warlords) will spring up to corner the resources and wealth even at the lowest levels, and it will be the same old story.

One of the challenges of the present democratic transition is connected with constitutional constraints. The 1999 Constitution has many provisions that are an affront to the rights of Nigerian citizens and these do not help matters in terms of the future of the country and its federalism. Femi Taiwo asks the question as to what sort of cosmopolitan constitution recognizes citizenship rights, on the one hand, and takes it away on the other, by making provision for consanguinity or ancestral origin as the basis of citizenship with a complex clause of being indigenous?[38] Talking about citizenship and at the same time emphasising being indigenous to a local community is contradictory. But even the perception of a Nigerian citizen in the communities is problematic. Meaning that in certain situations it is easier for a person to be accepted as an "abstract" Nigerian citizen than to be recognized as belonging to the area of residency, which leads to a denial of citizenship rights.

On the issue of gender, the citizenship provision of the 1999 Constitution has a retrogressive clause against Nigerian women. Foreign women married to Nigerian men are entitled to the country's citizenship. However, foreign men married to Nigerian women are not entitled to it. A leading legal expert I. F. Sagay succinctly argues that this provision is a contradiction. For it is obviously "discriminatory against Nigerian women and is therefore a violation of sections 17(2)(d), and 42(1) prohibiting discrimination on the basis of community, ethnic group, place of origin, sex, etc."[39]

A general tendency in the country is that people only get concerned about discriminatory practices when affecting them and not others. Claude Ake bitterly observes the tendency among most Nigerians to be indifferent to the rights of others being trampled on. His words in 1995 still remain true in the current circumstances:

> In Nigeria, we tend to be indifferent to the rights of those whom we have the power to oppress. We are only attentive to rights when we have less power than

our competitors. That underscores a lack of principled commitment to rights and equity. Southerners complain about Northern monopoly of political power and Northern oppression. But in every Southern state, ethnic groups which are dominant rigorously oppress the others. Similarly, the minorities who complain of oppression by those who control the state government are extremely oppressive in the local government areas which they control.[40]

Found in the 1999 Constitution are provisions for full rights of association and peaceful assembly. Yet, the number of political parties is restricted, whereas there are claims to multiparty system. For even in the context of the nationalist struggle against British colonialism, when Nigerians were subjects and not citizens, there was no enforcement of registration of political parties.[41] Prior to the ruling of the Supreme Court of Nigeria, in 2002, setting aside some of the electoral provisions as illegal, powers given to the Independent National Electoral Commission (INEC) included decisions to register parties and to limit them. The provision also stipulates that political parties must have physical presence and offices in two-thirds of the thirty-six states of the country and the federal capital Abuja. Scratching beyond the surface, it is glaring that this was paving the political space in favor of the rich and the powerful, and tilting the field against the dominated classes in society. Certainly, in a democracy, people concerned with desert encroachment in the far North or the environmentalists in the oil-producing Niger Delta have the right to form parties focusing on ecological devastation caused by the oil exploration. It should be up to the people in those regions to decide, within the democratic process, whether such political parties are relevant or not.

A major challenge to the Nigerian state and the people pertains to constitutionalism, which goes beyond having a constitution in place. Julius Ihonvbere succinctly and poignantly analyzes the key issues of constitutionalism as:

First, the *process* of constitution making and the extent to which it is popular, inclusive, participatory or process-led, and democratic; and second, the available openings, institutions and processes of making the constitution a *living* document by taking it to the people so that they are in a position not just to have access to it, but also to understand it, claim ownership and use it in defense of the democratic enterprise.[42]

Embarking on this will mean that constitutionalism will be an entirely embracing process, and all mechanisms will be in place to check the excesses of power wielders. Sovereignty will be in the hands of the citizenry as a collective, and the arbitrary rule of governments—that have the tendency of lifting themselves above the aspirations and wishes of the people—will not be the norm and practice any longer. As has been argued elsewhere, the problem of democracy in many countries in Africa is "that the states have been willing to have constitutions but have been unwilling to allow constitutionalism."[43] Throughout its history, Nigeria is yet to have a constitution coming from a national debate, inclusive participation by all segments of the people and based on their agreed consensus.

When the Nigerian pro-democracy movements started pushing the agenda for a Sovereign National Conference (SNC) in 1989, it was part of the agenda to battle the military dictatorship. This was a strategy within the project of a pro-democracy movement that was initiated and controlled by leftist and pan-Nigerian organizations. The core movement was the Socialist Congress of Nigeria (SCON). It was operating underground but using front organizations that were visible in the daily political struggles of the people. This was how the National Consultative Forum (NCF) and later the Committee for the Defense of Human Rights (CDHR) emerged. These organizations in collaboration with others did not only start calling for the SNC but attempted to hold a mock one in 1989, which the regime aborted. Conceptualization of the SNC was broadly mobilized for by SCON and canvassed for by the NCF and the CDHR, which later morphed into the Campaign for Democracy (CD), as an umbrella body for many radical and pro-democracy bodies. The focus of the struggle was for the SNC to be based on popular representation from labor unions, professional organizations, farmers, students, youth, women organizations, political movements, community organizations, religious bodies, and representation from the various electoral constituencies as enshrined in the 1979 Constitution.

New forces entered the battlefield when the military dragged Nigeria into further murky waters of ethnicization and regionalism, by annulment of the presumed victory of M. K. O. Abiola in the 1993 presidential election. One impact was that the annulment of the June 12 election was interpreted in ethnic terms in many quarters, as the determination of the North to deny a Southern presidency. Increasingly the agitation for the SNC was derailed, as it slipped from the control of its initiators completely as ethnicist and their militias gave the SNC a new definition and direction. The new entrants were now calling for the SNC to be composed of ethnic representation, to the exclusion of other identities, and placing as their main agenda the question of whether Nigeria should even remain as one country or whether the country should be dismembered.

A fact often overlooked by those solely advancing the ethnic line is that most parts of the country are multiethnic with no clear-cut territories demarcating peoples. Figures are not available, but any casual observer can see that people move around—the population of most towns in the North is significantly made up Yoruba, Igbo, and other people who are historically of Southern origin. It is the same in the South with a high population of Nupe, Hausa and so on that are historically of Northern origin. Many of the citizens have no trace of connection elsewhere apart from where they reside. One solution is to make it mandatory for Nigerians to have their citizenship rights where they reside. It is relevant to argue that contrary to the ghetto logic peddled by some undemocratic governance, ruining of national institutions, poverty, unemployment, and exclusion from the political process, and other ills in the country transcend ethnic boundaries. Another fact is that pluralism and democracy cannot entertain an exclusionist agenda. There are many identities in the country. The reality has to be appreciated that there are citizens without ethnic identity and some who will not want to be represented in those terms but at class, gender, professional and other levels of identity plurality.

Many are yet to grapple with the present development in connection with the political situation, and thus are still agitating for the SNC. In spite of the limitation of the present order, of what increasingly seems a never-ending transition from civilian rule to a democratic experiment, the political space is comparatively larger than what it used to be under military dictatorship. There is the need to deepen the process to be inclusive. In light of this, other means have to be employed to address the serious problems of constitutionalism, ethnicity, control and distribution of resources, religion, federalism, citizenship, and so on, so as to move the transition that is stagnated in civilian rule toward democracy. Since 1999, a component of the initial tendencies that advocated for the SNC has been advancing a new line. The summary of this position is advanced by Olisa Agbakoba:

> I am not sure that the "Sovereign National Conference" may be the appropriate forum for this dialogue. I have long advocated the SNC but I think that its advocates must take on board some of the objections of the opponents of the SNC. The fear of elected office-holders that there cannot be two sovereigns in the country must be taken into account. We need not insist on a dialogue taking the form of a "sovereign" conference, so long as its result will not be altered by anybody. . . . Obasanjo himself will do well to expand his own Constitutional Review Panel to include the National Assembly and civil society.[44]

However, it is precisely in this context that President Olusegun Obasanjo and the politicians in power, both in the executive and the legislature—and even down to the states and local governments—are playing partisan politics with the issue of reforms. Mainly, they have been following a narrowly guided path and not involving the citizens and civil society organizations. On a number of occasions, Obasanjo has even ridiculed the agitation for a national conference by saying that by being the president means that the people of Nigeria gave him the trust of their sovereignty.[45]

Given the whole nature of the national setting, and the tendency of most politicians, civil society must move ahead as part of the citizenry to wage struggle and mobilize stakeholders for reforms. Citizens have rights and should never wait for anyone in power when pushing their legitimate interests. There is a danger in waiting for government to take the first action on issues such as constitutionalism and reforms.

There has to be institutionalized guarantees and concrete measures taken to ensure group and cultural rights for all the peoples wherever they reside in the country. Constitutionally enshrined provisions stressing equality of practitioners of all religions, their freedom to articulate their positions, and to worship freely anywhere within the country, have to be practically implemented. In addition to this is the recognition of the plurality nature of society. Social provisioning, including education, health facilities and employment opportunities, should be made available to all citizens. Nigeria must strive to establish a genuine multiparty system based on pluralism, which forms the bedrock of class and ideological politics, and the building of genuine and representative democratic structures and institutions—both in the spheres of the state and civil society. The inclusion of people to reflect plurality of the polity, in the decision-making process should be seriously placed on the inclusive and participatory agenda. A pending attention has to be paid to the thorny question of citizenship. In concrete terms, it is still viewed within a primordial realm of local indigeneity, in which emphasis is on the tracing of a person's ancestral origin to a particular community rather than location/geography. People should get rights, and also carry out their duties and obligations to the Nigeria state, wherever they reside, work and pay taxes. Much ought to be done to transcend the present situation in which citizens having civil and cosmopolitan orientations are relatively at the receiving end in a plural society in which dominant classes have pushed sectarian politics to the front seat. The democratic question has to be seen beyond the realm of public governance to other spheres, such as strengthening civil society organizations, popular associations of the working people, organizations struggling for the rights of women and the independent press. Nobody or any group shall be allowed to come to power outside the constitutional means. Efforts should be made to ensure that settlements are cosmopolitan, meaning that no area should be established exclusively for people of particular ethnic and religious identities. Embarking on a path of genuine reforms in all aspects of national life is most likely to put Nigeria on a fresh start in the twenty-first century.

Conclusion

The analysis examines the efforts made, in the colonial phase, by pan-Nigerian nationalists to forge a united front toward putting a united independent country on course and how the British stifled this project by promoting conservative and counter-forces. The postcolonial stage was marked by remarkable struggles to democratize the political space and toward the realization of the meaning of independence. Despite the gains made, divisive and primordial identity politics, even at the highest level of national governance, further weakened the state and partly led to a violent military intervention that dragged the country toward disintegration, which culminated in a vicious civil war—with some of the negative consequences still surviving.

Prolonged decades of military dictatorship did not enable Nigerians to have continuous opportunities to learn and develop democracy. Remarkable was also the trend that public governance kept degenerating, especially in the last fifteen years of the twentieth century. Unpopular state policies, sponsored by imperialist financial institutions, led not only to deterioration and decay in the economy but also in all other sectors within the polity. Military authoritarianism was based and nurtured on repression and Nigerians did not have the avenue for an all-embracing national discourse and dialogue to make the state more relevant. However, this in itself brought out many organizations and forces in civil society that posed a challenge to the state and to the military, leading to the handover to civilians in 1999.

A major feature of the centralization was that a high degree of power was conferred in the office of the president. Not surprising, therefore, that many leaders presided over state affairs in a manner similar to that of managing a personal estate. The 1999 Constitution—which the military fashioned and imposed on the people without their participation in its making—has not significantly altered the concentration of power in the central government. This means that the 1999 Constitution is more in essence unitary, except in its theoretical claim of upholding federalism. Years of denial of significant autonomy to the lower units of federal structures, authoritarianism, the absence of governance based on the consent of the citizenry, and the lack of an enduring democratic culture and practice contributed in galvanizing various forces to pose challenges to the state and the ruling class.

In the wake of a civilian government that came to power on May 29, 1999, formerly suppressed grievances and anger have continued to erupt. Perceived injustice—real and imagined—and hate memories, with origins in the past and located in the limitations of the new democratic arrangements, are triggering up. People's fears, violence and entrenched narrow perceptions are surviving. All this suggests that both the state and civil society have a task to address the thorniest problems of the times. Worth recognizing is the fact that issues, as well as the discourse on the question of putting Nigeria on a democratic course, cannot be restricted to the exclusive confines of the ruling elite. Imperative is the need to seriously consider the concrete engagement and involvement of people—and their organizations—in the democratization and political processes.

Major surgical operations, beyond mere constitutional reforms, have to be embarked on. For Nigeria to survive the labor unions, professional bodies and various strands of popular and people's organizations in civil society have to be part of the initiative. Limiting the restructuring of constitutional reforms to a reluctant and tiny representative elite, to the exclusion of the people and their organizations in civil society, is not the best way.

Resolution of basic problems hindering the efforts toward erecting democratic structures and institutions requires serious attention. Neglecting this resolution puts impediments on the path of a proper transition to a democratic order and thus prevents the Nigerian state from becoming more relevant to the citizenry. First, the problems include the lack of real democracy but the existence of civilian in power. Second, there are no concrete negotiated guarantees of group and collective rights. Third, there is no adequate mechanism for tackling both the subtle and violent ethnic and religious problems. Fourth, prevailing is the failure to establish a true multiparty system based on pluralism, which forms the bedrock of class and ideological politics. Fifth, there is the near absence of genuine and representative democratic structures and institutions—both in the spheres of the state and civil society. Sixth, there are the crucial issues of the ownership, control and distribution of resources. Seventh, more than ever before Nigerians must debate the thorniest question of citizenship, which is constitutionally and fundamentally defined within a primordial and confused clause of indigenousness. Embarking on a path of genuine reforms in all aspects of national life may lead to beating the swords into ploughshares and pave the way to making the state more relevant for Nigerians and Africans.

Notes

1. Shades of public opinion in different fora and outlets point to this fact. For the author of this chapter, field interviews (in January and February 2000) covering the different geopolitical zones of Nigeria inform this conclusion.

2. Jibrin Ibrahim, "Democratic Transition in Africa: The Challenge of a New Agenda: Concluding Remarks," in *Democratization Processes in Africa: Problems and Prospects*, ed. Eshetu Chole and Jibrin Ibrahim (Dakar, Senegal: CODESRIA, 1995), 173–74.

3. See John Markakis, "Ethnicity and Conflict With Reference to Ethiopia and Sudan," in *Social Science and Conflict Resolution Analysis*, ed. Hurskainen Arvi Hurskainen and Mohammed Salih (Uppsala: Nordiska Afrikainstitutet, 1993).

4. Tim Sisk, *Power Sharing and International Mediation in Ethnic Conflicts* (Washington, DC: U.S. Institute of Peace Press, 1996), 21.

5. Marina Ottaway, "Ethnic Politics in Africa: Change and Continuity," in *State, Conflict and Democracy in Africa*, ed. Richard Joseph (Boulder, CO: Lynne Rienner Publishers, 1999), 299.

6. Julius Ihonvbere, "Avoiding Globalization: The State and Depolitization in Nigeria," in *Globalization and the Dilemmas of the State in the South*, ed. Francis Adams et al. (London: Macmillan Press, 1999), 155.

7. See Peter M. Lewis et al., *Stabilizing Nigeria: Sanctions, Incentives, and Support for Civil Society* (New York: Council on Foreign Relations and The Century Press, 1998).

8. See Okwudiba Nnoli, *Ethnicity and Development in Nigeria* (Aldershot, UK: Averbury, 1995), 158–59; Adebayo O. Olukoshi and Lisa Laakso, eds., *Challenges to the Nation State in Africa* (Uppsala: Nordiska Afrikainstituet, 1996); and Basil Davidson, *The Black Man's Burden: Africa and the Curse of Nation State* (London: James Curry, 1992), 228–313.

9. In the many postcolonial years, quite a number of Nigerian leaders (civilian and military) were ex-students of Katsina College (later named Kaduna College, then Government College Zaria, and now Barewa College Zaria). The President of the Northern People's Congress and Premier of Northern Nigeria, Sir Ahmadu Bello, attended the college. Former Nigerian Heads of State, who were educated at that college are: Sir Tafawa Balewa (Prime Minister, from 1960 to 1966), General Yakubu Gowon (Head of State from 1966 to 1975), General Murtala Ramat Mohammmed (Head of State, 1975–1976), and Alhaji Shehu Shagari (Executive President, 1979–1983). The college also produced Aminu Kano, who led the left wing, NEPU, from the anticolonial struggles to the end of the First Republic in 1966, as well as led its successor to the radical people's Redemption Party (PRP), 1978–1983.

10. For detailed information on the counteroffensive, anti-NEPU onslaught and propaganda, see the dense intelligence document, "NEPU SECURITY," National Archives, Kaduna (NAK), SNP, no. 349.

11. C. S. Whitaker, *The Politics of Tradition, Continuity and Change in Northern Nigeria 1946–1966* (Princeton, NJ: Princeton University Press, 1970), 380.

12. Bryan Sharwood-Smith served as a colonial officer in Northern Nigeria between 1927 and 1957, after an earlier service in the mandated colony of British Cameroons for six years. He held various positions and became the President of the Northern House of Assembly in 1952. Later that year, he was appointed Lieutenant Governor of the Northern Region, the capacity in which he served from 1952 to 1957. For further reading, see his political autobiography, *But Always as Friends: Northern Nigeria and the Cameroons* (London: George Allen and Unwin, 1969).

13. See Bill Freund, *The Making of Contemporary Africa: The Development of African Society Since 1800* (London: Macmillan Press, 1984), 216.

14. It was at that time that a cultural group officially used its Hausa name Jam 'iyar Mutamen Arewa. It was then opposed to any reference to it with the English transla-

tion of the name, which means Northern People's Congress, the NPC abbreviation that Sharwood-Smith used here. It only took the English name when it formally declared itself a political party.

15. See letter by Sharwood-Smith, Resident of Kano Province, to the Secretary of the Northern Provinces, in "NEPU-SECURITY."

16. See letter by Sharwood-Smith, in "NEPU-SECURITY."

17. The provinces referred to as the Cameroons (in colonial Nigeria) were part of the German colony of Cameroon before World War I. After the defeat of the Germans in the war, Western Cameroon and a part of Northern Cameroon were given to the British by the League of Nations collectively as a trust territory, which was incorporated into the British colony of Nigeria. Western Cameroon was in the Eastern Region of Nigeria and the portion of Northern Cameroon (later named Mubi Province) was in Northern Nigeria. After independence, a plebiscite was held in which the Northern Trust Province of Mubi, later renamed Sardauna Province, voted to remain part of Nigeria.

18. The politics of the census is part of the national debate with much protest and challenge. Allegations have been made about an inflated population in relation to the North by some elites in the South. There have been counter-responses by the Northern elites. The fact of the matter is that the issue of accurate census has been a controversial political matter in Nigeria, depending on the context (even between and among local communities). In 1976, the regime of General Murtala Mohammed rejected the 1973/1974 census that was conducted by the previous government of General Yakubu Gowon. Conducting an authentic national census is an issue that the new democratic project will have to face. For an example of the controversy concerning the census, see Okwudiba Nnoli, *Ethnic Politics in Nigeria*, (Enugu: Fourth Dimension, 1980), 255.

19. For a background on some of the party alliances of the time, see "Political Bodies in Nigeria, 19581964," NAK: ZAR PROF, No. c.45.

20. Obafemi Awolowo was the first premier of the Western Region. On the eve of independence, he relinquished the position and moved to the national parliament as leader of the opposition. He remained the leader of the Action Group (AC) while his deputy, Chief Ladoke Akintola, became the new premier of the Western Region. On this and other alliances in the context of the chaotic 1964/1965 controversial elections, see Adewale Ademoyega, *Why We Struck: The Story of the Nigerian Coup* (Ibadan: Evans Brothers, 1981), 19–22.

21. The coalition of UPGA was composed mainly of the AG, the NCNC, NEPU and the UMBC.

22. For some of the issues raised here, see Billy Dudley, *Parties and Politics in Northern Nigeria* (London: Frank Cass, 1968).

23. Remi Anifowose, *Violence and Politics in Nigeria* (Enugu: Nok Publishers, 1992), 155–77.

24. The leader of the coup d'etat was Major Kaduna Chukwuma Nzeogwu. His parents were of Midwestern Igbo origin. Nzeogwu himself was born and bred in the Northern Nigerian capital city of Kaduna, the name he was christened after. Various accounts point to the fact that he was a cosmopolitan officer. In terms of language and

other cultural factors, he was very much a product of the environment of his upbringing in Northern Nigeria. There are indications that incompatible forces representing divergent interests and working at cross-purposes took part in the coup. Forces operating in the coup were more complex beyond Major Nzeogwu's naivety and idealism. Major Nzeogwu carried out the operation and took over the seat of power in the North. A retired military officer with claim of some insights into the events of the January 1966 coup, who prefers being anonymous, says that some Northern soldiers welcomed the military putsch in Kaduna, while some Northern technocrats allegedly embraced Nzeogwu. It was when the realization came to them that no Igbo politician or military officer was killed that things changed. With the coup not completed, the Nzeogwu group did (or could) not take over power. The coupists were arrested and detained without trial. Rather, the Chief of Army Staff (an Igbo officer), Major-General Thomas Aguiyi Ironsi, emerged as the Head of State and Commander-In-Chief of the Nigerian Armed Forces. I have used discussions with an insider to some of the events, who wants to remain anonymous. On a detailed account of the first coup by one of its five core movers, See Ademoyega, *Why We Struck*, 71–105.

25. Nnoli, *Ethnicity and Development in Nigeria*, 242.

26. The July 1966 coup d' etat started as a mutiny by some Northern officers and soldiers. In that coup, there were the killings of some Igbo officers in the various barracks. Prominent among the leaders who were killed were the Head of State Major-General Aguiyi Ironsi, and the Military Governor of the Western Region Col. Adekunle Fajuyi (a Yoruba). Northern officers who played prominent roles in that operation included Majors Murtala Mohammed, T.Y. Danjuma and Martin Adamu. A Northern officer, the Chief of Army Staff, Lt. Col. Yakubu Gowon, took over as the Head of State. See Ademoyega, *Why We Struck*, 71–105.

27. Abubakar Momoh, "The Rise of Civil Associations, Militarism and Popular Struggles in Nigeria, 1986–1994," paper presented at the eighth General Assembly Conference on Crises and Transformation in Africa, CODESRIA, Dakar, Senegal, 1995.

28. Festus Eribo, "Higher Education in Nigeria: Decades of Development and Decline," *Issue: Journal of Opinion* 24, no. 1 (1996): 65.

29. Retired Major-General Mamman Kontagora was imposed as the sole administrator of Ahmadu Bello University, Zaria, after a major conflict at the university in 1995, with all of the powers of the university's council, senate and other organs conferred on him and personally backed by a special decree. After the death of General Sani Abacha, the military dictator in June 1998, General Kontagora remained in charge of the university for additional months.

30. Attahiru Jega, "Unions and Conflict Management in Nigeria's Tertiary Institutions," *Issue: Journal of Opinion* 24, no. 1 (1996): 62 and A. R. Mustapha, "The State of Academic Freedom in Nigeria," in *The State of Academic Freedom in Africa* (Dakar, Senegal: CODESRIA, 1996), 103.

31. Adebayo Olukoshi, "The Politics of Structural Adjustment in Nigeria," in Thandika Mkandawire and Adebayo Olukoshi (eds.), *Between Liberalization and Oppression: The Politics of Structural Adjustment in Africa*, (Dakar, Senegal: CODESRIA, 1995), 164.

32. Nninmo Bassey, "The Niger Delta and the Future of Democracy in Nigeria," paper presented for the Assessment of Democratic Reform in Nigeria, International-DEA, January 2000.

33. Many facts and items of evidence have come out clearly in the various investigations since the new civilian regime came to power. It has been established that Abacha and his allies stashed away billions of dollars in foreign banks. The new civilian government has recovered smaller portions of the loot.

34. The evidence and confessions from the trials of some of the key figures of the Abacha security apparatus are indisputable, revealing (especially by those who carried out his orders) as to how the assassinations were organized from the top. Generals and lower rank officers (that were in charge of the death squads) confronted and exposed each other and made revelations. This was more so at the Human Rights Investigation Commission (HRVIC), known as the Oputa Commission, which conducted hearings into cases of human rights violations during all of the previous military regimes in Nigeria. The findings of the Commission held some key military officers responsible for various human rights violations.

35. See Jibrin Ibrahim, "Religious and Political Turbulence in Nigeria, *Journal of Modern African Studies* 29, no. 1 (1991), and Matthew Kukah, "Religion and Politics of National Integration in Nigeria," in *Nigeria: The State of the Nation and the Way Forward*, ed. Mahadi Abdullahi et al. (Kaduna: Arewa House, 1994), 453.

36. This information is not directly cited from the 1963 Constitution, but is quoted from Bassey, "The Niger Delta and the Future of Democracy in Nigeria."

37. Bassey, "The Niger Delta and the Future of Democracy in Nigeria."

38. Femi Taiwo, "Of Citizens and Citizenship," in *Constitutionalism and the National Question in Nigeria* (Lagos: CENCOD, 2000), 89–98.

39. I. E. Sagay, "The 1999 Constitution: A Critique," in *Constitutionalism and the National Question in Nigeria*, 65.

40. Claude Aka, "A Plausible Transition," TELL, Lagos, September 25, 1995, 34.

41. Jibrin Ibrahim, "A Political Analysis of the 1999 Nigerian Constitution: Its Problems and Prospects," *Legislative Mandate* 2, no. 2 (1999): 18–24.

42. Julius Ihonvbere, "How to Make an Undemocratic Constitution: The Nigerian Example," *Third World Quarterly* 21, no. 2 (2000): 344.

43. Cited in Jibrin Ibrahim, "A Political Analysis of the 1999 Nigerian Constitution," 19.

44. Olisa Agbakoba, "The Missing Fundamentals," *THIS DAY*, February 6, 2000, 14.

45. The latest of this was widely broadcast on national radio and television and carried in the print media, while the president of Nigeria was on an official visit to Oyo State in 2001.

9

The Disintegration and Restoration of State Authority in Sierra Leone

Hashim Gibrill

God knows that we in Africa are sick and tired of war and strife.[1]

Kwame Nkrumah, 1957

THIS CHAPTER FOCUSES ON THE VIOLENT DISINTEGRATION of state authority in Sierra Leone, seeking to elicit lessons and imperatives intrinsic to averting the repeat of this national calamity. During the 1990s, governmental authority in this small West African country of 5.5 million people crumbled in a political context of sustained violent conflict among state forces, insurgent rebels, community militias, rebellious soldiers, hostile external forces, brigands, subregional and international peacekeepers, and mercenaries. This political violence occasioned acute human suffering and national dissonance. At the same time, and challenging the violence, vigorous national efforts have combined with regional and international military and humanitarian interventions to stop the fighting, re-impose state authority and services throughout the country, demilitarize society, reintegrate communities, confront immediate post-war recovery needs, and address the underlying causes of the national calamity. Numerous participants, domestic and external, have been involved in this effort of conflict resolution and political, economic, and social reconstruction.

The decade-long violent turmoil in Sierra Leone began as an insurgency against a discredited, fragile regime. It rapidly became a complicated, vicious war in which the armed forces of elected governments and military and insurgent regimes engaged in alliances and battles with an array of internal and external forces. Estimates of those killed in the war range from 50,000 up to 75,000.[2] Involved as advisors, observers, conciliators, rescuers, covert arms suppliers, and assistance providers have been forces and representatives of, notably, the Economic Community of West African states (ECOWAS),[3] most prominently Nigeria; the United Nations (UN); Britain; the Organization of African Unity (now African Union); the Commonwealth; and the United States. Other prominent actors have been the arms dealers and diamond and natural resources smugglers. In addition, many groups in civil society (religious organizations, youth and women's organizations, public intellectuals, professional groups, overseas communities), international organizations, and nongovernmental organizations have sought to provide refuge and help craft peace in the midst of conflict.

The internal war in Sierra Leone began on March 23, 1991. After more than a decade of violent regime transitions, sharply contested elections, armed insurrections, terror, trials and executions, economic decay, social disruption, and external interventions, Sierra Leone has arrived (as of 2004) at a precarious peace and stability still circumscribed by militarized realities on the ground, contentious politics, continued widespread disillusion and poverty, and ongoing conflicts in neighboring states (Cote d'Ivoire and Guinea).

The end of the internal war, officially declared on January 18, 2002, has prompted the return home of the many thousands of internally displaced Sierra Leoneans and refugees from Guinea, Liberia, and farther afield; estimates are that up to 2 million people were forced to flee the violence, anarchy, and privations of the war. There is also a fragile economic recovery spurred by foreign assistance, local expenditures occasioned by the 17,500-strong UN peacekeeping force (UNAMSIL),[4] growing official diamond sales, and the expansion of commercial activity in the wake of growing political stability. There is also the post-war reckoning—retribution and catharsis—proceeding overtly through the activities of a Special Court to try war crimes, and a Truth and Reconciliation Commission.[5] It is the current and past decade's political and economic realities, which resulted in Sierra Leone being regarded as a state, which have disintegrated. This disintegration was marked by a profound crisis of legitimacy, efficacy, and physical survival of the instruments, institutions, and personnel of government, such that the Sierra Leonean state no longer "ruled" its territory in any substantive way beyond localized enclaves. This disintegrated state is now undergoing an uncertain, fragile process of rebuilding. There is hope for the future and a somber realization that this progress can be halted and even reversed.

How did Sierra Leone arrive at this juncture? After all, Sierra Leone has a marked record of national achievement—in the history of pan-Africanism, in the resistance of Africans against the terror of the Atlantic trade in captives, in nationalist resistance to the colonial state, in indigenous and introduced systems of education, in agriculture, and in the arts and professions. Sierra Leone's human resources are diverse and capable. The country also has a broad, accessible material base. Mineral resources include diamonds, iron ore, chromite, gold, platinum, rutile, bauxite, and titanium. These minerals, together with coffee, cocoa, palm oil, timber, cattle, fish, and other animal and forest products, and a range of processing, consumer, and retail industries, provide Sierra Leone's economic foundation.

At the time of independence (April 27, 1961), most Sierra Leoneans and external observers saw the country as destined for political stability and economic growth.[6] Yet, by the mid-1970s, the country had experienced three military coups, disputed elections, disputed constitutions, treason trials, political hangings,[7] was listed among the most destitute in the world, and was increasingly dependent on external military forces to prop up the political regime and international financial institutions to bail out the national budget. And worse was to come. At the beginning of this new century, Sierra Leone is listed as the most destitute country in the world;[8] is seen as a country of barbarous conflict in which up to one-third of the population has been internally displaced or fled to neighboring states;[9] is the arena of a major regional and United Nations peacekeeping and state reconstruction effort; is a state that has exhibited Hobbesian characteristics: no security of life nor limb nor property, nor sustenance, nor relations between men and women, nor between adults and children, nor between the capital and the hinterland; and is a state that has nominal sovereignty and violently contested government authority.

What precipitated this political and economic implosion? How will Sierra Leone recreate authoritative political institutions, build national consensus, and pursue social and economic recovery? How will Sierra Leoneans "*join an fo mek Salone go bifo*"?[10]

The disintegration of state authority in Sierra Leone occasioned by the internal war has been widely reported on. The historical trajectory, prominent events, and participants in this process have been detailed. The overt and underlying political, social, and economic bases of the war remain, however, matters of conjecture and dispute. There is much richness and astuteness in existing discussions[11]; nevertheless, there remains room for continued reflection on the causes of state disintegration in Sierra Leone and what must be done to get beyond this national and regional tragedy. The analysis presented here reflects on the unfolding disintegration of state authority in Sierra Leone and the political lessons intrinsic to this disintegration that must be part of a sustained, viable struggle "to make the state relevant."[12] As the Association of African Political Scientists observe, "The causes of the myriad conflicts on the continent have probably not been thoroughly researched and understood."[13]

State Failure and Collapse

The process of state disintegration in Sierra Leone centers on the war that began in 1991. The decade-long turmoil made clear the limited capacity of the state to defend national borders, maintain internal control and security, protect and harness national resources, and administer government policy. However, the outbreak of the war and the subsequent state implosion can be seen as the culmination of thirty years of increasing political authoritarianism and violence, self-serving and sectional misuse of the power of the state, venal exploitation of the country's financial and natural resources, and thoroughgoing political and economic penetration by external actors.[14] By 1991, the state in Sierra Leone had been thoroughly undermined by domestic disunity, political strife, malfeasance, and greed, and thoroughly penetrated by external forces and interests. Sierra Leoneans were caught up in a crisis of both statecraft and material survival.

Africanist scholars in various ways have documented the slow disintegration of the state in Sierra Leone: from the militarized ending of the Albert Margai administration in 1967, through the increasing political violence, authoritarianism, and economic decline of the Siaka Probyn Stevens era (1968–1985), through the continuing economic decline, escalating violence and outbreak of the war during the administration of Joseph Saidu Momoh (1985–1992) culminating in the essential handing over of the government to the military in 1992, through the military interregnum of 1992–1996 and the heavy reliance on outside forces to prosecute the internal war, through to the establishment, violent overthrow and restoration of the civilian administration of Ahmed Tejan Kabbah (1996–), including the anarchic violence in Freetown, the capital city, in January 1999. There is much information, insight, and good political science in these discussions; this current analysis is indebted to them.[15]

The considered opinion of prominent analysts is that the roots of the war in Sierra Leone lie entrenched in political, economic, and social inequalities; that, crucially, the war was not simply a matter of struggle over criminal access to the country's renowned diamond beds. But this view is challenged by other commentators and activist groups who have posed the following important questions: Why has Sierra Leone imploded in this violent manner? What makes it different from other poorly run states? In this latter reading of events, diamonds are said to explain much of the violence and longevity of the war, if not the initial causes. Thus, the argument has been made: "Traditional economics, political science and military history are of little assistance in explaining Sierra Leone's conflict. The point of the war may not actually have been to win it, but to engage in profitable crime under the cover of warfare."[16]

An allied argument concludes, "the struggle for justice becomes a struggle to maintain an economic enterprise."[17] This reasoning cannot be ignored. Pillaging diamond deposits and other natural and agricultural resources (timber, cocoa, coffee) was always, or soon became, the key motivation for some combatant groups.[18] But clearly, while there are discernable trends, not all African states with significant deposits of accessible natural resources are wracked by war; nor are all of Africa's long-running conflicts in resource-rich states. From the outside perspective, the enabling conditions for the war—the roots of state disintegration—are to be found in the character of politics pursued in Sierra Leone that as a result steadily weakened the state and precipitated the implosion. More broadly, history, material resources, and contemporary political fault lines have combined in the causes of the war and the resultant disintegration of the state in Sierra Leone.

Within the chronology of state disintegration in Sierra Leone, it is possible to discern core political and economic tendencies and trends. These include, broadly:

1) The sharply contested, and often irregular character of political succession involving steadily increasing authoritarianism, militarization of the political process, and reliance on external actors to maintain or overturn the political status quo;
2) The venal misappropriation and exploitation of national resources, deepening economic crisis, growing mass hardship, and dependence on external sources for national sustenance;
3) The reassertion of the significance of historic loyalties and political formations, the violent insertion of the marginalized into political reckoning, and the clamor for change from many sides; and
4) Political penetration and contagious violence from external sources.

Over time, these tendencies and trends came to a head and resulted in the decade-long conflagration that the country is now struggling to get beyond. The analytical task is to elaborate and seek explanations for these tendencies and trends within the context of the historical development, structural limitations and stringencies of Sierra Leone's statehood. The place to begin is with a brief overview of the state in Sierra Leone. "Even though the postcolonial state's aim [in Africa] was to overcome 'old hierarchies,' relations of subjection were introduced and consolidated that broadly perpetuated those the colonial state had initiated."[19]

Situated on the west coast of Africa, bordered by Liberia to the south and east and Guinea to the north and east, Sierra Leone is one of Africa's smallest contemporary countries. Its boundaries, largely determined by the Berlin

Conference of imperialist states in 1884–1885, contain a population of approximately 5.5 million in a landmass of 27,699 square miles. The political evolution of the contemporary Sierra Leonean state encompassed the historic states and other political formations in this coastal West African region,[20] the colonial state (Crown Colony [1808] and Protectorate [1896]) established by British imperialism, and the current state largely fashioned in the transition to contemporary independence.

The political history involved in this state-creation process is dynamic, often dramatic. It includes the establishment of the original human settlements in the savannahs, forests, and along the coast of West Africa; the successive in-migrations and territorial stabilization of many of today's indigenous peoples spurred in significant part by the state-building activities and conflicts of the western Sudanic states; the penetration of trans-Saharan trade; European incursions beginning in the mid-fifteenth century, initially led and dominated by Portugal during the fifteenth and sixteenth centuries, and eventually dominated by the British from the eighteenth century, involving initially the exchange of commodities (gold, kola, spices, camwood, ivory, beeswax), and manufactures (cloth, weapons, luxuries), but eventually centering on the transatlantic trade in captive Africans; African returnees from Britain and the Americas (Jamaica, Nova Scotia) beginning in the 1780s; the liberated captive Africans (recaptives) who landed in Sierra Leone between 1807 and the 1870s; the transfer from imperial to national power culminating in independent statehood on April 27, 1961; and the politics of the current state that emerged from this historical process. There is much rich history here.[21]

In many ways, the contemporary state in Sierra Leone largely continues to reflect the balance of power established among indigenous social forces and between these indigenous forces and the departing imperial power, Britain, during the transition to formal independence.[22] This similarity is manifested in the philosophies of development, much of the educational and legal systems, external linkages and internal interests, urban and rural interests, class and gender pyramids, and ethnic relations. The contemporary state is not, however, simply the colonial state with indigenous instead of foreign functionaries. It has putative sovereignty, legitimacy, and more complex and broader governmental responsibilities and resources. And, crucially, it advances, accommodates, or suppresses the interests and aspirations of a wider range of social forces.

What are the core characteristics of the contemporary state in Sierra Leone? In summary, the Sierra Leonean state is a composite, penetrated, and contested state, existing upon a marginalized economic base, in a regional structure of unequal individual states. It is not a resource poor state, but is buffeted, constrained, and undermined by the structural imperatives of its marginalized, fragile existence.[23] It has exhibited various regime types (civilian and military, multiparty and one-party, and transitional), and ideological elaborations (nonaligned, socialist, democratic socialist, liberal democratic) and institutional structures (prime ministerial, presidential, republican, and anarchical).

To briefly elaborate, the contemporary Sierra Leonean state is a composite state because it co-exists with historic states and other political structures. These historic political formations, while no longer sovereign entities, commingle with and challenge the contemporary Sierra Leonean state in terms of loyalty, legitimacy, efficacy, law, administration, and salience to the political and economic lives of citizens. Current national boundaries cross-cut historical economic regions and ethnic groups, and constitutional provisions for paramount chiefs and regional subdivisions underscore, acknowledge, and "make real" this composite reality.[24]

Likewise, the contemporary Sierra Leonean state is a penetrated state, pressured by a range of external forces. These forces include representatives of the former colonial power, neighboring states, international organizations, nongovernmental organizations, mining and trading corporations, smugglers, diamond dealers, mercenaries, and brigands. Over the four decades since the end of colonial rule, these external forces have vitiated Sierra Leone's sovereignty via overt intervention, through their power to dictate national priorities and policies due to Sierra Leone's current subordinated position in the global political and economic order, using destabilization and pillage tactics.

The contemporary Sierra Leonean state is also, clearly, a contested state. It is the arena for, and the open objective of, deep-seated struggles among contradictory and fractious dominant and subordinate social forces in an ongoing struggle for hegemony. There are two aspects of this struggle for hegemony—facets of contestation and penetration. In all states, hegemony is something that has to be recreated and shored up on a daily basis through processes of socialization, indoctrination, legislation, and by police and military action.[25] In Sierra Leone, as in much of Africa, domestic hegemony, and the political, economic, and social hierarchies it encapsulates, are only tentatively in place, and, therefore, still up for broad contestation. In Sierra Leone, the struggle for hegemony is sharply ongoing in terms of the factions, fractions, perceptions, battlelines, and contentions within regularized politics. The struggle for hegemony became war when those holding state power were no longer able to manage or suppress the mounting challenges to their hegemony.

Related to this is the other aspect of hegemony that speaks to interstate relations. Sierra Leone exists in a network of West African states with a regional hegemon (Nigeria), contending or influential states (Cote d'Ivoire, Ghana,

Guinea, Senegal, Burkina Faso, and Libya), power brokers (France, Britain, the United States), and prominent regional and global agencies (ECOWAS, African Development Bank, Organization of African Unity/African Union, IMF, World Bank, and UNHCR). Struggles for interstate hegemony in West Africa, involving, most prominently, the Nigerians, French, Ivorians, and Libyans, and to a lesser degree, the Guineans, Liberians, Senegalese, Burkinabes, British, and Americans, have impacted domestic struggles for dominance in Sierra Leone via support, attack, and sustained intervention. This web of interstate relations is, therefore, also part of the reality of the contemporary state in Sierra Leone.

In many of its core facets (fracture, penetration, and contestation), the state in Sierra Leone mirrors that of other states in Africa and elsewhere. Yet the combination and growing intensity of these three political and political economic realities prompted a violent (temporary but profound) implosion of state authority witnessed in very few (Liberia, Democratic Republic of the Congo, and Somalia) other instances. What specifically unfolded in Sierra Leone that resulted in the disintegration of the state? This question is now pursued. As Isebill Gruhn notes, ". . . the interface between all the relevant forces in each catastrophe is so perplexing that only the ideologue claims to understand completely how and why things 'fall apart,' or how to put things back together again."[26]

In detailing and seeking to understand the disintegration of the state in Sierra Leone, what immediately seizes attention are the competing personalities and contending forces, the political and military clashes, the casualties, the profiteers, the conciliators, and the destruction. However, as noted above, within this rush of events, four broad political and political economic trends and tendencies are discernable. These should now be concisely elaborated.

The first trend, fundamentally political, centers on the sharply contested, often irregular character of regime change; growing authoritarianism and militarization of politics; and reliance on external actors to maintain or overturn the political status quo.

Since achieving independent statehood, authoritarianism, intolerance of opposition, ineffectual political institutions, maladministration, widespread discontent, and violent dissension have all marked Sierra Leonean politics. These politics have been highlighted by sharply contested regime transitions, tenuous stability, insertion of the military and external forces into the political reckoning, growing state violence, and political thuggery.

The capsule chronology and tenor of political succession and regime change in Sierra Leone reads as follows: Milton Margai, elected under the banner of the Sierra Leone People's Party (SLPP), assumed prime ministerial leadership of independent Sierra Leone in April 1961. He died in office in

April 1964, and was succeeded by his close relative, Albert Margai. The SLPP suffered electoral defeat in March 1967 at the hands of the All People's Congress (APC) led by Siaka Stevens. Stevens' swearing-in as prime minister was immediately followed by a coup d'etat led by Brigadier David Lansana. Subsequently, Lansana is replaced by Lt. Colonel Andrew Juxton Smith, who headed a National Reformation Council. A counter-coup in April 1968, initially led by privates under the banner of the Anti-Corruption Revolutionary Movement, then by Colonel Bangura and the National Interim Council, led to an almost immediate military handover to the elected leadership, Stevens and the ACP. A republican government was established in April 1971, severing constitutional ties with the British Crown. A one-party state was fashioned via further constitutional amendment and a referendum in June 1978. President Stevens retired in November 1985, handing over power to the decommissioned, former national army commander, Major General Joseph Saidu Momoh. Multiparty politics was reestablished, again via constitutional amendment and a referendum, in September 1991. A coup d'etat led by Captain Valentine Strasser ousted Momoh in April 1992, and established military rule under the National Provisional Ruling Council, later the Supreme Council of State. A palace coup in January 1996 replaced Strasser with Brigadier Julius Maada Bio. Following national elections in February 1996, civilian government was restored under the leadership of Ahmed Tejan Kabbah and the SLPP. Kabbah was ousted by an insurrection in May 1997 led by Major Johnny Paul Koroma. External forces, led by Nigeria, restored Kabbah to power in March 1998. A transitional government of national unity, headed by Kabbah and including representatives of various insurgent forces, was established in July 1999. Kabbah and the SLPP were returned to power by electoral victory in May 2002. These events and transitions involved much complex politics. A detailed elaboration cannot be attempted here; but core realities can be elucidated.

The twenty-four-year political hegemony of the All People's Congress under the leadership of Stevens and his hand-picked successor Momoh, encapsulated much of the character of the politics of fraction, penetration, and contestation. APC rule was marshaled in by a coup and counter-coup (1967, 1968) and brought to an end by the de facto handing over of the state to the military (April 1992). During the period of APC hegemony, the unfolding politics of state disintegration included attempted military coups; electoral violence; consolidation of a one-party state via enticements, intimidation, and constitutional manipulation; political trials and executions; recurring public demonstrations of discontent regarding corruption, inflation, political favoritism, and general deprivation; external intervention; and border incursions and skirmishes involving the armies and irregular forces from neighboring states.

Despite the warfare in neighboring Liberia, it can be argued reasonably that government authority in Sierra Leone would not have disintegrated had it not been for the fragility of the state occasioned by an authoritarian, self-serving, increasingly alienated regime that could no longer beat back challenges to its political hegemony. The transition from the seventeen-year rule of Stevens to Momoh estranged key members of the governing bloc who had themselves hoped to assume leadership of the state, cracked the façade of authoritarian rule providing dissenters and challengers opportunities to penetrate and destabilize the existing power bloc, and created an environment of political uncertainty. The succession battle lines seemingly were drawn between the two vice presidents, Francis Minah and S. I. Koroma; the anointing of Momoh by Stevens to be his successor as head of state and leader of the one political party flouted established constitutional mandates and political understandings.[27] Subsequently, Momoh oversaw the treason trial and execution of Minah and sidelined Koroma. This contested leadership transition increased factionalism and alienated key APC stalwarts, their business partners, and external backers. The internal fracturing of the APC establishment helped provide new political space. Leading voices from the professions, trade unions, student and youth organizations, religious groups, and external governments and international agencies argued and agitated for a return to multiparty politics. This growing dissent and clamor for change was given succor by the delegitimizing of the one-party state in Africa in the face of domestic struggles for popular participation, the collapse of one-party states in Eastern Europe, and pressure (often in the form of financial sanctions) from external providers.[28] Yet, another challenge to APC hegemony came from the disaffection of large segments of the population who perceived the APC as a Temne-dominated conclave. The agitation for multiparty politics provided an opportunity for competing ethnic groups to vie for state power.

The transition of power from Stevens to Momoh was unsuccessful because of the personalized, authoritarian nature of rule under Stevens. After obtaining his initial political legitimacy via electoral victory, Stevens proceeded to center political power around himself and his political and business allies, meeting every challenge to his authority with either blandishments or repression. He subordinated his party, maneuvered political competitors, terrorized the opposition and placated the general populace with a mixture of populism and manipulation. By undermining or manipulating state and government institutions (the constitution, parliament, judiciary, central bank, and political parties), Stevens became the embodiment of the state. But as he physically disintegrated, the state disintegrated around him. Although Stevens handed Momoh the state, he could not transfer his political acumen and prowess to his successor.

Another key legacy of Stevens' rule was the steady militarization of the political process to either prevent or permit change in the identity and makeup of the political class. Commencing with the transition from SLPP to APC political hegemony, increasingly the military was brought to the center stage in the political process to quell rising militant challenges to the political process, including student and worker demonstrations, to deal with border skirmishes and incursions, and, most significantly, to battle with the insurgency spearheaded by the Revolutionary United Front (RUF) beginning in March 1991. Despite this militarization of politics, there was also, ironically, a steady decline of the capacity of the state to defend the national territory and provide internal security. This was manifested in growing reliance on foreign regular and mercenary forces to prop up the APC regime, and, subsequently, to prosecute the war.

The April 1992 seizure of government power was the culmination of this increasing military involvement in politics. Since 1992, the alternating usurpation and restoration of civilian authority (including notably Koroma's "warlordism" coup against Kabbah and the subsequent reinstatement of civilian authority orchestrated by Nigerian forces) continued and typified the militarized character of politics in Sierra Leone.

All of these competing, increasingly hostile forces bludgeoned the state; eventually Momoh could no longer ward off the escalating challenges to state sovereignty and government authority. The unsteady and ultimately overturned authoritarian transition was both a product and a reflection of the contested, penetrated, and fragile nature of the state in Sierra Leone.

The second broad trend focuses on political and economic realities. It involves the venal misappropriation and exploitation of national resources, deepening economic crisis, growing mass hardship, and dependence on external sources for national finance. This trend led to national destitution and was a key catalyst of political disintegration.

Historically, the material bases of existence in Sierra Leone have involved a diverse, complex domestic economy comprising widespread, self-sufficient subsistence farming, supplemented by regional and trans-Saharan trade, later by the trade in captives, gold, and ivory, then the transition to cash crop production and mining. Significantly, British colonial hegemony was marked by unequal development between the colony (Freetown) and the protectorate (hinterland); most commerce, infrastructures, and public goods were centered in Freetown. British and French imperialism in this corner of West Africa also involved the rerouting of historic trans-Saharan trade routes, further reinforcing the underdevelopment of the hinterland. In Sierra Leone, all the minutiae of political events take place within a solidly capitalist social formation and development thrust. Colonialism left Sierra Leone with an economic legacy of mineral extraction, exploitation, and marginalization of the hinterland, and a "peripheral" combination of petty, merchant, and transnational capitalism.[29] Economic relations with the West were never severed and no attempts were made at transcending peripheral capitalism as was at least debated in neighboring Guinea, Ghana, and Burkina Faso.

In spite of increasing demands made on the economy to meet postcolonial development aspirations, the political class largely misused public resources and ignored its responsibilities to the people. For instance, when the APC assumed power in 1968, it promised new directions in internal and external affairs. The party voiced commitment to a populist reform agenda involving, in the economic sphere, social justice, an attack on corruption, a mixed economy with greater indigenous control, an emphasis on rural development including the encouragement of village consolidation and the rehabilitation and expansion of the co-operatives network.[30] Instead of making good on its promises, the political class permitted the continuous rifling of national resources by internal and external actors. Political offices were used to build an economic base by favoritism, nepotism, contract fees, diversion of public funds, facilitating the activities of high-profile business partners, and, notably, resource smuggling.

Indeed, resource smuggling became part and parcel of the rewards of governing as officials sought out domestic and foreign partners to facilitate their nefarious activities. Estimates are that up to 95 percent of diamonds mined have been routinely smuggled out of the country,[31] denying Sierra Leone sorely needed development funds and prompting the widely noted enigma of a country so rich in resources, yet mired in poverty. This intertwining of government office with illicit exploitation of national resources put a premium on access to or sidelining of state power; it became a central part of the contestation, penetration, and fragility of the state in Sierra Leone.

Prominent among the business partners of the political class have been the Lebanese, a controversial group of immigrants in Sierra Leone. Under British imperial hegemony, the Lebanese became traders and middlemen all over West Africa. In Sierra Leone, they largely replaced the Krios as the commercial class. In the postcolonial era, Siaka Stevens notably used prominent Lebanese as financial backers for party and personal activities. For example, Jamil Sherif Mohammed became a major business advisor, partner, and shareholder in government parastatals. The Lebanese in turn have used their relationship with the political class to facilitate and legitimize their commercial activities (legal and illicit) and to provide political cover.[32] Most Lebanese merchants feign a disinterest in politics though there are a few who have been prominent power wielders. Despite intermarriage and the existence of an Afro-Lebanese community, the overall primary economic and political allegiance of this community appears to be to Lebanon. The activities of the Lebanese can be seen as modern-day mercantilism. They transact business in Sierra Leone but repatriate their proceeds to Lebanon.[33] The commercial prominence of the Lebanese community has long given rise to popular resentment, which as far back as World War I had prompted violent demonstrations. As mass immiseration deepened in the postcolonial period, increasing instances of anti-Lebanese demonstrations have occurred. For example, a serious riot against Lebanese nationals took place in Kono in 1977 forcing many of them to flee the diamond-mining town.[34] Even today, popular sentiment is that the Lebanese have a stranglehold on Sierra Leone's economy, with the resultant political clout that this brings.[35] At times, in response to popular antipathy, the government of Sierra Leone has sought to regulate the cavalier business practices and reduce the commercial prominence of the Lebanese. Arguably, after his ascendancy to state power, Momoh tried to dislodge the Lebanese's hold on Sierra Leone's political economy. The sincerity of this and similar regulatory efforts were, however, questionable, as over the decades too many government officials have colluded with this mercantilist group to smuggle diamonds and gold.[36]

Gradually, during the 1970s and 1980s, Sierra Leone witnessed economic decline highlighted by growing national budget deficits, public services decline, growing poverty, and mass resentment.[37] The suffering of the general populace was only compounded by the International Financial Institutions' (IFIs) imposed structural adjustment policies on Sierra Leone in the early 1980s. The policies soon occasioned major currency depreciation, inflation, government employee retrenchment, and removal of consumer subsidies.[38] Already widespread economic privation deepened, prompting public protests and government repression.

Once government authority crumbled in the 1990s in the context of war, established chains of venality were broken and a free-for-all ensued for exploitation of Sierra Leone's natural bounty, involving local miners, insurgent forces, soldiers, mercenaries, brigands, and the clients for the diamonds and other prized resources. External illicit diamond traders, smugglers, and procurers included most prominently the Lebanese, but also Israelis, Russians, South Africans, Nigerians, Guineans, and Indians.

Now we have the post-war economy with new dynamics, continuing demands, and straightened resources: former belligerents struggling to maintain illicit diamond-mining operations; the central government trying to regain control of mines; the expenditures and commercial activity engendered by the presence of foreign troops, nongovernmental and international aid agencies and financial organizations; and the pressing needs for post-conflict rehabilitation and growth of the public infrastructure. All in all, this provides a complex and tenuous political economic basis upon which to rebuild the state.

The third broad trend, in large part sociopolitical, centers on the violent insertion of the marginalized into political reckoning, the reassertion of the significance of historic loyalties and political formations, and the clamor for political change from many sides.

The political and economic history of Sierra Leone shaped and was shaped by the social structure. If we regard politics as the competition and conflict among differentiated socioeconomic groups (social forces), factions, and prominent individuals, to advance or defend their material and ideological interests, and that in this politics, the state most often takes the side of the dominant forces and powerful individuals, rather than standing by impartially, then it is necessary to delineate whose interests the state is defending and advancing and whose interests are subordinated by state activities.

Under British imperial hegemony in Sierra Leone, the Crown Colony of Krios dominated the protectorate of indigenous groups. This colonial ordering of immigrants versus indigenes was largely replaced during the transition to independence by electoral and political rivalry between the Mende and Temne ethnic groups, each with allies among the smaller ethnic communities. These ethnic rivalries are overlain and complicated by class, urban-rural, and racial cleavages involving the Lebanese presence.

For over twenty-four years, the APC, perceived as a Temne-dominated institution, controlled the state along with their indigenous and non-national partners. As elaborated above, following Stevens' endorsement of Momoh and the resulting fracture of the APC, new political space opened up. The agitation for multiparty politics provided opportunities for competing ethnic and political groups. Entering into the political fray came students and professionals, the unemployed and underemployed, the overseas community, external observers, and diverse others. Widespread popular alienation had long engendered calls for the reinstitution of multiparty politics, and the desire in some quarters for a populist armed insurrection, to break the political dominance of the single ruling party.

The growing popular clamor for political change was eclipsed by the outbreak of the war, occasioned by the RUF insurgency. Although this insurgency soon became a vicious, rapacious, self-serving campaign of terror and pillage, its original rationale spoke to the growing alienation of the general populace from the political class. Others have pointed to the fact that the RUF initially sought to attract to its fight for "democratic empowerment" a "very broad coalition of the déclassé elements in society, unemployed workers, excluded intellectuals, members of the armed forces, pan-Africanists students, traders, farmers, chiefs and elders and all people who were prepared for the sustained struggle against the decadent APC system."[39] In the violent turmoil and the state disintegration that the war engendered, erstwhile marginalized ethnic hunters and warriors formed themselves into militias, such as the Kamajors, Kapra, and Tomaboros.[40] Vigilante groups such as the West End Boys also emerged. All these groups found new roles in terms of refuge, self-defense, community policing, and brigandage in the context of the disintegrating state in Sierra Leone. This violent, sustained insertion of Sierra Leone's heretofore marginalized groups into the center of the political arena spoke to the fragility and contested character of a state erected on contradictory amalgam of personalized authoritarianism, class, and ethnicity.

The final broad trend concerns the political penetration and contagious violence from external sources. As previously stated, Sierra Leone exists in a subregion of generally small states, but with a regional hegemon, Nigeria, and other influential states and transnational actors. Ongoing political turmoil in neighboring states and struggles for interstate hegemony in West Africa have impacted domestic political struggles in Sierra Leone via contagion, intervention, and connivance.

For instance, the 1966 coups in Ghana and Nigeria are generally regarded as having influenced the 1967 coup in Sierra Leone. More significantly, a continuous thread in Sierra Leonean politics has been the reliance on external forces to prop up, or overturn, the political status quo. Guinea intervened in Sierra Leone in 1971, 1973, and 1979 to secure Stevens' regime. Guinea was also called upon in 1991 to confront the RUF insurgency, and again in 1992 in a vain attempt to reverse the coup that brought an end to Momoh's regime. The resort to South African and British mercenary forces (Executive Outcomes and Sandline International), West African peacekeeping forces, British regular forces, and, finally, United Nations peacekeepers to help prosecute the internal war underscored the declining capacity of the Sierra Leonean state to defend its national territory and provide internal security.

In Africa's wars, while the domestic territory may serve as the primary location for conflict, neighboring states are often involved as safe bases for insurgent forces, havens for fleeing populations, conduits for forces and arms, smuggling routes, supporters of factions, and conciliators between belligerents.[41] In the case of Sierra Leone, Foday Sankoh, leader of the RUF, trained in Libya, supported Charles Taylor's insurgency in Liberia, and returned home to launch insurrection in 1991. The spread of conflict from Liberia to Sierra Leone was spurred in good measure by Taylor's determination to punish Liberia's neighbor for providing the rear base for ECOMOG forces, during their intervention in Liberia's civil war. What made this counterstrike possible, however, was the enabling environment of decaying authoritarianism in Sierra Leone. Aside from Liberia, Libya was implicated in the Sierra Leonean civil war as a sponsor of the RUF. Earlier, Libya had supported Taylor's National Patriotic Front of Liberia insurgency. Libya's adventurist foreign policy centering on belligerence against the state and people, which may have been grounded in some inchoate notions of a radical transnational political project, was ill-advised, and has been ruinous to Sierra Leonean and subregional stability. On the other hand, Nigeria's intervention, although at times beset with charges of illicit diamond mining, indiscipline, and abuse, was ultimately a stabilizing and positive move.[42]

The foregoing historical, political, economic, and social trends come together in a complex but understandable way to explain the disintegration of the state in Sierra Leone, and provide the context for recovery strategies and efforts. The origins of the disintegration of the state in Sierra Leone lie within the character of the politics pursued by those who have wielded or resisted state power; misappropriated state resources and vitiated state sovereignty. The internal fracturing of APC hegemony, the spillover of the conflict in Liberia, and the RUF insurgency sounded the death knell of the APC regime in 1992 and the beginning of the disintegration of the state in Sierra Leone. From 1992, the insurgency gathered steam as state forces were unable to defend much of the national territory. The state became increasingly unable to exercise governmental authority in any meaningful way outside of localized enclaves; prosecuting the war was largely delegated to mercenaries and subsequently to regional and international peacekeepers; the exploitation of priced national resources was taken over by insurgent forces and domestic and external looters and smugglers; and policing authority essentially became the province of community militia and self-appointed vigilantes.

Making the State Relevant: The Imperatives and Challenges

Given the tragic politics outlined above, what are the imperatives that arise from the disintegration of the state in Sierra Leone? How will Sierra Leone "build a sustainable peace?" The importance of this task is captured in the local expression "*Leh we join an fo mek Salone go bifo.*"[43] Any answers proffered must be grounded in an understanding of what went wrong. Blame has been apportioned for this descent into chaos and destruction, and clearly there is much to be spread around. During the protracted implosion of the state, seemingly popular advocates and good intentions were stymied or turned bad, and external forces pursued nefarious agendas. At the heart of the disintegration of the state in Sierra Leone was the ongoing, open struggle for hegemony which could not be contained within the structural limitations of a fragile, penetrated state governed by a decaying, authoritarian regime. Once the authoritarian power bloc fractured, due to internal discord and mounting popular disaffection, alienated social forces and malevolent, opportunistic domestic and external actors bludgeoned the state apparatus and personnel. In the process, a vicious mayhem ensued.

In seeking to rebuild the state and society, much of what is required appears axiomatic. A core conclusion of the Secretary-General's eleventh report on the United Nations Mission in Sierra Leone reads: "A durable solution to the conflict in Sierra Leone can be based only on restoration of government authority throughout the country, tangible progress towards economic recovery, full reintegration of ex-combatants, national reconciliation and participatory democracy."[44] Broad efforts in these regards are underway, orchestrated by the national government, domestic nongovernmental organizations, and international agencies.[45] But much remains to be done. In pursuing this recovery agenda, salient imperatives include breaking the political hold of historic and new enmities, fashioning principled pan-African statecraft, and articulating world responsibilities.

Sierra Leoneans must seek to get their own house in order. The constant resort to external forces and agencies to beat back domestic opposition, defend the nation, and bail out the economy has to an end if sovereignty and government authority are to be anything other than a cruel chimera. Sustained peace and state security are the first priority. Without peace, all else will be derailed. Peace has to be fought for with as much determination as the war. Peace education and peace activism are central in this regard. Traditional and contemporary institutions and the process of socialization, conflict resolution, and healing must all figure in this effort.

The issues of national reconciliation and consensus building will take center stage in the struggle to create a durable peace. What is required is reconciliation at the level of the people, rather than simply elite agreement. This will involve reconciliation between belligerents and victims, rural and urban communities, the capital and hinterland, immigrants and indigenes, and between the generations. There also needs to be hope for the next generation, rather than the plundering of its national birthright. At the heart of such reconciliation will be concrete and sustained strategies for poverty alleviation and national wealth creation grounded in growing national self-reliance. As is constantly remarked, Sierra Leone is replete with resources that should serve as the basis for economic recovery and substantial growth. Development plans must utilize its natural resources to energize its human capital. Also, the economies of some neighboring West African states, especially Ghana, are buoyed by the remittances, portfolio investments, and tourism of their overseas communities. The state, business class, and migrants can do much more to realize similar benefits for Sierra Leone.

On a political track, electoral politics need to be recast as part of the struggle for the future. Elections in Sierra Leone have largely served to entrench divisions and fuel animosities. The long history of disputed elections, violent campaigns, and winner-takes-all, ethnic political conclaves must be confronted. The May 2002 innovations in the electoral process, including proportional representation and party candidate slates, did little to break the hold of class and ethnic politics. What is required is diversity in governance rather than class, ethnic, and gender exclusions. Allied to this is the need for good governance and transparent public management in the context of a reinvigorated state pursuing a popular, as opposed to hegemonic, project.

On a regional, pan-African terrain, political adventurism, fortune-seeking, and hegemonic struggles have to be contained within the rubrics of good neighborliness. ECOWAS and the African Union must find the wherewithal to ward off the cavalier attacks on vulnerable populations. Peacekeeping strategies and resources must evolve to meet the diverse challenges of Africa's internal wars. Requirements include sanctions against belligerent states, early intervention in simmering conflicts aimed at countering war-talk and preventing the escalation of initial clashes into sustained warfare.[46]

On a global level, other imperatives include the ban on small arms trade and the pursuit of the traders in 'blood diamonds' in more than rhetoric. Global responsibilities must be met in these regards. The diamond and resource smugglers, arms dealers, and financiers are not from Mars—African, Asian, and European countries and the United States must show greater diligence regarding countering the rapacious activities of their nationals in Africa's war zones. They must develop the political will, or more realistically be pressured, to sanction their own nationals once evidence is gathered of nefarious involvement in Africa's conflicts. Activist organizations that are gathering the evidence and disseminating their findings have to be encouraged and supported.[47]

The complexities and emergent exigencies of state disintegration in Sierra Leone have been elaborated. Political and economic strategies have to be fashioned that recognize and confront the various facets of the disintegration. The crux of the matter: the struggle for hegemony has to be transformed into broad national consensus, and the structural weaknesses and tensions of the current state have to be transcended.

Conclusion

The chapter has attempted to examine the causes of the disintegration of the state in Sierra Leone, and the possibilities for reconstituting the state in Sierra Leone so that it can be made relevant to the lives of the majority of the people. In the case of the roots of state failure and state collapse, several contributing factors were identified including the colonial legacy, the dismal performance of the various regimes in Sierra, and the devastating civil war.

In order to make the state relevant in Sierra Leone, the core of state failure would have to be addressed. This would include addressing the economic, social, and political problems such as unemployment, corruption, low standard of living, education, health care, the respect for human rights, accountability, transparency, and the rule of law. If these myriad problems can be successfully addressed, then state authority would be restored with legitimacy and the state would then become relevant to the lives of the majority of the Sierra Leonean people.

Notes

1. Kwame Nkrumah, "Broadcast to the Nation, December 24, 1957," *Axioms of Kwame Nkrumah* (London: Panaf Books, 1972), 105.

2. Ian Smillie, Lansana Gberie, and Ralph Hazleton, *The Heart of the Matter: Sierra Leone, Diamonds and Human Security* (Ottawa: Partnership Africa Canada, 2000).

3. The ECOWAS force, officially the ECOWAS Monitoring Group, went by the appellation ECOMOG.

4. UNAMSIL is the acronym for the United Nations Mission in Sierra Leone.

5. See the reports of the UN Secretary-General on the United Nations' Mission in Sierra Leone. See, for example, United Nations Security Council, *Eleventh Report of the Secretary-General on the United Nations' Mission in Sierra Leone* (S/2001/857), September 2001.

6. See Peter K. Mitchell, Richard Synge, Christopher Clapham, and Linda Van Buren, "Sierra Leone," in *Africa South of the Sahara*, 32nd edition (London: Europa Publications, 2003), 916–35; John I. Clarke, "Sierra Leone in Africa," in *Sierra Leone in Maps* (London: University of London Press, Ltd., 1966), 10; Humphrey J. Fisher, "Elections and Coups in Sierra Leone, 1967," *Journal of Modern African Studies* 7, no. 4 (1969): 61136.

7. Sierra Leone became known as a country of "coups, attempted coups and treason trials." *Africa Confidential* 16, no. 4 (Februrary 21, 1975): 6.

8. UNDP *Human Development Report 2002*, Country Table, Sierra Leone.

9. United Nations High Commissioner for Refugees, *2002 UNHCR Statistical Yearbook*, Sierra Leone, Table F1.

10. The charge of the Sierra Leone National Recovery Strategy 2002–2003 reads "*Leh we join an fo mek Salone go bifo*" [Let us work together to make Sierra Leone progress].

11. Reporting on the war has been notable. The award-winning Sierra Leone Web site, allAfrica.com, the BBC, and CNN have all provided systematic reporting. The award-winning photo journal and documentary *Cry Freetown* by Sorious Samura provided firsthand images and reflections. The depth of coverage is reflected in the sad

fact that in March 2000 Sierra Leone was declared the most dangerous country for journalists by the New York–based Committee to Protect Journalists. There is also a substantial academic discourse.

12. An earlier draft of this chapter was presented at the International Conference, "Beyond State Failure and Collapse: Making the State Relevant in Africa," held March 16–19, 2000, Monrovia, Liberia.

13. The Editors, "Commentary: Peace and Security in Africa," *Association of African Political Scientists Newsletter* 2, no. 2 (May–August 1997): 1.

14. This reading of events, while not without many nuances, and while not the official or diplomatic assessment, is confirmed by leading analysts and dispassionate observation.

15. Some notable or interesting works include the essays on various facets of the War in Sierra Leone in Ibrahim Abdullah et al., "Lumpen Youth Culture and Political Violence: Some Sierra Leoneans Debate the RUF and the Civil War," *African Development* 22, nos. 3 and 4 (1997): 171–216; Christopher Clapham, *Sierra Leone: The Political Economy of Internal Conflict*, Working Paper 20, Netherlands Institute of International Relations, "Clingendael" Conflict Research Unit, July 2003; Fred M. Hayward, "Political Leadership, Power, and the State: Generalizations from the Case of Sierra Leone," *African Studies Review* 27, no. 3 (September 1984): 19–39; Jimmy D. Kandeh, "Ransoming the State: Elite Origins of Subaltern Terror in Sierra Leone," *Review of African Political Economy* 26, no. 8, (September 1999): 349–66; George K. Kieh, "The Crisis of the Neo-Colonial State and the Sierra Leonean Civil War," *African Strategic Review* 1, no. 1 (2005) 6, 47–68; Frank Ly, "Sierra Leone: The Paradox of Economic Decline and Political Stability," *Monthly Review* 32, no. 2 (June 1980): 10–26; William Reno, *Corruption and State Politics in Sierra Leone* (New York: Cambridge University Press, 1995); A. Zack-Williams, "Child Soldiers in the Civil War in Sierra Leone," paper presented at the Development Studies Association Conference, September 12–14, 1999, University of Bath.

16. Smillie, Gberie, and Hazleton, *The Heart of the Matter: Sierra Leone, Diamonds and Human Security.*

17. George Gedda, "Diamond Trade in Africa Fuels Insurgencies, National Conflicts," *Atlanta Journal Constitution*, Oct. 17, 1999, A20.

18. It can be noted in this regard that Foday Sankoh, the leader of the Revolutionary United Front (RUF), became the Minister of Natural Resources in 1999, during the short-lived transitional government of national unity. This portfolio was a de facto recognition of RUF control of many of the diamond fields and other areas of prized natural resources, and RUF determination not to cede control of the lucrative illicit trade. See also David J. Francis, "Diamonds and the Civil War in Sierra Leone," *The Courier*, July–August 2001, 73–75.

19. Achille Mbembe, *On the Postcolony* (Berkeley: University of California Press, 2001), 40.

20. By political formations, we have in mind the numerous self-governing and vassal villages, loose associations of communities, and small kingdoms which composed the array of governing structures.

21. A sure overview of this history can be obtained from the following: Arthur Abraham, *An Introduction to the Pre-Colonial History of the Mende of Sierra Leone* (Lewiston, NY: Edwin Mellen Press, 2003); Christopher Fyfe, *A Short History of Sierra Leone* (London: Longman Group Limited, 1962); John I. Clarke, *Sierra Leone in Maps* (London: University of London Press, Ltd., 1966); Walter Rodney, *History of the Upper Guinea Coast 1545–1800* (London: Oxford University Press, 1970); Ken Post, *The New States of West Africa* (Harmondsworth, UK: Penguin Books Ltd., 1970); A. G. Hopkins, *An Economic History of West Africa* (London: Longman Group Limited, 1973); A. P. Kup, *Sierra Leone: A Concise History* (New York: St. Martin's Press, 1975); Toyin Falola and A. D. Roberts, "West Africa," in *The Twentieth Century: Volume IV, The Oxford History of the British Empire*, ed. Judith M. Brown and Wm. Roger Lewis (Oxford, & New York: Oxford University Press, 1999), 515–29.

22. Frantz Fanon provided a most incisive commentary on this period of Africa's history:

> Some decades ago, the colonialist rulers could indefinitely propound the highly civilizing intentions of their countries. The concessions, the expropriations, the exploitation of the workers, the great wretchedness of the peoples, were traditionally conjured away and denied. Afterwards, when the time came to withdraw from the territory, the colonialists were forced to discard their masks. In the negotiations on independence, the first matters at issue were the economic interests: banks, monetary areas, research permits, commercial concessions, inviolability of properties stolen from the peasants at the time of conquest, etc. . . . of civilizing, religious, or cultural works, there was no longer any question. The time had come for serious things, and trivialities had to be left behind.

Toward the African Revolution (Harmondsworth, UK: Penguin Books Ltd., 1970), 130–31.

23. By "structural imperatives," we are referencing Hamza Alavi's classic essay "State and Class under Peripheral Capitalism," in *Sociology of Developing Societies*, ed. Hamza Alavi and Teodor Shanin (New York: Monthly Review Press, 1982).

24. Roselyn Adele Walker, "The Paramount Chieftaincy in Sierra Leone," introductory essay in *Paramount Chiefs of Sierra Leone: Photographic Portraits by Vera Viditz-Ward*, by the National Museum of African Art (Washington, DC: Smithsonian Institution, 1990).

25. See Michael Parenti, *Inventing Reality* (New York: St. Martin's Press, 1993); Alan Wolfe, *Limits of Legitimacy: Political Contradictions of Contemporary Capitalism* (New York: Free Press, 1997).

26. Isebill V. Gruhn, "Land Mines: An African Tragedy," *The Journal of Modern African Studies* 34, no. 4 (1996): 687. However, see the concept of the "ideological critique" in Samir Amin, "The Crisis of the State," in *Maldevelopment: Anatomy of a Global Failure* (London: Zed Books Ltd., 1990), 76.

27. Interview with Dr. A. Kaakyire D. Frempong, Department of Political Science, University of Ghana, Legon, on July 8, 2004.

28. Similar pressure for "democratic" opening was applied to President Daniel Arap Moi in Kenya and President Kenneth Kaunda in Zambia.

29. A. M. Howard, "Economic History," in Clarke, *Sierra Leone in Maps*, 74; A. G. Hopkins, *An Economic History of West Africa*, (London: Longman Group Ltd., 1973).

30. See "Address by the Prime Minister, Dr. Siaka Stevens, to the Third National Delegates Conference of the All People's Congress Party held at the Brookfields Stadium, Freetown, May 1970," appended in The A. P. C. Secretariat, *The Rising Sun: A History of the All People's Congress Party of Sierra Leone* (Freetown, Sierra Leone: A.P.C. Publications, 1982).

31. "Sierra Leone: Economic Emergency," *Africa Research Bulletin* (November 30, 1987): 8887.

32. It was reported in 1979 that Lebanese financial groups covered almost every corner of public finance in Sierra Leone such that no major contract was issued without passing through the hands of the middlemen, who organized the deals to the advantage of themselves and foreign contractors. *Africa Confidential* 20, no. 9 (April 25, 1979): 7.

33. The hometowns of Lebanese in Lebanon provide many examples of mansions built with profits from trade in Sierra Leone's diamonds.

34. "Sierra Leone: Currency Conflicts," *Africa Confidential* 20, no. 9 (April 25, 1979); "Sierra Leone: Rape," *Africa Confidential* 25, no. 24 (November 28, 1984); "Constitutional Changes: Sierra Leone," *Africa Research Bulletin* (December 15, 1985): 7851; "Sierra Leone: Lebanon's Shadow," *Africa Confidential* 27, no. 17 (August 20, 1986).

35. Interview with Sierra Leonean refugees in Accra, Ghana, July 17, 2004.

36. A recent assessment of the trade in Sierra Leone diamonds concludes, quoting UN sources, that "the contraband diamond trade of West Africa is controlled by the Lebanese." Emmanuel Goujon and Kelvin Lewis, "Bin Laden's Network May Have Brought Sierra Leone 'Blood Diamonds,'" AFP, Freetown, November 13, 2001.

37. For a concise overview of the growing economic crisis, see David Fashole Luke and Stephen P. Riley, "The Politics of Economic Decline in Sierra Leone," *The Journal of Modern African Studies* 27, no. 1 (1989): 133–41.

38. Samadu Sesay, "Rapid Decline in Economy," *African Concord* (May 7, 1987): 9–10.

39. A. Zack-Williams, "Child Soldiers in the Civil War in Sierra Leone," paper presented at the Development Studies Association Conference, September 12–14, 1999, University of Bath, 10–14.

40. Zack-Williams, "Child Soldiers in the Civil War in Sierra Leone." See also Jimmy D. Kandeh, "Ransoming the State: Elite Origins of Subaltern Terror in Sierra Leone," *Review of African Political Economy* 26, no. 8 (September 1999): 349–66.

41. Hashim Gibrill, "War and Recovery in Africa: Getting Beyond the Bitter Lessons," *Endarch* (Spring 2000): 7.

42. The politics of intervention in the war, involving, notably, Nigeria, Guinea, Ghana, Burkina Faso, Cote d'Ivoire, Libya, Britain, the United Nations, the Organization of African Unity/African Union, and the United States, require sustained elaboration and reflection. This is attempted in a forthcoming paper.

43. National Recovery Committee, *National Recovery Strategy 2002–2003,* May 2002.

44. United Nations Security Council, *Eleventh Report of the Secretary-General on the United Nations' Mission in Sierra Leone* (S/2001/857), September 7, 2001.

45. See United Nations Security Council, *Twenty-Second Report of the Secretary-General on the United Nations' Mission in Sierra Leone* (S/2004/536), July 6, 2004; *National Recovery Strategy 2002–2003.*

46. See my earlier discussion in "War and Recovery in Africa," 16–18.

47. Gibrill, "War and Recovery in Africa."

10

Somalia: State Failure, State Collapse, and the Possibilities for State Reconstitution

Alice B. Hashim

ELSEWHERE I HAVE SPOKEN OF "VIRUSES" that attacked the body politic in Somalia over an extended period of time. Here I will illuminate some of the factors that led to the failure and collapse of the Somali state and suggest a model for redesigning the governing formula that should better suit Somali proclivities. After reviewing possibilities and forms for reconstituting the Somali state, I decided that the Swiss canton model might most appropriately serve this purpose. I will present features of the Somali culture that, I believe, make this a reasonable assumption. Somalis seek local self-government as well as opportunities for individual expression. Community is especially important to the pastoralists who live in a "Malthusian" environment.

The central argument of this chapter is that federalism offers the best framework of democratic governance for Somalia. In other words, federalism would provide the best route for reconstituting the state in Somalia and making it relevant.

Sociocultural Background

Somali society is composed of two main bloodlines of the descendants of Abu Taalib of the Quraysh people of Arabia. There are the Soomale from which the Dir, Issaq, Hawiye and Darood clan families of the north are descended and the Sab composed of the Digil and Rahanwien of the south. The clan-family provides the broadest and most inclusive membership for the Somali people. Members of clan-families are said to be able to count back thirty generations in the recitation of their ancestral chain. The second tier of inclusion is the clan, which frequently acts as a corporate political unit. In the north, where the people are primarily pastoralist, nomadic herdsmen, have for generations relied on their well-established governing skills for survival.

One of their most important institutions is *Heer*, which means agreement. It is a compact or bilateral treaty as well as an administrative and adjudicatory organ. *Heer* works in conjunction with *Hidird* or "roots," a forum, which includes male in-laws. These two institutions work to ensure the orderly functioning of society and cement political cohesion. *Heer* decisions are binding and the group is collectively responsible for enforcement. The treaties are enforced through the Somali *diya* system which requires "blood wealth" to compensate an aggrieved party. Material compensation is, more often than not, in the form of animal wealth, although other forms of compensation are possible.[1] The interdependency of this system provides the basis for clan loyalty that is essential for survival in the Malthusian environment of northern Somalia. These arrangements are generally related to collective defense. Thus, not only did the interrelationship of *Heer*, *Hidird* and *diya* provide for a method of conflict resolution, but it was also a collective method of addressing problems related to economic hardship, deprivation and safety. These sociocultural institutions, while enabling group survival in the harshest of environments, had the effect of enforcing small group particularism conducive to societal fragmentation. While the Somalis have been able to enforce group loyalty, they have not been able to counter the divisive tendencies this encourages. This "centrifugal" tendency became especially salient in the efforts to build and maintain an independent nation-state.

Many of the areas of the south have Darood clans living in proximity to the Digil or Rahanwien, in particular the Marehan subclan, but the southern clans have a different sociocultural background. Many are settled in agriculture or are only seminomadic. As such, they are not a part of the major clan networks. Moreover, being apart historically, they did not play a major or active role in the political or economic events that led to state failure and collapse. Therefore, they are not a part of the analysis here. However, the south is relevant insofar as it bears on the analysis of how the nascent Somali state was called upon to integrate two very different systems of administration from Britain and Italy at the time of independence from colonial authorities, and it will be relevant in the future when considering the reconstitution of the state.

Colonialism

Like most other African nations, European cultural values were infused into the colonized populace. In the case of Somalia, there were serious disruptions to the historical Somali way of life. First, Somalis had to cope with several foreign languages. The British had colonized the north in what was known as British Somaliland. Italy had colonized the south in an attempt to make it an "Italian garden." Thus the Somali people, who had already differentiated between the Soomale and Sab lines in the north and south respectively, had these divisions reinforced through Western colonization. The French were in an area that Somalia would later claim as having been historically a part of the greater Somali nation. There were the Ogadeni (a subclan of Darood) in eastern Ethiopia. Furthermore, the Somalis had to cope with the Arabic tongue as trade across the Red Sea had existed for hundreds, perhaps thousands of years. Third, there was the problem of economic dislocations. Within the north, the Issaq had a long history of trade with outsiders and because of their contact with foreigners were perhaps more outward looking than others. This contact continued as the north supplied British Aden with fresh meat. However, the British did not invest money or time in Somalia per se. Their presence was to maintain their influence in the region and corner the market on the livestock trade. It has been argued that British trade worked to the detriment of the local economy since the British believed it was unimportant as Somalia "was being inserted into the capitalist world system."[2] With European colonialism came the commodification of herds. Grazing lands were abused as attempts were made to keep up with demand for more meat. Environmental abuse resulted from the overgrazing of ecologically fragile lands. Transhumance, the seasonal migrations that were so necessary to preventing overgrazing, was interrupted. The uncertainty of whether nomadic groups would be able to follow the regular seasonal grazing patterns increased anxiety. The increased anxiety led to increased tensions between clans.

Third, the Somalis had *not* historically depended on a central governing authority. As outlined above, Somali social order is informed through its clan structure.[3] The demands for rapid conversion from a decentralized self-governing system based on generations of understanding and acquiescence, to acceptance of a foreign one that was thousands of miles away would prove most difficult if not impossible. I would argue that this was the precursor to inevitable state failure and collapse. In the actual events that followed independence, it did not matter whether the government was the experimental parliamentary regime that lasted nine years nor the military one instituted by Colonel (later General) Mohammed Siad Barre in 1969; power resided in the hands of a few. Whether the people were pastoral or agrarian, merchant or trader, religious leader or community elder, they had not been given an opportunity to be heard nor contribute to the formulation of government. It is therefore instructive to briefly review the character of the parliamentary regime that followed independence.

Independence and the Parliamentary Regime

The governing formula patched together by the British and the Italians on the eve of Independence in 1960[4] was put to the test during the first ten years of Somali self-rule. One of the initial problems was that the constitution had not been sufficiently debated by representatives of the various clan families. Perhaps the first elected parliament should have sat as a sort of "constituent assembly" to debate and ratify the constitution, but nothing of this sort was done. The Somali National League (SNL), a political party representative of the Issaq in the north, boycotted a referendum held in June 1961 to ratify the new constitution. Of those Issaq who did attend, over half opposed it. Generally speaking, those who were to be governed by the governing instrument had little if any input into it.

At the outset of the parliamentary period that ran just short of a decade (1960–1969), representatives of two larger clan families attempted a mode of "consociational democracy." In this model, elite cooperation by leaders of different groups might transcend segmental cleavage. In this case, Jamma Qalib, a leading member of the SNL became president and Dr. Abdirashid Shirmarke (Darood and Somali Youth League leader) was prime minister. This arrangement adhered to a constitutional provision that the prime minister and the president should not be from the same clan. Clan representation through particular political parties was an essential feature of the parliamentary period.[5] These men did try to hold a central government together. However, a few persons representing the largest clans continually rotated in and out of office. Less populous clans felt left out and so created a multiplicity of parties to represent their interests. As Lucian Pye argued "political development in general cannot advance without a sense of deep identification with the total system."[6] However, attempts to be represented in the government led to small group factionalism as increasingly smaller groups contended for parliamentary seats. As a matter of fact, although there were regulations against the practice, there were sixty-two one-man lineage parties fielding 1,002 candidates in the March 1969 election.[7]

This aberrant application of "proportional representation" was evidence that the Western model given to Somalia could not be appropriately transferred. As Basil Davidson argued:

> Proportional representation might work well in Italy, where people were divided into classes but . . . nearly all Somalis were farmers or cattle people. They were not divided into classes. They were divided into clans. These clan divisions were very old, but colonial rule had deepened them . . . [and] colonial rule used the old clan divisions as a way of preventing Somalis from uniting together, while Somali habits of thought reinforced disunity.[8]

As alluded to above, this analysis confirms what other scholars have observed about Somali society: there are at work both centrifugal and centripetal forces. On the one hand, small group particularism pulls Somalis away from unity of thought and purpose; on the other, they may form a series of alliances that enable them to overcome enemies with supposedly far superior resources. The tendency toward distinct clan or lineage identity, but an overarching sense of oneness when facing outsiders, can be seen in other parts of Africa albeit in relation to larger groups known as tribes—for example, in the federation of Nigeria or among the riverine tribes of Sudan.

The system of proportional representation described above had the net effect of exacerbating the centrifugal propensities of the Somali clans. There were a dizzying array of alignments and realignments as the various clans and subclans sought a place at the governing table. By the time the 1969 elections came, there were claims of abuse of power and accusations of corruption and nepotism. Among the deputies in the National Assembly, unruliness abounded. Votes were bought and sold and there was little if any accountability to constituents because representatives could rely on clan support. That was possible because of the patrimonial nature of clan politics. The temptations for gain had overcome the nationalist fervor of the early years.[9] Deciding to put an end to further parliamentary-governing chaos, Colonel Mohammad Siad Barre began a reign of power through a military coup d'etat in October 1969.

The Military Regime of Mohammad Siad Barre

Siad Barre had been trained for military service during the Italian administration and had served as a police inspector during the post–World War II British Military Administration (1940–1950). Some scholars argued that in the early stages of political modernization, military officers could play a progressive role. However, as happened throughout Africa during the decades of the 1970s and 1980s, either the military-leader-cum-president became strictly authoritarian or became a pathological tyrant akin to Idi Amin of Uganda. In either case, there was little possibility of independent thought from those surrounding the leader and no possibility of political participation by the populace. Barre exhibited all of the traits of a prophet, prince, autocrat and finally tyrant. However, these personas were to develop slowly through evolutionary stages, as the fortunes of the president and the nation went through the stresses and strains of attempted rapid industrial development.

In the beginning, Barre, who was from the Marehan, a small subclan of the Darood clan family, and reputedly a cousin of the turn-of-the-century Somali nationalist, Sayid Abdille Hassan, took on the persona of "soldier-reformer." Barre had charisma. He was known to have been well versed in the poetry and oral literature for which the Somali people are justly famed and he was an accomplished orator. It might also be said that he was perceived as a "radical revolutionary," bringing with him, as he came to power, other high-ranking military officers. In the manner of Jamal Abdel Nasser of Egypt, whom he admired, he sought to base his revolution on the principles of socialism, Islam and pan-Somalism. In the early years, he often spoke of the compatibility of Islam and socialism and the need to bring "oneness" to the Somali nation. This *oneness* would discourage and seek to eliminate differentiation based on wealth, education or social status. Barre's philosophy during the first eight years of his rule (up until 1977) developed the ideology of "Scientific Socialism" through which he proclaimed that he would reorganize society by eliminating clan consciousness, promote "self-help" projects and pursue literacy and universal economic improvement.

Barre was impatient to get development off the ground. Through a strategy called "crash programs" he sought to "prioritize" many sectors for simultaneous development. These included livestock, agriculture, industry, water resources development, mineral exploration and exploitation, tourism and training.[10] The crash programs would also seek to institute economic policies of import substitution, resistance to foreign aid "with strings," and the organization of cooperatives through which the Somali people would "pool their resources."[11] By way of implementing this policy, the First Development Program, 1971–1973, put a freeze on prices of basic essentials such as maize. It instituted an Agricultural Development Agency and reduced government salaries by 40 percent. An increased tax was levied on luxury and building items, and a National Banana Agency was established to control exports and seek buyers other than Italy.

As a prophet, idealist and soldier-reformer, Barre was sincere in his desire to bring about the overarching goals of the regime. However, as a practical governing leader, there were many traditional ways of doing things that he left intact. For example, he left the livestock trade that provided most of the indigenously created revenue in the hands of the pastoral nomads who, in the mid-1970s, were 70 percent of the population. There were others who profited from the efforts of the nomad producer. These were the traditional drovers and brokers and the middlemen traders. In fact, these agents received as much as 25 to 30 percent of the price paid by the hard currency importer.[12] Leaving this important sector of the economy in private hands was a matter of practical survival for Barre, despite his impassioned speeches about the need to implement socialism. Aside from the trade's middlemen, there were government collaborators in the livestock trade, who, if frustrated, might prove to be powerful adversaries.

Although the framework, plans and policies were laid out, implementation would prove extremely difficult. Nature, never kind to Somalia, intervened with successive years of minimal rain and one of the worst droughts in memory during 1973–1974. To Barre's credit, he established a rural campaign for massive famine relief. Schools were closed and students, who were sent into the countryside to teach the new Somali orthography, shouldered this effort. Multilateral aid in cash and kind poured in from many countries and the government was able to save tens of thousands of lives. These events were a serious set back for the economy and the regime's development plans. Nevertheless, Barre persevered with resettlement schemes for the nomads and the establishment of "orientation centers." These centers taught socialist values and reliance on institutions of government for welfare, justice and protection. The goal of the orientation centers was to replace the old "tribal" identity with one that was Somali nationalist. In the resettlement areas, weekly meetings were designed to replace lineage structure socialization. Furthermore, women were to be uplifted and made "equal with men." A Proclamation was issued to this effect and the Somali Women's Democratic Organization (SWDO) was created.

Mohammad Siad Barre's laudable intentions to build a self-sufficient nation-state were defeated for a number of reasons. The years of drought certainly took their toll and while Barre tried to lessen the devastation by sending in the young people to help, this was a setback for development. Second, there was considerable resistance to the replacement of traditional community values with foreign socialist ones. As many as ten sheikhs, who condemned the new laws establishing equal rights for women and banning polygamy, were executed. Third, many clans, especially the Issaq, resented the incursion of Barre's military officers into leadership positions that replaced local governing elders. Even though the regime during its golden years made significant social achievements,[13] they came at a high cost to human rights and civil liberties. In addition to indoctrination that was carried out in the orientation centers, there was a newly created Somali Revolutionary Socialist Party (SRSP) in June 1976 for the purpose of instilling the political values, goals and ideology of the regime.

As Barre became ever more eager and determined to instill the new ideology, he became increasingly more impatient with any form of dissent. His style of personal rule was transformed as he slipped from the lofty roles of prophet, soldier-reformer, father figure, and prince of accommodation, to the earthier one of autocrat. The creation of the National Security Service (NSS) was evidence of this transformation. Those who continued to point to problems or difficulties were subject to arbitrary arrest and imprisonment. There was no hope of a fair public trial. As the decade of the 1970s came to a close, and throughout the 1980s, freedom of political association, personal liberty and movement, public expression, and the right to form unions and strike were severely curtailed or prohibited. Ironically, while the government continued to rely on the foreign exchange the nomadic pastoral producer provided, very little was done to improve the rangelands. The Issaq in the north particularly were affected by the deterioration of the range and the infrastructure of the northern capital, Hargeisa. Furthermore, the regime developed a preference for Marehan and Ogadeni and Darood concerns to the extent that those from other clans, and especially the Issaq, could not be heard. This situation presaged the northern Issaq rebellion against Barre's rule that would eventually engulf the whole nation in civil war. Although there was still some promise left in the regime during the 1970s despite the defeat of Somalia in the war with Ethiopia (1977–1978), by the middle of the next decade the rapid downward spiral of the economy left no doubt that the regime was in serious trouble. We will turn to that period now to discuss the aftermath of the war, loss of the regime's popularity, the continuing economic catastrophe and the ultimate loss of legitimacy of Siad Barre's rule.

At independence, it had been the intention of Somali patriots and nationalists to reconstitute greater Somalia by reintegrating the Somali nation under one administration. This irredentism was particularly focused on the Ogaden that had been ceded to Ethiopia by Britain in 1947. Barre decided to make his move in 1977 during a period when Ethiopia was trying to consolidate the revolution that had overthrown Haile Selassie and wage war against Eritrea. Thus, together, Somali regular troops and the Western Somali Liberation Front (WSLF) succeeded in gaining effective control of the region. The Soviet Union had decided to adopt Ethiopia after its Marxist revolution. Although the Soviets wanted to keep both states as clients, Barre refused this arrangement and looked toward the West for support. The Soviet Union gave massive amounts of support in materiel and advisors to Ethiopia and even sent in Cuban troops to help. Somalia could not persuade the United States nor the Middle Eastern states to support its cause and so, having been outgunned and outmanned, was defeated. The reaction to this defeat among his countrymen was disappointment and disillusion with the regime. Others reacted in despair or outrage.

The "October Revolution," as the regime was known, had been losing momentum because of the difficulties discussed above as well as other problems. One such problem was the one million refugees that streamed into Somalia from the Ogaden. This migration placed enormous burdens on an already overextended government. Approximately half of these refugees were placed in the northern community of the Issaq. Despite their general disapproval of the government, the Issaq tried to accommodate the refugees. The economic situation continued to deteriorate and worsen. With Ogaden failure, criticism of the government and of Barre's personal leadership escalated. Somalis from all clans began to view him as unreliable and ineffective. They reasoned that a leader with military training should not fail so utterly in this important, indeed crucial military undertaking. The more Barre was criticized the more sour his mood became. A vicious circle was set in motion as Barre became even more of an autocrat and more tyrannical in his attempt to stifle criticism.

In an effort to mollify some of his supporters, Barre increased his decided preference for those in the Marehan/Ogaden/Darood circle. He was beginning to turn away from his avowed aim of eliminating "tribalism" by openly giving them employment, business and educational opportunities to the exclusion of others. By 1983, the Issaq who had become embittered over being left out of government and development projects, as well as the government's attempt to implement controls over the livestock trade and expatriate labor remittances, mounted a protest through the Somali National Movement (SNM) that had been formed in 1980. In 1986, a critical event, the assassination of the northern region's national security service chief resulted in a full government crackdown. In the meantime, Barre decided to offer amnesty to the Majerteen, (subclan of Darood, of whom important leaders were estranged from and unsympathetic toward the regime) officers who had defected during the Ogaden war and were in exile in Ethiopia. In an effort to counteract the Issaq rebellion, he offered them lucrative business opportunities and positions in the national army, if they would return home and support the regime. The deliberate ploy of playing one clan off against the other was fully activated, as his 180-degree turn away from pan-Somalism in favor of regime survival became a reality.[14]

There is one area left to discuss in this review of the causes of failure and collapse of the Somali state under the leadership of Mohammad Siad Barre. It is necessary to look at the economic problems that were, in and of themselves, enough to wreck any nation-state still in its infancy and still quite fragile.

The Fragile Economy

Economic slowdown was a fact as early as 1975. The economy continued to flag until there was a complete standstill by the early 1980s. The Barre regime had been indifferent to the development of the rural economy, preferring instead to build up the government's bureaucratic cadres of the urban center, agriculture and industry, pretty much in that order of priority. The anomaly here was that the rural pastoral producers provided as much as 80 percent of foreign currency earnings. The government had inherited from the former colonial administration a system whereby it could extract resources without involving the rural producer. This was done through marketing boards, banking systems and other forms of institutional facilities. As Abdi Samatar pointed out, there were no reciprocal obligations between the state and society.[15] In a subsistence economy controlled by the producer, the government would not have had such extensive control. However, in Somalia, a collusion of wealthy traders and the government gave the producer a minimal return on production. This small mercantile class of traders narrowed the base of capital accumulation and increased dependency on foreign strategies of development. As I have argued elsewhere, the omission of the producer from consideration, as the commodification of livestock production increased, was to invite the ultimate failure of strategies to develop or improve the economy.

The livestock trade peaked in 1982. As discussed above, the Issaq in the North who were most successful in this sector were in rebellion against the government. Furthermore, in 1983, Saudi Arabia declared a health ban on Somali livestock. Barre's inattention to the needs of the pastoral producer and nature, which again and again tended to exacerbate Somali problems, combined to bring the valuable livestock trade to a virtual standstill. By 1984, inflation had spiraled to 100 percent. The government, in response to austerity measures dictated by the IMF, limited access to government jobs that it had formerly guaranteed to high school and college graduates and devalued the Somali shilling by more than 70 percent. Exports earned $58 million only and imports totaled $408 million, putting the trade deficit at $350 million. In 1986, foreign debt had grown to $172 million and was rescheduled in 1987 to be paid over twenty years.[16]

Food aid and other assistance amounted to 75 percent of the operating budgets of all social and economic ministries. There was also "security assistance" provided by the United States at $50 million in 1985 and $75 million in 1986, mostly to purchase U.S.-made military equipment. The United States reportedly suspended military aid in 1988 because of reports of human rights abuses by the regime against the Issaqs, also known as Somali National Movement rebels.[17] Before briefly recounting their rebellion and that of other clans who joined in to bring Barre's rule to an end, a summary of economic as well as other factors leading to the failure and collapse of the Somali state has been succinctly put by a United Nations official, and is worth noting here:

> Economic problems have their roots in a number of factors that can be attributed to Somalia's limited institutional capability, low skilled human resources, inefficient management (production and otherwise), harsh climate (frequent natural disasters and the inability to control them), insufficient investments in physical infrastructure and inappropriate development strategies and policies of

its past and present. As a consequence, the economy of Somalia has become increasingly dependent on foreign aid.[18]

Thus, in addition to the lack of popular civic participation that the Barre regime forbade, there was the ever-present clan competition and politics as well as the full range of economic problems. All of these issues came to a head in 1988, which by this time witnessed widespread dislike of the regime. Other clan families and subclans in a show of Somali centripetal force quickly joined the Issaq rebellion. In May 1988, the SNM forces seized control of the northern capital of Hargeisa and the town of Burao. Government troops responded with systematic shelling and bombing until both towns were flattened by the end of August. The Issaq had to defend their land against refugees from the Ogaden, government troops and paid mercenaries. However, Colonel Omer Jess, an Ogadeni, refused to take part in the sacking of the north, turned his troops toward the southwest where he later joined forces with General Mohamed Farah Aideed. Aideed had the backing of the Hawiye clan. In this concerted effort, the clans, showing that they could rally to bring Siad Barre down, did so, and freed Somalia of his rule.

When Siad Barre was driven out of Villa Somalia by the United Somali Forces on January 26, 1991, it was not evident what or who would replace him. In the aftermath of that struggle, there was again great divisiveness that led to the breakaway of the Issaq from the Somali Republic. They have reformed "Somaliland" as it had been known when the British held it. There is also an ongoing attempt to form "Puntland." Instead of reinserting the formerly lost lands of the Northern Frontier District of Kenya, the Ogaden and Djibouti, the former British North and the Italian South into a greater Somalia, there was splintering. It is my belief that it is possible to save Somalia from further disintegration through an adjustment of governing formulae and mechanisms. In the same manner that the Somalis have adapted in the past to English, French and Arab influences and made Islam their own, they also adopted a Latin orthography for the written expression of their language. It is therefore not unreasonable to expect that they can adapt a foreign model of federalism, if it is appropriate to their needs. Here we may usefully review some working definitions of federalism and later evaluate a model for use in Somalia.

Making the State Relevant: Federal Solutions for Survival, Growth, and Development

One definition of federalism is a division of public authority between constitutionally defined orders of government. Carl J. Friedrich recognized five levels of government: the local community, the tribal or regional community, the national community, the supranational culture, and the global world community.[19] Federalism, regionalism and decentralization have all increased in importance as possible ways of dealing with the political issues resulting from such interaction. Ivo D. Duchacek posited that " . . . self-ruling territorial communities that have decided to form a higher supranational union from 'below,' delegating power to a central authority for some purposes while retaining local self-rule for other purposes . . . are usually called *confederal* or *federal* systems."[20] According to Preston King, " . . . federalism constitutes a variable response to opposing demands for the centralization and decentralization of power on a specifically territorial basis."[21]

In the age of globalization, larger political units have the best opportunity for influence in the world arena. This argument augments what I believe to be true for Somalia. Splitting into small self-contained units such as "Somaliland" and "Puntland" cannot be expected to serve the Somalis in the age of globalism.

Paraphrasing Ursula Hick's view, preserving the integrity of the units that the nation's identity, culture and tradition dictate is the inherently democratic objective of a federation that is inherently "democratic."[22] The question is, do the Somalis seek to maintain their culture and tradition in an overarching Somali nation?

The Somalis have traditionally used methods of interclan collaboration and coping mechanisms that make some form of federalism plausible. One is the traditional indigenous method of building alliances and the other is in regional drought response. As both rely on regionalism, they seem to suggest the best possibility for reconstituting the Somali state.

The System of Alliances

Within a given territory, a clan or subclan will probably not have all the resources it needs for survival. As discussed above, the primary concern of the *diya*-paying group, the subclan or clan, is the need to maintain solidarity to meet an external threat. Alliances are contracted with other clans and neighboring subclans which may include marriages. These groups often split up, regroup and form new *Heer* alliances or treaties. Thus clan alliance configurations may change. A *reer* (herding group) is generally not less than two to three hundred men with sizeable stock-wealth. Below this level they would not be able to function as a viable jural and political unit. Furthermore, the larger the group is, the less the sacrifice is for individual members in fulfilling *Heer*-treaty obligations. Based on the above description of building alliance structures, it is clear that large federations may develop.

Alliances may be formed among smaller Somali groups who live interspersed among larger clans and lineages. Those who have been completely separated from their lineages of origin must enter into alliances from a position of weakness. "Either be a mountain or attach yourself to one" is a Somali proverb that summarizes the dependent relationship of such alliances.[23] In this connection, the term *gaasgaanbuur*, meaning "pile of shields," is used. It refers to alliances that may be made outside the kinship group or those made simply to increase fighting strength against potential enemies. The Somalis use the same term in describing alliances among other nations such as NATO and the former Warsaw Pact. These alliances come into full play when the rangelands are in drought condition. Somalis then employ "drought response mechanisms."

Drought Response Mechanisms

The "drought response model" employed for hundreds of years to ensure survival has been fully described by Lee V. Cassanelli.[24] This systematized action in defense of pastoralism as a way of life required no overarching central authority, until the Barre regime intervened in any but a marginal way in the practices of the nomads. I find the drought response model compelling and useful in arguing for regionalism or a loose form of federalism as a starting point toward reconstituting the Somali state. Somali social structure, with its ever-widening concentric circles of group commitment, as well as traditional drought response mechanisms, corresponds well to Swiss-type cantonal and federal levels of government. According to scholars of pastoralism, there are characteristically definite responses to drought: dispersal, depletion, exchange and temporary settlement outside the pastoral sector.[25] In the drought response model, the political processes of adaptation and accommodation are employed as well as decision-making and organizational skills. Networks of kinship and credit are called upon. The laws of clientage and alliances are executed. The Somali nomad's "drought-confrontation strategy" explains the resiliency of pastoralism. The coping techniques include maintaining sizeable herds of livestock above and beyond what would normally be needed as a method of insurance against inevitable drought. Next, when drought is apparent, ecological strategies are initiated. Animals are separated according to their ability to cope with the drought. Stock is reduced by increased exports of both live animals as well as hides. Sturdier stock will be maintained while the weaker animals will be slaughtered (sheep and goats first) and sold, so that herdsmen can obtain other foodstuffs such as dates, rice and grains. These will replace coffee, tobacco and imported cloth that is generally bought during good years. In dire circumstances, the cattle and finally the camels will go.

The next step is to keep only what we could call "essential personnel" in the pasturelands to lessen the pressure on the remaining herds and improve their chances for survival. A small group of younger men watch over the herds while women, children, the elderly and infirmed are sent to urban kinsman or predetermined agricultural allies. These allies are part of a long existing "symbiotic relationship between pastoralists and agriculturalists." A lineage may need to accept clientele status (*sheegad*) of a nearby clan. In this arrangement, the client group works and fights alongside the patron clan in exchange for protection that includes access to the "patron's" water and pasture. By use of these techniques, the strategy is meant to ensure the survival of the family and the lineage group, the preservation of the reproductive potential of the family livestock, and the conservation of the grazing and water resources of the clan. These strategies make it possible for the nomads to reconstitute their herds once the drought has dissipated. "This resiliency is all the more remarkable if it is realized that no central government until the present one [Siad Barre's rule] intervened in any but a marginal way in the practices of the nomads."[26]

The traditional drought response methods were proven to be superior to the drought responses organized by the more recently formulated state policies. The government response under Siad Barre simply encouraged settlement in agricultural lands. Barre wanted to diffuse the practice of clan alliances as well as get more people settled into agriculture. When international help was sought, agencies were unable to carry out drought relief as efficiently. There were redundancies, duplication of effort and huge expenses. Rather than permanent settlement advocated by the Barre regime, pastoralists normally wished to return to pastoralism and did so generally without the help of centralized authority or foreign assistance. As the drought-response methods show, the Somali community is interdependent and the community is the level at which Somalis should begin to reorganize their state. It will do no good at all to design a top-down state for Somalia. Siad Barre tried to replace the *diya* system with state courts. He was however, unable to replace the indigenous, traditional system of *diya* with a strong centralized authority thousands of miles away.

The Swiss Canton Model of State

Given the Somali predilection for decentralized governing authority, an examination of the Swiss model as a possibility for Somalia seems appropriate. The Swiss confederation was originally composed of twenty-two (now twenty-six)[27] sovereign cantons that were self-governing states and not provinces of a centralized state. Three of the states were further subdivided based on the configuration of the country (the valleys of Obwalden and Nidwalden), or religious reasons (Inner Rhodes and Outer Rhodes, Catholic and Protestant respectively) or rural versus urban (Basletown and Basle country). One of Switzerland's most important governing features was the communal citizenship upon which canton citizenship was based. This is still true today although since 1848 the Swiss Confederation was converted into a federation.

The Swiss called themselves "an alliance between sovereign states," and the first article of the Constitution spoke of "twenty-two sovereign cantons." Swiss cantons originally had a unicameral parliamentary system as there was felt to be no need for the control of one chamber by another.[28] Prior to the annual canton meeting that might be held in a public square or meadow near the capital, the local council prepared the agenda that has been vetted through previous public debates with "complete freedom of speech" for every person.[29] The deliberations in the annual cantonal gathering could then only deal with points appearing on the agenda. This process made it possible for the meeting to move smoothly along, avoiding disruptions, heated conflict and rash decisions.

Prior to looking at the relationship of the cantons to the federal government, I would like at this point to examine this grassroots approach to the state in the context of the Somali sociopolitical structure. Today, the Swiss still have three layers of political identity: the commune, canton and Swiss federation. In like manner, each Somali is connected through layers of identity, namely, the herding group, subclan and clan family. In the Somali case, lineage permeates all three levels, strengthening the ties. Just as membership in a lineage group or clan cannot be abrogated, civic and political participation designed on this basis would provide the Somali with inalienable rights of citizenship.

A unicameral legislative body as in the Swiss cantonal model would be appropriate to consider when analyzing the homogeneous Somali grassroots governing unit, since it closely approximates the traditional Somali *Heer* treaty or contract with its explicitly formulated body of obligations, rights and duties to which all are bound. Furthermore, the unicameral legislative model discourages unnecessary differentiation. The Swiss annual canton meetings approximate the coming together of Somali herdsmen during the *gu* season when social exchanges take place on a grand scale involving religious rituals, marriages, literary exchanges and the recitation of ancestral genealogy. The parliamentary period might be an extension of that gathering.

Generally clan gatherings are perforce economic, social and political. Gatherings are democratic and free, allowing all persons opportunities to speak and contribute ideas. However, in the case of parliamentary debate, there needs to be a clear-cut focus on the issues that affect all the people. Therefore it is suggested that the traditional *Shir*, the councils of elders, convene just prior to the *gu* festivities to discuss the agenda that will follow it.

It may be that because the Somalis are in fact homogeneous—as that term is commonly applied to groups within the same historical experience, race, culture, language and religion—they may not need the hundreds of years it took the heterogeneous Swiss to build their federation. Somali federation may similarly not require a civil war as occurred in the American model, since there is no large collectivity with a way of life that seeks to defend itself against a progressive majority. Moreover where the Swiss were divided because of language (German, French, Italian and Romance), the Somalis have one unifying Somali language. Where the Swiss were divided because of religion (Catholic, Protestant, Jew, Orthodox, Old Catholic, agnostic or atheist), the Somalis have the unifying force of Islam.

The Swiss federation was developed in response to the need for the original three cantons—Uri, Schwyz and Unterwalden—to come together in 1291 for self-defense.[30] This Swiss version of *gaasgaanbuur* was established for resistance to oppressive feudal overlords. At a time when Europeans could unabashedly be referred to as *tribes*, it was said that they knew something of Roman law and administration, but rather more about "the democratic practices of German tribes."[31] Each family held a small area of land, making each family to a large extent self-reliant, but forest and pastures were owned communally and everyone took part in the decisions about their management.[32]

Shared decision-making is a hallmark of *Xeer*, a system of customary law embedded in Somali culture that guides kinship group governance and relations with other Somali groups, clans or communities. In a pastoral society that prides itself on simplicity, government should follow the predilections of the people, since it is meant to serve the people and not the people serving the government. With *Xeer*, Somalis have enforceable rules and regulations and mechanisms of conflict control. Therefore through *Xeer* and *diya*, as well as *Hidird* (male forums) and *Heer*, the ground rules and framework are already in place. If the Somalis want to replace *diya*, it should be left to them to work out a suitable replacement over time. The social relations of production that is important to pastoral and agrarian societies alike need to be understood and respected.

Impenetrable monolithic structures are not what are needed in Somalia. That is not to say standards and procedures are not necessary, but they must be appropriate to conditions and circumstances. The Somali state will have to be reconstituted incrementally through a process of experimentation that takes place over a number of years, probably a decade or even a generation. Having said that, it is still possible to offer guidelines for bringing the Somalis back into attitudes of collaboration and cooperation. They will need to present a united front against those who would scatter the clans and conquer the land. This is an age-old concern because of Somalia's strategic location at the juncture of the Red Sea and Indian Oceans.

Somalia may still be vulnerable to incursions from abroad. A vulnerable nation might face aggression, territorial incursions and other, subtler forms of trespass. One of the problems that has plagued Africa over the last forty years is the intense and pervasive monetarization and commodification of goods and services formerly used for sustenance or furthering the health and viability of the larger society.

At this juncture of their history, all Somali clans and clan families need to have a giant "pow-wow" which includes men and women, intellectuals and religious leaders. Those who have a predisposition to war and those who seek peace must call on their elders and statesmen for guidance. Former warriors need to lay down their arms, for survival can no longer be sought through violence. Should Somalia continue to be broken up piecemeal into parcels of land, the Somali people will, in the process, lose much of what has over the last two millennia, made them the people they are.

For the benefit of all Somalis, there are certain matters of trans-clan importance that need to be monitored by an overarching specifically constituted authority. Among these are defense, a monetary system (currency), a postal system, and foreign policy. Armed action should only be carried out in defense of outside aggression, and then only when many and all attempts for solutions have been sought through neutral international, multinational and multilateral mediation. Just as a national army had to be foresworn in post–World War II Japan, Somalia needs a respite from conflict in order to create space for development.

According to Daniel Elazar, the term "'federal arrangements' suggests that there is more than one way to apply federal principles. . . . [Fe]deralism can be considered a genus of political organization of which there are several species."[33] In the search for ways and means for Somalia, a certain "species" of federalism that considers the cultural factors that are peculiar to Somalia within a larger African context would be needed.

It would seem, therefore, that if Somalis chose this type of federalism, democratic participation would depend heavily on local government, as the overarching common government would be filled with pre-chosen delegates from the "constituencies" or localities. Based on what has been said above about indigenous Somali local government, this would not, a priori appear to be a problem. The United States (1776–1789) and Switzerland (1291–1847) both started out as confederations, later tightening the structure by changing over to federal systems wherein the federal government was given more power. In the case of Switzerland, it took six centuries for the Swiss to develop enough confidence to strengthen central authority, having had so much success with local self-government to solve most of their problems.

Some might argue the looseness of a federation may not provide enough structure for Somalis. This argument might have credence if we were speaking uniformly of settled agriculturalists. However, as possibly two-thirds or more Somalis are still nomadic herdsmen engaged in transhumance, it could be reasonably argued that decision-making at the local level of *reer* is absolutely essential. Given the above explanations about drought-response mechanisms lineage, *reer* and clan government, the Somali must be free to create alliances and cooperative unions as the ecology dictates. Furthermore, the Somali nation has been traumatized by the recent civil war that continues to smolder. It is necessary for them to have time to regroup and think about their options.

Conclusion

The chapter discussed the factors that caused state failure and collapse in Somalia. Specifically, the chapter examined the numerous shortcomings of the parliamentary democratic experiment in Somalia during the immediate post-independence period. The democratic experiment was aborted by a military coup that brought Siad Barre to power. Initially, Barre was committed to the reconstitution of the Somali state. But, overtime, Barre became a tyrant and established a repressive and authoritarian state. The failures of the Barre regime precipitated the formation of various clan-based militias with the common goal of ousting Barre from power. The conflicts between the Barre regime and the various clan-based militias eventually led to a civil war, which brought about the collapse of the state and the removal of the Barre regime.

Since the collapse of the state, Somalia continues to experience violence and disintegration. For example, the northern portion of the country has seceded and established the Republic of Somaliland, although it has not been recognized as a sovereign state in the international system.

Finally, in order to reconstitute the Somali state, including addressing the problem of violence and disintegration, the chapter suggests the adoption of a federalist system of governance similar to the Swiss cantons. Under such an arrangement, Somalia would remain a unified state, but the various clans would have local autonomy.

Notes

1. For a detailed study of this and other aspects of the Somali patrilineal clan system see I. M. Lewis, *A Pastoral Democracy* (Oxford: Oxford University Press, 1961).

2. Ahmed Samatar, *Socialist Somalia, Rhetoric and Reality* (London: Zed Books, 1988).

3. See the works of Lewis, *A Pastoral Democracy*; I. M. Lewis, *A Modern History of Somalia: Nation and State in the Horn of Africa* (Boulder, CO: Westview Press, 1988); David Latin and Said Samatar, *Somalia: Nation in Search of a State* (Boulder, CO: Westview Press, 1987); Abdi Samatar, *The State and Rural Transformation in Northern Somalia, 1884–1986* (Madison: The University of Wisconsin Press, 1989); Samatar, *Socialist Somalia*; and Alice B. Hashim, *The Fallen State: Dissonance, Dictatorship and Death in Somalia* (Lanham, MD: University Press of America, 1997) for discussions on the decentralized self-governing modes of the Somali clans.

4. One study of this arrangement is Paolo Contini's *The Somali Republican Experiment in Legal Integration* (London: Frank Cass, 1969); another is that of Mark Karp, *The Economics of Trusteeship in Somalia* (Boston: African Studies Program: Boston University Press, 1960).

5. A. A. Castagno Jr. discusses the Somali situation in *Political Parties and National Integration in Tropical Africa*, ed. James S. Coleman and Carl G. Rosberg Jr. (Berkeley: University of California Press, 1970).

6. Quoted in Arend Lijphart, *Democracy in Plural Societies* (New Haven, CT: Yale University Press, 1977), 19.

7. I. M. Lewis, "The Politics of the 1969 Somali Coup," *Journal of Modern African Studies* 10, no. 3 (1972).

8. Basil Davidson, *Modern Africa* (London: Longman Group, 1983), 177.

9. For a fuller discussion of these events, see Lewis, *A Pastoral Democracy*.

10. From Siad Barre, *My Country and My People* (Mogadishu: State Printing Agency, 1974). This was a collection of Barre's speeches published from time to time by the Ministry of Information and compiled in the above publication.

11. Barre, *My Country and My People*.

12. See Hashim, *The Fallen State*, 85.

13. For example, health centers and infirmaries were built throughout the countryside. Vaccination campaigns against cholera (1970) and smallpox (1977) were effective. School enrollment increased from 42,000 in 1969 to 243,000 in 1978 and 60 percent literacy was obtained. See Jan M. Haakosen, *Scientific Socialism and Self-Reliance* (Bergen, Norway: University of Bergen Press, 1984).

14. A detailed discussion of this fascinating period of the Barre regime can be found in Hashim, *The Fallen State*.

15. Abdi Samatar, *The State and Rural Transformation in Northern Somalia, 1884–1986*.

16. Figures taken from Samatar, *The State and Rural Transformation*, 149–53.

17. See Samatar, *The State and Rural Transformation*, and The Heritage Foundation, *Preserving American Security Ties to Somalia*, No. 745 (Washington, DC: The Heritage Foundation, 1989), 7.

18. Office of the Resident Representative of the UNDP, Special Country Report to the Administrator-Confidential, Mogadishu, Somalia, 1990, 7.

19. Carl J. Friedrick, *Trends of Federalism in Theory and Practice* (New York: Frederick Praeger, 1969), 3–4.

20. Ivo Duchacek, *Comparative Federalism: The Territorial Dimension of Politics* (New York: Holt, Rinehart and Winston, 1970), 2.

21. Preston King, *Federalism and Federation* (Baltimore: Johns Hopkins University Press, 1982), 21.

22. Ursula Hicks, *Federalism: Failure and Success* (Oxford, UK: Oxford University Press, 1978), 4.

23. There are categories into which these weaker partners may fall: *deris* or neighbor; *saar* or appendage; *sooraa* or followers; and *sheegard* or pretenders, or those who say or claim to be something they are not. Also, see Lewis, "The Politics of the 1969 Somali Coup," 189.

24. Lee Cassanelli, *The Shaping of Somali Society: Restructuring the History of a Pastoral People, 1600–1900* (Philadelphia: University of Pennsylvania Press, 1982), 60–63.

25. See Cassanelli, *The Shaping of Somali Society.*

26. Cassanelli, *The Shaping of Somali Society*, 64.

27. Italics are mine.

28. George Sauser-Hall, *The Political Institutions of Switzerland* (Bern: Swiss National Tourist Office Publishing Department, 1946), 145.

29. Sauser-Hall, *The Political Institutions of Switzerland.*

30. Nicholas Gillett, *The Swiss Constitution: Can It Be Exported?* (Bern: Yes Publication, 1989), 12.

31. Gillett, *The Swiss Constitution: Can It Be Exported?*

32. Gillett, *The Swiss Constitution: Can It Be Exported?*

33. Daniel Elazar, *Exporting Federalism* (Tuscaloosa: University of Alabama Press, 987), 6.

11

Making the State Relevant in South Africa

Owen Sichone

SOUTH AFRICA HAS A LONG HISTORY OF MODERN STATE FORMATION. Much of this history, however, has been dominated by colonial rule and apartheid, both of which excluded the majority indigenous population and other peoples of color from participation in political life. It was only with the elections of 1994 that the whole population was able to enjoy universal franchise under a liberal constitution. The aim of this chapter is to review the experience of state failure in South Africa and show how the current struggles to make the state relevant in citizens' lives grapple with the legacy of apartheid.

According to the somewhat selective generalizations of prominent American political thinker Robert I. Rotberg, "Nation-states fail because they can no longer deliver positive political goods to their people. Their governments lose legitimacy and, in the eyes and hearts of a growing plurality of its citizens, the nation-state itself becomes illegitimate."[1] This general definition is only partially true for South Africa, where the colonial state was never legitimate from the point of view of the disenfranchised majority but was able to deliver to the white minority on the basis of systematic racial discrimination policies of segregation and apartheid.

Africa entered the twenty-first century with a lot of optimism, despite the fact that the fate of most Africans in reality showed little sign of improvement. The reason for the hope of a better future was partly the political changes that took place in Nigeria and South Africa, two of the continent's most powerful states. As President Mbeki consolidated the reconstruction of South African society after half a century of apartheid, an "African Renaissance" was proclaimed that promised to put the continent on a new footing. Focusing initially on the leading role of South Africa, but also recognizing the importance of a new generation of African leaders in Ghana, Uganda and Rwanda, who were promising to bring a new seriousness to the business of African statecraft. President Thabo Mbeki, the leading spokesperson for the "African Renaissance" seeks to make this the "African Century" and reverse all of the negative political and economic crises that have bedeviled the continent for so long.

The nonracial, nonsexist democratic society that the ANC-led government seeks to establish is meant to be very different from the apartheid society, but also has the unenviable task of correcting the many social problems it inherited from the previous regime. A further disadvantage is that the end of apartheid coincided with the triumph of neoliberalism on a global scale. Whereas many ANC supporters had hoped for a post-apartheid society in which the state would implement socialist policies or, at the very least, welfare capitalism, their hopes were not realized. Privatization rather than nationalization is the basis of the ANC's economic policies.

The exact methods of creating the new society are a much-debated topic. At present, there is an uneasy combination of pragmatism, reconciliation, and redistribution in the government's macro-economic policy framework. The state continues to play the leading role in the provision of social services and construction of infrastructures. There is, however, pressure from global economic forces for South Africa to accelerate the pace of privatization and structural adjustment even though the inherited racial, gender and regional inequalities have not yet been corrected. It is doubtful whether the private sector can uplift the quality of life of the black majority in the short or even medium term. Apartheid was, after all, state-driven economic and political discrimination designed to make Africans the servants of European settlers.

This chapter will give an overview of the South African situation; highlight the economic and social problems created by apartheid and the extent to which the ANC-led government has put in place the policies to remedy the situation. I will then use the example of crime and violence to show how important the role of the state is in the maintenance of law and order in South Africa and the region and how this might contribute to the development of the southern African region as a whole. Then, I will suggest some ways in which the post-apartheid South African state could be made relevant.

The Apartheid Legacy

Apartheid or racial segregation was the policy of the National Party regime, which ruled South Africa from 1948 until it lost the democratic elections held in 1994. This was not a system of "separate development" as the NP spin-doctors used to argue, but racial discrimination and preferential treatment of European settlers in all areas of human development. The result has been that white South Africans enjoy a high standard of living, while the lives of close to half the black population are characterized by abject poverty, in what is an ostensibly a wealthy country.

Any discussion of South African life cannot escape the reality of having a well-developed white society side by side with a poverty-stricken black majority or what President Mbeki called the "two nations." Thus, although the concept of state failure or collapse does not describe the situation in "white" South Africa, whose economy and bureaucracy generally functioned well, the apartheid state was illegitimate from the perspective of black South Africans. In my discussion, I will focus on the high levels of violent crime to show that beneath the veneer of a stable and efficient state lurks a society under pressure. In matters of crime prevention and citizens' security, the state in South Africa is battling to assert its authority.

In the five years that the ANC has been in power, the country continues to be racially divided but the pace at which racial discrimination and privilege have been dismantled has been impressive. Although the black majority suffers high levels of poverty, the provisions of houses, clean water, electricity and basic services are being provided to communities that were discriminated against under apartheid. The Reconstruction and Development Program (RDP) and Growth, Employment and Redistribution (GEAR) are the macroeconomic policy instruments that the ANC-led government has been using to bring about change. The basic ideas of economic justice are as old as the liberation movement's earliest manifestos, most notably the Freedom Charter of 1955, but are also in harmony with current global economic ideologies.[2]

For many years the Freedom Charter was the manifesto of the liberation movement in South Africa. For the youth who campaigned for the release of Nelson Mandela and other political prisoners, it also provided the promise of a better life. Learning the sections of the Charter by heart, the young people expected that "The doors of learning and of culture shall be opened" and that "education shall be free, compulsory, universal and equal for all children."[3] Many of the promises contained in the Charter have not been delivered and the demoralization of a generation of young South Africans, whose hopes of a better life appear bleak, is cause for concern.

The Two Nations

Poverty and wealth coexist uneasily in South Africa and this has serious implications for the country and Southern Africa as a whole.[4] The October

Household Surveys found an official unemployment in 1996 of 20.3 percent and an expanded unemployment rate (which includes those who have not looked for work in the past four weeks) of 34.4 percent.[5] By 1998, official unemployment had risen to 26.1 percent and the expanded unemployment rate to 38.6 percent; predictably, young Africans are the worst hit by the lack of jobs with 50 percent of those aged 15 to 30 likely to be unemployed.[6]

The lack of employment opportunities is the single most important economic problem facing the ANC-led government and will certainly add to the state's security and crime problems that I will discuss in the rest of the chapter. This will serve to illustrate why it is important to expect the state to play the leading role in the process of poverty alleviation as well as in the control over the means of violence.

Although liberal political parties and the owners of capital blame high unemployment on rigid labor laws, and thus on the state, the trade unions have also been critical of the government's economic policies, which they view as more supportive of big business than of the workers. The racial character of the unemployment problem, however, is clearly a legacy of the past and one from which the employers of cheap labor such as the mines and farms have profited immensely in the past. The social inequalities created by the apartheid system will not be eradicated in the near future. The inability of the state to implement the policies needed to improve education, health and other social services in the current global setting compounds an already desperate situation. As table 11.1 shows, the previously disadvantaged population continues to be at a disadvantage in the economy.

In 1996, there were about 9.1 million employed people in South Africa out of an economically active population of 13 million. As the job market changes in favor of skilled workers in the private sector, so will the problem of unemployment worsen among women and Africans who are concentrated in public sector and unskilled jobs.

It is generally feared that this bleak job scenario has contributed to the crime wave that has gripped much of urban South Africa and affected some

Table 11.1. Economically Active Population in South Africa by Race and Sex, 1996

	African	*White*
Employed		
Male	3,506,509	1,060,736
Female	2,175,968	795,716
Unemployed		
Male	1,810,570	45,938
Female	2,395,421	43,127

Source: Statistics South Africa[7]

rural areas as well. The failure of the police to cope with the high crime rate has caused South Africa to become a heavily armed society. Furthermore, the private sector plays a leading role in the crime prevention business due to the perceived inadequacies of the police. But it is debatable whether the privatization of policing can improve the security situation in the country.

South Africa's Culture of Violence

Although South Africa is a violent society and guns are used in many reported crimes, it does not really have a gun culture. Much of the domestic and criminal violence that plagues the country does involve the use of guns. Reports in the news media about women who have been killed by abusive partners, policemen killed for their service pistols, drive-by shootings, contract killings, and random shootings in schools, army bases and even hospitals reveal the extent of this crime problem. The culture of violence shows no particular love for or understanding of firearms and merely uses guns as a means to evil ends. This culture of violence cannot be fully understood without referring to the combined impact of economic crisis, illicit drugs, and alcohol abuse and apartheid's violence on the society as a whole.

There is no denying the scale of the problem, but there is no agreement on the solutions. South Africa does not yet have a powerful gun lobby similar to the 6 million-member American National Rifle Association, but new gun control legislation is being resisted by groups of gun owners countrywide. So far, South African politicians have not been held ransom by this pressure group. Unlike in America, there is no network of gun enthusiasts who take their baby sons to the shooting range and buy them guns as birthday presents, as soon as they are able to walk. South Africa does however have a well-armed population. If there is a gun culture, it is based on the claims to a frontier tradition on the part of Boere-Afrikaners whose ancestors always carried guns. In this sense, it is a nationalist claim similar to the Zulu claim for the right to carry "traditional weapons," a right defined and so resolutely defended by IFP leader Mangosuthu Buthelezi. The loudest pro-gun noises have tended to come from the predominantly white owners of licensed firearms, who have come to link their safety and security to the possession of weapons. A survey of farmers found, for instance, that although most of the respondents lived alone with their spouses, they had five or more firearms in the house. "One farmer with two safes full of weapons and other weapons concealed in the attic and other places admitted that he had too many weapons but did not know what to do with them."[8] This faith in guns is inherited from the apartheid past, when a siege mentality was promoted by the National Party but has recently become part of the post-apartheid society's language of disappointment. The failure of the South African Police Service to check the rising crime levels—to put it bluntly, the state's failure to protect citizens—has led many citizens to look for ways of protecting themselves. Guns are one of these solutions.

The right to carry guns as a means of defending lives, cars and other property has taken on a new significance as the perception has grown that people were safer under apartheid. Indeed apartheid encouraged the white population to become heavily armed and prepare for the total onslaught. Today, South Africans still carry identity documents that bear pages for endorsing driving as well as gun licenses. Seemingly, when South African citizens come of age, they are expected to have guns with which to protect their cars. This war mentality was very much part of the apartheid culture of the laager (defensive position) put up by the National Party in its attempt to convince white families that they were part of an army defending Christian civilization from communists and agitators.

In post-apartheid South Africa, total onslaught siege mentality has been redirected from the communist to the criminal threat. As in other parts of the world, cutbacks in police budgets have spawned a boom in private police forces and vigilantism. In urban South Africa especially, there is a growing reliance on non-state security firms. There are estimated 180,000 registered security guards in the country—at least 40,000 of whom are armed. There are also approximately 100,000 unregistered guards.[9]

The end of apartheid saw a significant reduction in levels of political violence. Criminal activity against person and property though it has not escalated, nevertheless has been reported in a manner designed to alarm. I am not saying that the crime situation is exaggerated, but only that it has not been made worse by the end of apartheid, as many people longing for a return to the apartheid order believe. The crime statistics are such that even the best police force in the world would not be able to cope:

1. Over two million (2,154,570) crimes were reported to the SAPS in 1998.
2. More police are killed in the line of duty in South Africa than in any other country in the world.
3. Johannesburg's inner-city flatland Hillbrow, with a population of half a million and more than a million commuters passing through every day, has 375 police on the beat.
4. In Cape Town, Mitchell's Plain, home to the most violent drug gangs in the world, has one police station and one satellite station for 1.2 million people spread over 70 square kilometers. Of the 323 police officers, based at the station, only 105 are involved in active policing.[10]

During the apartheid years, South Africa became well armed and developed a formidable weapons industry comparable to none in Africa. White families also became well armed and it was more or less taken for granted that guns were *needed* for the survival of the volk. Thus, whereas the right to bear arms is made a big issue in America, with numerous state agencies specializing in the protection of people and property, the apartheid regime was engaged in a deliberate strategy to arm the whites and keep the blacks unarmed.

Without guns, violent crimes still occur. Rapes, murder, arson and robbery can still occur with knives, petrol and matches, *knob-kerries* and other traditional weapons. So in looking at the problem of guns in South Africa, we have to separate the issue of gun control from that of South Africa's culture of violence. The solutions for these closely related problems are not easy.

Crime and the Human Security Challenge

South Africa is a world leader in violent crime. Serial killers emerge on a regular basis in both big cities and rural towns. Other violent offenses including gang rape and murder are part of routine gang initiation rituals. The frequent killings of the very law enforcement officers, who are supposed to protect society, also contribute to the view of many citizens that law and order have all but collapsed. The use of violence to settle personal and group differences has almost become normal. Even business competition and sports rivalries usually turn into violent confrontations. When a profitable taxi route becomes over-subscribed and incomes start to fall, "taxi-violence" follows resulting in the deaths of the passengers upon whom the industry depends. In the past, killing of business rivals in this industry was linked to "Third Force" violence designed to sow terror among the black population. That some policemen were also taxi owners further complicated the problem because there was no trust between the public, rival taxi organizations and police charged with investigating crimes. Both licensed and illegal guns have been used in most of the taxi-violence.

Armed robberies, especially cash in transit heists and car hijacking have also involved the use of guns. They occur with such frequency that they are indeed part of the culture of crime. The large number of private armed security companies, alarm and electric fencing and other specialist firms in the security industry shows the extent to which the society has been traumatized. Where else in the world do you find anti-robbery flame-throwers fitted on a car to burn would be carjackers? The architecture of the urban home has been altered completely with panic buttons and other electronic gadgets reinforcing the sense of siege in this traumatized society.

Unfortunately, guns that are one of the main causes of the wound are also seen as a cure and frightened people acquire guns in order to feel safe. Criminals thus need to be well armed to overpower their victims, and the first thing they do when they break into a house is look for the gun cabinet. Indeed the killing of policemen and traffic officers appears to be mainly aimed at obtaining their service pistols.

What is well known but rarely discussed is the close association between violence, drugs and alcohol. Every weekend, the city trauma clinics prepare themselves for knife wounds and bullet wounds and it would be quite easy to prove the existence of a predictable pattern of weekend violence as an alcohol-related complex of senseless drinking, rape, child abuse and murder. Civilian doctors at big township hospitals have more experience in treating stab and gunshot wounds than even military doctors in other countries.

Although the Western Cape together with Gauteng and Kwazulu-Natal are more prone to violence than the other provinces, table 11.2 shows that the steady increase in violent crimes for the region is representative of the national trend.

In many of these crimes, guns are an essential part of the criminals' toolkit. Certainly, the gangs that carry out attacks on cash in transit vans use armor piercing ammunition and carry out their crimes with military precision, suggesting that they may have a military background. The link between the recent wars in Southern Africa as a whole and rising crime and insecurity is not limited to South Africa. The general public's perception that security has worsened under the ANC government is reflected in the crime statistics that show an increase in property-related robberies. Contrary to some politicians' views that corruption has increased under majority rule, between 1994 and 1998 there was actually a decline in commercial crimes like forgery and fraud, although there may well have been an increase in news reports on high profile cases involving the new political leaders.

Table 11.2. Violent Crimes in the Western Cape, January 1994–December 1998

Crime	*1994*	*1995*	*1996*	*1997*	*1998*
Rape and attempted rape	5,371	5,681	6,228	6,658	6,204
Murder	2,667	3,095	3,259	3,129	3,534
Attempted murder	2,679	2,910	3,254	3,639	4,105
Carjacking	—	—	288	322	399
Hijacking of trucks	—	—	52	43	61
Robbery of cash in transit in vans	—	—	21	20	15
Bank robbery	—	—	33	31	35

Source: Crime Information Analysis Center, 1999, Annexure B, p. 13.

Reported cases of murder, rape and assault were already high under apartheid and statistics show that the incidence of such crimes has not decreased since 1994.[11] Despite this fact, the feeling of insecurity among the people has continued to rise. Whites emigrating to Australia or America cite crime as one of their motivations. Blacks setting up vigilante groups like the Cape Town–based People Against Gangsterism and Drugs (PAGAD) or the Northern Province–based *Mapogo a Mataga* and numerous smaller street–level instant justice mobs have emerged. These reinforce the perception that the police are ineffective or corrupt and that the courts are lenient. Businesses protected by *Mapogo* for example have publicly stated that the police is incapable of providing the security that they have gratefully accepted from the vigilantes. The challenge to the state have created stress between the democratic constitution that guarantees numerous human rights, including those of suspected and even convicted criminals on the one hand, and a still traumatized population, on the other. The state has no choice but to protect criminals in a situation, for example, where vigilante groups have been known to collect money from neighbors in order to pay the bail for a suspected rapist or murderer, in order to execute the suspect once he is out of police custody. Clearly, there is something wrong with the South African criminal justice system.

The easy access to firearms among both the criminals and the vigilante self-protection groups is in part a result of the commercialization and mass production of weapons in South Africa. Denel (formerly part of Armscor) is South Africa's state-owned arms manufacturer, some of whose many subsidiaries are involved in the production of handguns. These are aggressively marketed through the national media and sustain a sizeable legal gun trade. The armaments industry is also undergoing privatization and foreign companies have shown interest in acquiring some of these forms. On the classified pages of local dailies, adverts like the ones below appear next to others for liquor licenses, security training courses and tombstones:

IT'S TIME STOP CRIME!!
WE BUY GUNS FOR CASH

Lorcin 7.65mm . . . R855
Lorcin 9mm SHORT . . . R890
Norinco 9mm PARA . . . R875
Russell 337-3665
Shooting Courses Available

USED GUN EXCHANGE
BEST PRICES AND VALUE EVER

Pistols from . . . R495
Revolvers from . . . R795
Shooting Course with Certificate
Best Prices[12]

Needless to say, the more legal guns there are, the easier it is for the illegal market to obtain stolen firearms. The campaign by the government to increase gun control regulations, which are supported by groups like the Gun Free Society of South Africa, is clearly on the right track. What is lagging behind is the political will to apply the gun free philosophy to South Africa's neighbors, many of whose wars are supplied by South African war materiel dealers.

Making the State Relevant in South Africa

In April 2004, South Africa held its third democratic elections and for the first time European and American elections observers did not bother to send any official delegations. This vote of confidence proved not only that South Africans have institutionalized democratic elections but also that the Independent Electoral Commission (IEC) and related structures such as the elections courts and constitutional court of appeal are indeed able to prevent unfair practices.

Although the ANC won close to 70 percent of the votes, there was still a sense of anticipation on the part of both the voters and the ANC leadership that the job of making a better life for all in South Africa has yet to be done. As table 11.3 shows, the voters not only gave a big mandate to the ruling party but the many small parties failed to make any big impact in parliament. In part, this is because only the ANC has managed to represent the nonracial, nonsexist and anti-apartheid ideals that have come to symbolize the hopes and aspirations of the New South Africa. Most of the opposition parties have narrow ethnic, racial and ideological support bases, while the ANC has kept the mass democratic appeal it won as the main anti-apartheid movement.

This transition from national liberation movement to governing party is not without contradictions. Since the beginning of the anti-colonial struggle, there have been some in the African population who accepted a qualified franchise for "civilized men." These black elites have long fought only for equality with their white counterparts and not for social justice as such. Their main complaint against segregation and apartheid was that they were required to share the same inferior quality social services as their fellow blacks from the villages. In a way, their participation in the liberation struggle has been a reluctant one for these assimilados. The end of apartheid as can be imagined marked the end of the struggle for such elites, while for the majority unemployed and unskilled workers and landless dispossessed, it marked the minimum achievement of basic democracy. Democracy for South Africans has come at a very high cost, but it nevertheless is not the only thing people were fighting for. What still remains to be done?

The ANC put out a post-election billboard, which said: "Thank you South Africa, Only the ANC can." Only the ANC can do what? Clearly, this refers to

Table 11.3. The Results of the 2004 General Elections in South Africa

Party Abbreviation	Total Votes	Percentage
ACDP	250,272	1.60%
ANC	10,878,251	69.68%
AZAPO	41,776	0.27%
CDP	17,619	0.11%
DA	1,931,201	12.37%
ID	269,765	1.73%
IFP	1,088,664	6.97%
KISS	6,514	0.04%
MF	55,267	0.35%
NA	15,804	0.10%
NLP	13,318	0.09%
NNP	257,824	1.65%
PAC	113,512	0.73%
PJC	15,187	0.10%
EMSA	10,446	0.07%
TOP	7,531	0.05%
SOPA	14,853	0.10%
UCDP	117,792	0.75%
UDM	355,717	2.28%
UF	11,889	0.08%
VF Plus	139,465	0.89%
Valid Votes	15,612,667	100%
Spoilt Votes	250,887	
% Poll	76.73%	
# of Voters	15,863,554	

Source: www.elections.org.za/elections2004_static.asp

the unfinished business of creating employment, providing education and other basic services and repairing the damage inflicted by the long years of state-sponsored terror and apartheid. Critics of ANC policies have accused it of collaborating with global capital and suggest that it is the ANC that has now become the standard-bearer of liberal democracy in South Africa and the African continent. But, the founders of the South African Native National Congress were not communists. The ANC has always had in its leadership mission educated elites, who were completely liberal and pro-capitalist in their convictions. Their counterparts in West and East Africa were no different. It is not accurate to accuse African elites of selling out, when they are trying to buy in and have a regular capitalist economy in which racism will not work to their disadvantage. The program of building a socialist state is for other social groups to champion.

In South Africa, there exists a strong labor movement and communist party. Both of these working class tendencies have deep roots in urban South

Africa and both are still closely aligned with the ANC. If at times there appears to be tensions in the movement, the unity seems to hold in part because the alliance is still committed to implementing a national liberation agenda. In achieving a better life for all, the state has proven to be more effective than the market in South Africa long before the ANC came to power. The rapid transformation of Afrikaners, who were predominantly rural folk struggling side by side with their black neighbors a hundred years ago, into an educated and prosperous urban middle class has been due to state-managed impoverishment of the black majority, but also state-sponsored welfare for the whites.

In the rest of the African continent as well, efficient state managers have proven more important than the invisible hand of the market in building schools and hospitals and providing stable employment opportunities for the poor. For the ANC government however, making the state the leading economic and social player has not been possible given the hostile neoliberal global political climate prevailing since the 1980s. After the 2004 elections, nevertheless, there has been a slowing down of the privatization campaign and a growing willingness to attempt state-led public works programs as a means of poverty alleviation and job creation. If the ANC were not a movement of diverse social groupings, such an endeavor to make the state relevant to the majority of citizens would probably not have been feasible, and narrow black empowerment schemes designed to promote the interests of black managers and capitalists would have been the goal of the government.

If the goal of national reconciliation and normalization of a society damaged by racist policies has not yet been achieved, it nevertheless has almost been accomplished as the holding of the 2004 national elections suggest. What still remains to be done in making the state relevant—and thereby entrenching its legitimacy in the eyes of the public—is responding to the challenge of poverty.

Given the impact of settler colonialism, it should come as no surprise that among the key areas of government intervention that the 2002 UNDP Human Development Report for South Africa highlighted were:

1. More serious land reform coupled with supportive services not unlike those provided by the apartheid and colonial states to resolve the problem of poverty among white South Africans.
2. More consistent government policies and involvement in the fight against HIV.
3. Providing social grants to both old and poor youth and making such support realistic in terms of real poverty needs.

The three main issues of land, HIV and jobs affect the African population and are directly linked to poverty. It follows therefore that the state must focus its resources on eradicating black poverty, because the white poor who were the concern of the colonial and apartheid governments since 1910, have by and large already been catered to.

In a way, this confirms the old national liberation adage that the primary aim of the liberation movement in South Africa required making black liberation paramount. If the majority is free, the country is also free.

The policies of the ANC government—although not moving rapidly enough to cover everyone—are nevertheless not opposed to looking after the interests of the black majority. This explains the electoral victory discussed previously; it also suggests that the process of making the state relevant has almost been accomplished and the legitimacy of the South African state is as strong as it can be in any regular democracy.

Conclusion

In this chapter, I have argued that colonialism and apartheid created a state that was illegitimate and irrelevant by definition for the black majority in South Africa. Throughout its long years of presenting itself to the outside world as the most advanced state in Africa, it carried the baggage of illegitimacy and minority rule. The very success it claimed for itself in the area of economic and technological development were made possible by the deliberate exclusion of the black majority from power.

In 1994, the South African state embarked upon the road to normalization and—with a combination of national reconciliation, democratization and some affirmative action, restitution and compensation for previous state oppression—started to dismantle the apartheid legacy of racial divisions and ethnic conflict.

By 2004, the democratic credentials of South Africa appeared secure. This was reflected in the fact, among other things, that various state and civil society institutions were in place to promote the further democratization of society and to protect the basic human rights of all.

Despite this achievement of political normalcy, South Africa continues to retain the economic features of a country divided into rich white and poor black populations, even though there is a growing black middle class. If there is any area of state activity that may lead to doubts about the state's legitimacy, it is the problem of black poverty. It would appear that the ANC government is aware of this challenge and has thus put in place policies to ensure that job creation, the tackling of HIV and AIDS and the provision of welfare support for the most vulnerable members of society will not be left to the unpredictable forces of the global markets but will be based on deliberate state policies.

Notes

1. Robert I. Rotberg, "The New Nature of Nation-State Failure," *The Washington Quarterly* 25, no. 3 (2002): 85–96; also at www.thewashingtonquarterly.com/02summer/rotberg.pdf, accessed February 18, 2004.

2. World Bank, *Reducing Poverty in South Africa: Options for Equitable and Sustainable Development*, The World Bank Papers on South Africa (Washington DC: The World Bank, 1994). See also Republic of South Africa, White Paper on Reconstruction and Development, Ministry in the Office of the President, Government Gazette, vol. 353 (16085), 1994.

3. ANC, *Selected Writings on the Freedom Charter 1955–1985*, a Sechaba Commemorative Publication (London, 1985), 3.

4. L. A. Deng and E. N. Tønneland, eds., *South Africa: Poverty and Reconstruction* (Bergen, Norway: Chr Michelsen Institute, 1996).

5. Statistics South Africa, 1998 October Household Survey, May 2000.

6. South African Institute of Race Relations, South Africa Survey 1999/2000 Millennium Edition (Johannesburg: SAIRR, 2000).

7. Extracted from South Africa Survey 1999/2000 Millennium Edition, 2000, 251.

8. Crime Information Analysis Center, The Incidence of Serious Crime, January–December 1998, 1999, 38.

9. Adele Kirsten, "Stopping Gun Violence in South Africa," AFRICANEWS, June 1997, South Africa, www.freeworld.it/peacelink/afrinews.html.

10. *Siyaya*, issue 5 (Winter 1999): *passim.*

11. Crime Information Management Center, "Quarterly Report 3/98: The Incidence of Serious Crime, January–June 1998," 2.

12. See, for example, *The Sowetan*, Monday, September 20, 1999, 25.

12

Making the State Relevant: The Politics of State Reconstruction in Uganda

Paul Omach

THERE HAS BEEN A CONSIDERABLE AMOUNT OF DEBATE about the state and state formation in the African context. There are various perspectives and positions on this debate. Notwithstanding these variations, there is a general consensus that the challenge of building strong, viable, and relevant states is quite profound in Africa. Two broad trends can be discerned from these debates. First, there are those who focus on the problem of internal management of African states. Second, there are works that focus on historical legacy as the explanation of the problem of the African state. In this category belong explanations that examine the international context that has bred the failure of the African state: colonialism and the Cold War power struggle to the present-day international economy.

Those who focus on the internal management of the state in Africa view it in contrast to the state in Europe. It is thus argued that the African state lacks attributes of "empirical statehood" associated with the modern state. The state in Africa has variously been described as "quasi state,"[1] "lame leviathan,"[2] "fictive,"[3] and "soft."[4] Central to all is the notion that the African state is different from the conventional state. It lacks legitimacy, suffers from insufficient structural autonomy from societal actors and influences, and is dependent externally. It is unable to consolidate state sovereignty and assert hegemony. The state in Africa is patrimonial, based on networks of patron-client relations, coercion, and institutionalized corruption. Thus, it has largely been irrelevant to needs of the population. Of recent, there has been greater focus on the phenomenon of state collapse. However, the trend in the literature has also been shifting toward examination of the process of state reconstruction.[5]

One country that has featured prominently in these debates is Uganda. It is lauded for its success in reversing state collapse and its efforts at state reconstruction. This chapter joins the debate at this point. It examines whether the steps that have been taken to reconstruct the state in Uganda can ultimately lead to the building of a state that can galvanize its diverse peoples into a single entity and serve their aspirations and general wellbeing. State reconstruction in Uganda has been carried out using the "hegemonic exchange approach,"[6] combining use of coercion and co-optation of domestic opponents. Although, thus far, this approach has yielded some success given the circumstance that obtained at the time, in the long run it is not a viable path to reconstruction. It is here argued that to successfully reconstruct the state and make it viable and relevant to the lives of the people, the state-building process must be separated from regime consolidation or the consolidation of personal power. This requires a process based on open debates, negotiation, and political consensus, as opposed to machinations and chicanery aimed at giving particular groups privileged position and advantage over others, which could lead to tension and rock the boat of the state. Lastly, the process must endeavour to reflect the aspirations of the citizens, based on the recognition of social, cultural, and political diversity of the society.

Laying the Foundation of a Weak and Irrelevant State: Collapse of the State in Uganda

Like many other African countries, the frontier of Uganda was determined by the colonial powers, and encompassed diverse ethnic nationalities, with distinctive pre-colonial political legacies. Uganda was thus an "artificial creation."[7] It is an ethnically heterogeneous and fragmented society. Therefore, the inability to integrate the different ethnic nationalities and groups into one state has been responsible for state collapse in Uganda. This has been attributed to political and economic policies pursued by the colonial and the successive postcolonial regimes.[8] The colonial state had a dual structure. It was characterized by the existence of a European administrative polity, which was only partly accessible to a small indigenous elite, and a heterogeneous society organized around various traditional structures or Native Authorities defined in terms of colonial conception of tribal criteria. These were linked to the central authority by the principle of indirect rule. Thus in Uganda there were the Kingdoms of Buganda, Bunyoro, Nkore, Toro, and the non-Kingdom areas. These entities, the Kingdom areas enjoyed greater autonomy than the non-Kingdom areas. Buganda especially enjoyed a privileged status, which incited envy and hatred among the other ethnic nationalities. Indirect rule thus encouraged ethnic compartmentalization and impeded national integration. The situation was further complicated by the penetration of religion into the traditional political and social systems.[9] Not only is politics in Uganda afflicted by religious cleavage between Protestants and Catholics, which came to correspond with the two major political parties—the Uganda People's Congress (UPC) and the Democratic Party (DP)—but also rivalry between Christianity and Islam. Religion thus came to play a disintegrative role. Furthermore, colonial policies resulted in regional, ethnic, and class inequalities and unequal development. Colonial policies favored southern Uganda by concentrating social and economic infrastructure, especially in Buganda and Busoga. Thus, social services, cash crops production, and communication networks were largely concentrated in the south while the north lagged behind in terms of development. Unbalanced social and economic development affected relations between ethnic groups and this has had a negative impact on the development of the state in Uganda.

Therefore, pre-independence politics in Uganda were characterized by the jostling for position and privileges of the different groups, which explains why the "form of government" appropriate for independent Uganda was a major preoccupation in the years leading to independence. Central to these debates was the role of traditional polities and their relations with the central government. The position and role of the Buganda Kingdom was a big issue because of its continued claim to privileged position, which it enjoyed under colonial rule. This resulted in the coalescence of new social forces antagonistic to traditional polities, specifically, the formation of the Uganda People's Congress (UPC), a multiethnic political party. The 1962 Constitution reflected these conflicting interests. It was a compromise document, a "manifestly opportunistic alliance and the demands of aristocracy in Buganda," which "left many issues unresolved" and "badly settled" others."[10] It provided for a federal status for Buganda and a semi-federal status for the other kingdom areas, placing the districts in a unitary relation with the central government. The powers and authorities of the Buganda state vis-à-vis the central government regarding such issues like finance were ill defined—as were the powers and authorities of the ceremonial President, Sir Frederick Edward Mutesa II, who was at the same time the Kabaka (King) of Buganda, vis-à-vis those of the Executive Prime Minister, Apollo Milton Obote. The emphasis on traditional or local polities enshrined in the constitution had a negative impact on the construction of the state. It led to a situation where national political institutions "were simply regarded as forum for power bargaining, means to be used in the accumulation of the resources necessary to strengthen local power bases or as instruments for the allocation of rewards to supporters and denial of rewards to opponents."[11] This impacted economic management since the state became the primary means of accumulation of wealth. This explains increased state intervention in the economy in the 1960s, which was primarily done through nationalization and the joint ventures between the Uganda Development Co-operation (UDC) and private companies, a policy designed to accelerate African control of the economy. However, as Nelson Kasfir observed, those with state political power were also careful not to design policies that, though beneficial to entrepreneurs, would consolidate the advantage of the Baganda who already had a head start due to colonial policies. This was an issue that generated ethnic hostility between the government and the Baganda.[12]

It was against such a background that the 1966 crisis occurred. In that year, the government of Prime Minister Milton Obote overthrew the constitution, abolished kingdoms, declared Uganda a republic with himself as Executive President, and centralized power. The army stormed the Kabaka's palace and forced him into exile in Britain where he later died. This resulted in a crisis of legitimacy for the UPC regime of Milton Obote and heightened ethnic animosity from the aggrieved Baganda against the ethnic nationalities associated with Milton Obote, especially the Acholi and Langi from the North. It also led to the culture of violence and militarism in the politics of Uganda, especially after the declaration of a state of emergency after the 1966 crisis and the assassination attempt on the life of President Milton Obote. Thus, by the time the army under Idi Amin overthrew the civilian government of Milton Obote, state coercion was already entrenched.

The military takeover of January 1971 marked the beginning of eight years of brutal and autocratic rule under dictator Idi Amin. The state adopted violence, repression, and terror as methods of control. Many were killed, or simply "disappeared," while others fled to exile. The country experienced social dislocation, institutional decay, paralysis, and impoverishment. The "economic war" policies of the regime and the expulsion of Asians deprived the country of entrepreneurs, managers, and other professionals who were the backbone of the economic and social infrastructure. Amin nationalized the economy and transferred ownership to Africans; mostly his henchmen and supporters. The mismanagement that followed led to a breakdown with implications for the political, economic, and social systems.[13] The state became less consequential to the economy, resulting into disengagement[14] from the state by producers. The "*magendo*," a black market network, came to dominate.[15]

Such was the legacy of the Idi Amin regime, which confronted the successive regimes with the insurmountable problem of reestablishing societal and political order. The situation was complicated by that fact that the old issues of state-building were still unresolved; namely, ethnic and regional rivalries, form of constitution, monarchical or republican form of state, and the economy —socialist or capitalist.[16] Furthermore, there were bitter feelings between those elite who stayed behind and survived and returnee exiles whose claim to a stake in national politics rested on their "roles" in the "liberation" of the country. Even the returnees were deeply divided among themselves.

Under the circumstances discussed above, the successive regimes after the overthrow of Idi Amin were short-lived and unable to cope with the challenges of reestablishing social and political order. Hence violence and disorder continued, with the threat of an imminent fully fledged civil war. This was the atmosphere under which the multiparty elections that returned Milton Obote to power were held in December 1980. The results of the elections were contested, with some claims that they were rigged in favor of the UPC.[17] Yoweri Museveni, who at the time of the election was the Vice-Chairman and Minister of Defense in the ruling Military Commission, contested the elections as a member of the Uganda Patriotic Movement (UPM), a political party he formed. The UPM lost and even Museveni lost the contest for a constituency to a Democratic Party (DP) candidate. Museveni cried foul and went to the bush and launched a guerrilla campaign against the UPC government in early 1981.

The failure of state reconstruction during Obote's second regime should therefore be understood in the context of the legacy of Idi Amin's eight-year rule. Obote inherited a collapsed state where formal institutions, authority, and law and order had been severely eroded. Further, "the extent of economic decay prevented even the most intensive rehabilitation efforts from making any perceptible difference in peoples' lives."[18] Secondly, the rise in political violence in the aftermath of the disputed 1980 elections that returned Milton Obote to power also impeded reconstruction efforts. Besides Yoweri Museveni's National Resistance Army/Movement (NRA/M), numerous other guerrilla movements—namely, the Uganda National Rescue Front (UNRF), the Former Uganda National Army (FUNA), the Uganda Freedom Movement (UFM), and the Federal Democratic Movement (FEDEMO)—launched armed attacks against Obote's government. This led to the rise in political violence and increased ethnic animosity. Faced with increasing threat from these guerrilla groups, the army was used as the instrument of state penetration and arbiter of political conflicts. The Uganda National Liberation Army (UNLA), the government army, carried out a brutal anti-insurgency campaign, with cynical disregard for human rights. In this way, the state failed to guarantee physical security for Ugandans, which undermined the legitimacy of Obote's second regime and its ability to consolidate authority.

Subsequently, the UNLA split along ethnic lines, which resulted in the overthrow of the government by faction loyal to renegade generals, Tito Okello and Bazillio Okello in July 1985. The Military junta under General Tito Okello invited the dissident groups that had fought against the regime of Milton Obote to join the government. The UNRF and FUNA, which were active in the west Nile region, responded positively. Similarly, the Federal Democratic Movement (FEDEMU) and Uganda Freedom Movement (UFM) joined the government. The NRA however opted to continue with the armed struggle. After some months of negotiations under the chairmanship of President Daniel Arap Moi of Kenya, the military junta under General Tito Okello and the NRA under Yoweri Museveni signed a power-sharing agreement in December 1985. However, in January 1986, the NRA captured state power, thus unilaterally abrogating the agreement. The UNLA disintegrated; the majority fled north to Acholi and to exile in Sudan, from where they planned to recapture power from the NRA. The capture of state power by the NRA disturbed the sociopolitical equilibrium and led to a shift in the locus of power, together with the concomitant economic benefits—an issue which is important in state reconstruction in Uganda.

Out of the Doldrums: The NRM and State Reconstruction in Uganda

At his inauguration in January 1986, a triumphant Yoweri Museveni pledged to effect "a fundamental change in the politics of our country."[19] The program of his administration was set out in the Ten-Point Program.[20] Top on the agenda was the issue of security. To this end, the NRA/M government embarked on the process of restoration of security and to rid the country of violence, lawlessness, and state terrorism that had become the norm in Uganda. This required addressing the role of the military. Right from the colonial era, the army had been used to maintain law and order, which translated into the suppression of internal revolts. This trend continued after independence when the army was manipulated by politicians and used to settle political rivalry and suppress opposition. In due course, the military degenerated into rival armed factions depicting the ethnic fractionalization of the wider society. Furthermore, recruitment into the army was mainly from the marginal groups in society, peasants, and semi-lumpens from the urban areas and other riffraff elements. In the absence of efforts to mould it into a disciplined force, it often degenerated into rival armed gangs that became a danger to society. It had become a predatory institution. Any attempt to reconstruct the state and make it relevant for the ordinary people thus necessitated addressing the question of the military and to make it the guarantor of security of life and property of the citizens. It is only through this that confidence can be reinstated in the state.

The NRM government attempted to do this through a mixture of political and military means. Combatants from the defeated UNLA and the other armed groups were co-opted into the NRA. At the same time, armed opposition was dealt with militarily. A code of conduct prescribing high discipline for NRA soldiers was enforced. Thus, the government succeeded in moulding the NRA into a relatively disciplined-armed force. This improved civil-military relations, and went a long way to restore confidence in the state as the custodian of security of life and property of its citizens. Further, in a move aimed at improving the respect for human rights in Uganda, the Uganda Human Rights Commission was established to investigate cases of human rights violations. This was an important confidence building measure in the state.

The NRM was not however without shortcomings. In the north and north east of the country where there was armed opposition, the state failed to guarantee security of life and property. The high-handed and militarist approach alienated many, as cases of human rights violation were reported with many people killed and others detained in military camps as "lodgers." The military approach also deprived the NRM of the opportunity to construct a nationwide base, and arrive at a political consensus as a state-building process. Thus, civil-military relations not only worsened, but attitudes were hardened. Besides, the NRA which was renamed the Ugandan People's Defense Force under the 1995 constitution is far from having evolved into a truly national army. It is still viewed as a partisan army owing it loyalty and allegiance first and foremost to Yoweri Museveni. It is therefore largely perceived as a personal army. Furthermore, the Human Rights Commission was mandated to investigate human rights violations up to 1986 only, that is, before the assumption of state power by the NRM government.

As part of its objective to establish national unity, a broad-based government was established. Personalities representing different political groups and shades of opinion were co-opted into the NRM government. Through a "gentlemen's agreement," political parties' activities were restricted during the four-year interim period to allow for a national reconciliation and reconstruction. This innovation was hailed as a model for state reconstruction in conflict-torn societies. However, soon the continuation of the restriction on political party activities began to irk party leaders, who protested at what they saw as an attempt by the NRM to muzzle opposition and establish a one-party state. Matters were not helped by the extension of NRM rule to 1995, by the National Resistance Council (NRC), without elections, at the end of the interim period in 1989.

It is thus worth noting that as much as these measures were important in reconstruction of the state on the basis of a broad political consensus, they were undermined by fact that they were used to consolidate the NRM regime and to neutralize the opposition. The much-acclaimed broad-based arrangement was nothing other than the old-fashioned co-optation strategy in which those members of the opposition participated in government in their individual capacities, and could not therefore act in a unified manner as members of a political organization. Besides, as Mahmood Mamdani argued, the broad base created by the NRM "was not organized around a minimum program, but around a distribution of offices."[21] Thus members from the opposition political organizations who joined the government did so, not necessarily for altruistic reasons, but due to the "politics of poverty," as James Katalikawe puts it.[22] This model cannot therefore, in the long run, lead to the reconstruction of a viable and relevant state.

The NRM government also established new political institutions and structures of governance, both at the national and local levels, albeit in an extralegal manner.[23] The National Resistance Movement Secretariat, headed by the National Political Commissar, was set up. The National Resistance Council (NRC), the ruling organ of the NRM, was transformed into a national legislature and its membership expanded to include newly appointed ministers and deputy ministers, and an ombudsman, in the form of Inspector General of Government (IGG), was appointed. Special District Administrators (SDAs) were introduced to replace District Commissioners. These were charged with, among other things, the supervision of Resistance Councils and Committees (RCs). These councils and committees were first introduced during the guerrilla war by the NRA/M as a method of mobilizing support, and later as administrative structures in "liberated" areas. It was argued by the NRM that RCs would be instruments of popular participation and thus foster popular democracy. The RC system was a hierarchical structure directly elected from the village or RC1 level, by every resident of eighteen years and above; and indirectly elected for the parish or RC2; sub-county or RC3; county or RC4; and the district or RC5. In the 1995 Constitution, RCs were renamed Local Councils (LCs), and became part of the local government structure under the decentralization system adopted by the government.

The introduction of these political structures was important for the reestablishment of state authority. The RCs in particular served the important purpose of reestablishing state structures and authority at the local or grassroots level. It has to be noted however that these political institutions and structures were not intended for state reconstruction per se, but for the consolidation of the NRA/M regime, or to "regularize NRM power." In this connection, the introduction of RCs should not therefore be taken as attempts to promote popular democracy, as presented by the NRM,[24] but to establish local structures of authority and support. Thus the boundary between state reconstruction and regime consolidation was blurred. This had a negative impact and served to undermine the process of state reconstruction. This was particularly the case in the north and northeast of Uganda where armed opposition groups contested the legitimacy of the NRA/M regime. In these areas, armed insurgents murdered some RC officials as a means of discouraging people from participating in RC system and preventing the NRM from establishing grassroots support structures.

A major step at state reconstruction was taken in 1988 with the appointment of the Uganda Constitutional Commission, which was mandated "to consult the people and make proposals for a popular and lasting constitution based on national consensus."[25] This was envisaged as a "nation-building" process that would galvanize the people of Uganda into a cohesive force.[26]

However, although the constitution making was viewed as an "opportunity to make a fresh start," not all agreed on the need for a new constitution. Some people argued that there was nothing wrong with the 1967 Constitution, while others argued for the reinstatement of the 1962 Constitution, which they considered to be the country's authentic constitution.[27] The mandate of the NRM government to embark on a constitution-making process was also questioned since it was not elected, but had "shot its way to power." Furthermore, the fact that the president appointed the chairman and members of the Commission did not go well with critics. Thus, the process was hounded by the perception, in some quarters of the Ugandan society that "the whole exercise was a gimmick," as the government "had already made a Constitution and was only seeking legitimacy for it." At the same time, although the government pledged "to create an atmosphere of peace, security and freedom necessary for fruitful discussion and debate," such an atmosphere could hardly be said to exist in the north and northeast of the country where a vicious civil war was at its peak. It is doubtful therefore that people in these parts of the country could freely contribute to the constitutional debate, contrary to the claims of the Commission that the people of the north and northeast participated in the debate. Although the Commission was scheduled to complete its work by 1991, its progress was slow and it was not until 1993 that it submitted its final report to the government. This slow pace of progress by the Commission led to concern that the whole process was a ploy to keep the NRM government in power indefinitely. The situation was not helped by the extension of NRM rule for a further five years, which was partly justified on the grounds that the process of writing a new constitution was not yet over.

When it finally submitted a draft constitution to the government, the Commission left some people disappointed. It avoided making decisions on some controversial issues such as those relating to the nature of the political system. The Commission recommended a national referendum to decide on whether the country should adopt a multiparty system or retain the "Movement System" favored by the government. This dented its credibility as it was seen as leaning rather closely on the position favored by the NRM government. To its credit, the Commission recommended that a democratically elected Constituent Assembly (CA) and not the NRC should debate the draft constitution. However, the CA was not without critics, some of whom argued that a constitution enacted under the CA statute was unlikely to create a conducive environment for political stability, sustainable economic development leading to prosperity.[28] The CA statute and rules of procedure were perceived to have been designed in such a way as to benefit the NRM. Besides, CA deliberations were manipulated and the conduct of the CA regarding contentious issues did not encourage consensus, which led to the criticism that its deliberations were already fixed in advance.[29] For instance, the question on whether Uganda should become a federal state was rejected firmly without a vote. And on the question of the political system, the CA, which was dominated by supporters of the NRM, voted by a margin of 199 votes to 68 to retain the "movement" not the party system for another five years. This prompted delegates who wanted an immediate return to multiparty politics to walk out of the house. Ultimately, the interests of the NRM triumphed and the movement political system was enshrined in the constitution—and together with it, a provision for the people of Uganda to determine the political system of their choice during the last month of the end of the fourth year of the parliament elected under the constitution.[30] The controversial referendum was held in June 2000, and the results reaffirmed the continued existence of the movement political system. This however has not settled the debate on the political system. By institutionalizing the movement, the NRM behaved in away that could discourage reconciliation and national consensus. Thus short-term political interests triumphed over state-building.

The NRM government was also confronted with the age-old problem that has since confronted state-builders in Africa; namely, the role of traditional structures and institutions in the modern states that state-builders aspire to establish. Traditional leaders enjoy a lot of legitimacy, which is not easily bestowed on national leaders. Unfortunately, the existence of traditional structures and institutions in multicultural and heterogeneous societies tend to complicate the process of nation-building. One option of dealing with this problem, which proved attractive to many who view traditional structures and institutions as anachronistic to the modern era, has been to suppress it, at times violently. This is what happened in Uganda in 1966 when Prime Minister Milton Obote overthrew the constitution, abolished kingdoms, and declared Uganda a republic with himself as executive president. However, as has been observed above, this action undermines the legitimacy of national leaders and impedes the process of state-building.

This issue, which had remained unresolved (or had only temporarily been swept under the carpet) came to confront the NRM government. Once again, the debate centered on the place of the Buganda Kingdom, and its relations to the Ugandan state. Buganda had been alienated due to the abolition of monarchies and the death of the Kabaka in exile in Britain. It was thus at the heart of support to opposition groups that waged the armed struggle against Obote's second regime. The issue of traditional institutions was therefore one of the issues that the Ugandan Constitutional Commission dealt with and expected to be debated, along with other constitutional issues by the Constituent Assembly (CA). However, the NRM government went ahead to introduce constitutional amendments that restored traditional rulers and institutions.[31] By acting opportunistically to gain the political support of the Baganda, the NRM government deprived the country of the opportunity to openly debate, negotiate, and come to an openly agreed position on these institutions. Thus, the feelings of mutual suspicions, and other sentiments that different groups hold, continued to linger. The manner in which this issue was handled has not therefore resolved the question of the role of traditional institutions in Uganda.

Reconstructing the Economy

When it took over the mantles of state power in January 1986, the NRM government inherited a shattered economy. There was high and rising inflation and production was at a rock-bottom level with most industrial enterprises either idle or producing at 10–20 percent of their installed capacity. The country's infrastructure was in a very poor state, and institutions were in a state of virtual collapse. The "magendo" informal economy had become so big, relegating the state to play a less consequential role.[32] The government's Emergency Relief and Rehabilitation Program presented in May 1986 reflected the grim reality. Thus, "it summed up a long list of acute needs."[33] However, the leaders of the NRM government, most of whom were heavily influenced by Marxist and dependency theories, and were therefore critical of IMF and World Bank free market policies, adopted interventionist economic policies. They abolished the dual exchange rate, re-valued the currency, and established price controls for essential imported commodities. These measures did not arrest the economic malaise. Donors withheld aid and inflation increased from 120 percent in May 1986 to 380 percent in May 1987.[34]

In an abrupt change of strategy, the NRM government dropped its interventionist policies. In May 1987, it presented its Rehabilitation and Development Plan, together with a comprehensive macro-economic policy package that agreed with the World Bank and the IMF. The program was supported by the IMF Structural Adjustment Facility (SDR 46.8 million over three years plus SDR 25 million under the Compensatory Financing Facility) and an Economic Recovery Credit of the World Bank (SDR 50.9 million plus 18.8 million under the African Facility).[35] The main aim of the Rehabilitation and Development Plan was rehabilitation and reconstruction of economic and social infrastructure to restore the productive capacity of key sectors of the economy. Meanwhile, the economic policy package was aimed at providing the economic framework for growth and development. To this end, the government adopted tight fiscal and monetary policy. A new currency was introduced and the shilling was devalued from new Uganda shillings 14 to shillings 60 per United States dollar.[36] There were also considerable increases in producer prices for traditional and nontraditional cash crops, liberalization of agriculture marketing and international trade, and the dismantling of buying monopolies—thus freeing producers from the excessive and exploitative control of state owned buying monopolies. Since then, reconstruction of the economy has proceeded along the lines of free market economic reforms supported by the IMF, World Bank, and Western donors.

In an effort to address institutional weaknesses, institutional and structural reforms have been carried out. Under the Civil Service Reform Program (CSRP), the civil service, which had become bloated, inefficient, and demoralized, had to be reformed to make it responsive to the country's needs.[37] This entailed rationalization of ministries, strengthening capacity to manage change, salary increase and introduction of a minimum wage, and the introduction of results oriented management. Accordingly, the overall size of the civil service had been reduced from 320,000 to 170,000 employees by the end of 1994. At the same time, to improve institutional efficiency, the Ugandan Revenue Authority (URA) and the Ugandan Investment Authority (UIA) were created and given semi-autonomous status, thus removing them from the control of the civil service. Furthermore, the government embarked on reform and privatization of public enterprises. As state control over the economy increased after independence, the public sector grew out of proportion without the corresponding managerial capability. Public enterprises were thus mismanaged since they came to be increasingly used for patronage. They therefore became largely unproductive and unprofitable and a financial burden.

However, the privatization of public enterprises has not been without problems. A Report of the Parliamentary Select Committee on Privatization expressed concern about the privatization process. It cited the lack of transparency, influence peddling by politicians, nepotism, corruption, and mismanagement of the process and its proceeds.[38] This may in the long run undermine the sustainability of economic reconstruction.

A number of questions have been raised about the appropriateness and sustainability of the economic reconstruction in the Ugandan. First, the weakness of the private sector has raised concern about the declining role of the state and the promotion of market oriented strategy. Second, the high level of poverty, which in 1997 was measured at 44 percent,[39] raises crucial questions about the sustainability of the economic reforms, especially about the role of the state. Moreover, to a large extent, the rural producers of food crop have not benefited from the liberalization of agricultural marketing. This has raised questions about the declining role of the state. Third, economic reconstruction in Uganda is overwhelmingly dependent on donor support. For instance in 1999/2000 financial year, total government expenditure was 20.7 percent of GDP and yet domestic revenue was 11.5 percent of GDP,[40] with the shortfall funded by donors.

Making the State Relevant

There is no doubt that the NRM government has achieved some successes in reversing state decay and embarking on the process of state reconstruction in Uganda. This showed that state reconstruction is indeed possible and rekindled hope for many states in Africa that are at different stages of decay. It is thus possible to look beyond state collapse. What needs to be asked however is whether the "Ugandan model" can lead to the construction of a state that is viable and relevant to the lives of its citizens. This chapter is skeptical about such a prospect.

Against this background, I argue that several steps need to be taken in order to make the state relevant to the lives of the majority of the people of Uganda. The issue of the "Museveni Cult of Personality" needs to be addressed. This is because state reconstruction in Uganda has largely revolved around the personality of the NRM leader Yoweri Museveni, and the process has reflected his vision and interest. The NRM leadership has been so preoccupied with regime consolidation and political survival that it closely controlled and guided the process of state reconstruction to ensure that outcomes are amenable to its interests. In the process, ideas, views, and interests of other groups have been muzzled. This deprived the country of the opportunity to build national consensus as the basis of state construction. At the same time, preoccupation with regime survival meant that the NRM adopted such strategies like the reward of certain groups at times at the expense of institution building. Accordingly, many issues remain unresolved, such as those regarding political form or system and the role of traditional institutions.

Another issue is the overreliance on external support. There has been overdependence on external support in the reconstruction of the state. This raises practical problems of the viability of the reconstructed state, especially in regard to its capability. There is a danger that the state may mirror the image of the external actors and lose sight of the unique sociocultural context. Overdependence on external actors risks creating a fragile state with shallow roots in the society, thereby making it susceptible to external forces.

One of the vexing problems that requires a serious solution is ethnicity. Steps need to be taken to create an enabling environment in which ethnic pluralism is one of the major centerpieces. This would be critical in the process of building a viable democratic state.

Another problem is political repression. The state reconstruction process must pay keen attention to addressing the age-old problem of the violation of human rights both at the individual and group levels. In order for the state to be made relevant, Ugandans whether as individuals or groups must enjoy and exercise the full battery of political and civil rights—the freedoms of speech, of the press, of association, of thought, and so on.

Closely intertwined with the need for the promotion of human rights is the creation of a viable multiparty system. Ugandans should have the right to establish political parties and to use them as the vehicles for legally contesting the control of state power. Unfortunately, the current "one-party system" established under the aegis of a "no-party system" undermines political democratization.

Also, it is exigent that the issue of traditional systems of government be addressed. Toward this end, based on national discussions and consultations, the role of the traditional rulers, including their relationship to the national government, need to be clearly delineated.

Central to the state reconstruction project is the establishment of an economic system that provides employment opportunities, addresses the vexing problems of poverty and ultimately serves as the motor force for improving the standard of living of Ugandans. The establishment of such an economic system would require the abandoning of the neoliberal economic prescriptions that are both anti-people and anti-development.

Uganda is also in desperate need of institutional revitalization. The agencies of the state need to be structured in ways that would make them functional, efficient, and effective. As part of this process, there is a need to clearly define the mission and functions of the various state agencies.

Efforts need to be directed toward the provision of social services—quality public education, health care, and other basic social services are critical to the process of endearing the people to the state.

Conclusion

In this chapter, I have attempted to discuss the factors, forces, and dynamics of state failure, collapse, and reconstitution in Uganda. Specifically, I examined the travails of both the colonial and postcolonial state in Uganda. In the case of the latter, I assessed the role of the various regimes in creating the conditions that led to state failure and collapse in Uganda. I then discussed the efforts of the Museveni regime to reconstruct the Ugandan state and to make it relevant to the lives of the majority of the Ugandans.

Finally, I identified some of the basic issues that must be addressed as preconditions for making the state relevant to the lives of the majority of the Ugandan people—the "personality cult," external dependence, ethnicity, political repression, the traditional systems of governance, the economy, institutional revitalization, and the provision of social services. It would not be sufficient to address one of two of these issues as separate matters. Instead, all of them must be addressed as interlocking and interrelated matters that are germane to the building of a democratic state in Uganda.

Notes

1. Robert Jackson, *Quasi State: Sovereignty, International Relations and the Third World* (Cambridge, UK: Cambridge University Press, 1990).
2. Thomas Callaghy, "The State as Lame Leviathan: The Patrimonial Administrative State in Africa," in *The African State in Transition*, ed. Zaki Ergas (London: Macmillan, 1987), 87–116.
3. Richard Sanbrook, *The Politics of Africa's Economic Stagnation* (Cambridge, UK: Cambridge University Press, 1985).
4. Donald Rothchild, "Hegemony and State Softness: Some Variation in Elite Responses," in *The African State in Transition*, ed. Zaki Ergas, 117–48.
5. See, for instance, Leonardo A. Villalon and Phillip A. Huxtable, *The African State at a Critical Juncture: Between Disintegration and Reconfiguration* (Boulder, CO: Lynne Rienner, 1998); I. William Zartman, ed., *Collapsed States: The Disintegration and Restoration of Legitimate Authority* (Boulder, CO: Lynne Rienner, 1995); Terrence Lyons and Ahmed I. Samatar, *Somalia: State Collapse, Multilateral Intervention and Strategies for Political Reconstruction* (Washington, DC: The Brookings Institution, 1995); Jeffrey Herbst, "Responding to State Failure in Africa," *International Security* 21, no. 3 (Winter 1996–1997): 120–44.
6. Donald Rothchild, "Hegemony and State Softness," 117–48.
7. D. A. Low, "The Dislocated Polity," *Uganda Now: Between Decay and Development*, ed. H. M. Hansen and Twaddle (London: James Currey, 1998).
8. Amii Omara-Otunnu, "The Dynamics of Conflict in Uganda," in *Conflict in Africa*, ed. Oliver Furley (London: Tauris Academic Studies, 1995), 223–36.
9. W. Senteza-Kajubi, "The Historical Background to the Uganda Crisis, 1966–1986," in *Beyond Crisis: Development Issues in Uganda*, ed. Paul D. Wiebe and Cole P. Dodge (Kampala: MISR/ Cross Roads Press, 1987), 25–40.
10. J. Oloka-Onyango, "Constitutional Transitions in Museveni's Uganda: New Horizons or Another False Start?" *Journal of African Law* 39, no. 2 (1995): 158.

11. Dan Mudoola, "The Problems of Institution Building: The Case of Uganda," in *Beyond Crisis*, ed. Wiebe and Dodge, 58.

12. Nelson Kasfir, "State, *Magendo*, and Class Formation in Uganda," *The Journal of Commonwealth and Comparative Politics* 21, no. 3 (1983): 87–89.

13. J. J. Jorgensen, *Uganda: A Modern History* (London: Croom Helm, 1981).

14. Victor Azarya and Naomi Chazan, "Disengagement from the State in Africa: Reflections on the Experiences of Ghana and Guinea," *Comparative Study in Society and History* 27 (1987): 106–31.

15. Nelson Kasfir, "State, *Magendo*, and Class Formation in Uganda," *The Journal of Commonwealth and Comparative Politics* 21, no. 3 (1983): 84–103.

16. Aidan Southall, "Social Disorganization in Uganda: Before, During, and After Amin," *Journal of Modern African Studies* 18, no. 4 (1980): 645.

17. F. W. Bwengye, *The Agony of Uganda: From Idi Amin to Obote* (London: Regency Press, 1985); D. W. Nabudere, "External and Internal Crisis in Uganda's Continuing Crisis," in *Uganda Now*, ed. Hansen and Twaddle.

18. John Kiyaga-Nsubuga, "From 'Communist' to 'Neo-Liberal': The Transformation of the National Resistance Movement (NRM) Regime's Economic Policy 1986–1989," Departmental Seminar Paper No. 5, 1997/98, Department of Political Science and Public Administration, Makerere University, Kampala, November 27, 1997.

19. President Museveni's swearing-in address, January 29, 1986, reprinted in Yoweri K. Museveni, *What Is Africa's Problem?* (Kampala: NRM Publications, 1992), 21–27.

20. *Ten-Point Program of NRM* (Kampala: NRM Publications, 1986).

21. Mahmood Mamdani, "Uganda in Transition: Two Years of the NRA/NRM," *Third World Quarterly* 10, no. 3 (July 1988): 1168.

22. J. W. R Katalikawe, "The Freedom of Association, the 'Museveni' Movement Political System and the Referendum 2000: The Great Debate," a paper presented at a Seminar at the Center for Basic Research (CBR), Kampala, June 15, 2000.

23. The Report of the Uganda Constitutional Commission: Analysis and Recommendations (Entebbe: UPPC, 1993), 54.

24. Tukahebwa B. Geoffrey, "Contradictions in the Democratization Program in Uganda under the National Resistance Movement," a paper presented at a conference organized by the Faculty of Social Sciences, Makerere University, Kampala, October 25–27, 2000.

25. Uganda Constitutional Commission Statute (Statute 5 of 1988).

26. Yoweri K. Museveni, address at a seminar on political systems, organized by the Uganda Think Tank Foundation in conjunction with The Frederich Ebert Foundation, Kampala, December 13, 1994.

27. The report of the Uganda Constitutional Commission, 1993, 85.

28. Uganda People's Congress, *The 1994 Constituent Assembly Elections: The UPC Position*, Kampala, 1994.

29. Dani Wadada Nabudere, *Uganda Referendum 2000: Winners and Losers* (Kampala: Monitor Publications, 2000).

30. Republic of Uganda, *Constitution of the Republic of Uganda* (Entebbe: Government Printer, 1995), articles, 69, 269 and 271.

31. See J. Oloka-Onyango, "Constitutional Transitions in Museveni's Uganda."
32. United Nations Development Program, Report on Development Cooperation in Uganda 1987, Kampala, July 1988, 12.
33. United Nations Development Program, Report on Development Cooperation in Uganda 1987, Kampala, July 1988, 13.
34. Charles Harvey and Mark Robinson, "Economic Reform and Political Liberalization in Uganda," IDS Research Report 29, November 1995, 4.
35. United Nations Development Program, Report on Development Cooperation in Uganda 1987, Kampala, July 1988, 13.
36. United Nations Development Program, Report on Development Cooperation in Uganda 1987, Kampala, July 1988, 14.
37. Republic of Uganda, Report of the Public Service Review and Reorganization Commission 1989–1990 (Kampala: Ministry of Public Service and Cabinet Affairs).
38. Republic of Uganda, Report of the Select Committee on Privatization, 1999.
39. Republic of Uganda, Background to the Budget 2000/2001, Kampala, June 1999.
40. Background to the Budget 2000/2001.

III

FUTURE PROSPECTS

13

Creating a Relevant State in Africa: The Lessons

George Klay Kieh Jr.

THE VARIOUS CHAPTERS IN THIS VOLUME HAVE DISCUSSED the crises engendered by the failure of the neocolonial state in various African countries. Additionally, the chapters have mapped out modalities for rethinking and reconstituting the failed and in some cases collapsed states, so as to make them relevant to the lives of the majority of the African peoples. Clearly, despite the pantomimes of the neocolonial state, the state as the overarching construct is still critical to the establishment of stable, democratic and prosperous societies in the continent. Hence, there is the exigency to fashion a different type of state architecture that is relevant to the lives of ordinary Africans. Omotoye Olorode provides an excellent summation of the salience of the state relevance project in Africa:

> The reconstruction of the "state" is considered necessary because some wounds are believed to have been inflicted on the state and its apparatus: some wounds that create crisis and debilitate the state and how their effects sustain the observed crisis.[1]

Against this background, drawing from the various case studies in this volume, the purpose of this chapter is to map out a general trajectory that would help make the state relevant in Africa. In other words, this chapter seeks to address the question of how the state in Africa can transcend failure and collapse and become relevant to the lives of ordinary Africans.

The Framework

The sine qua non for making the state relevant is the deconstruction, rethinking and reconstitution of the neocolonial construct. Generally, this would entail systematic efforts to purge the state of its colonially inherited nature, character and mission. As argued in chapter 1, the postcolonial state in Africa is a colonial construct fashioned on the interests and agendas of the European colonial and imperial powers.

The neocolonial state has a multidimensional character that has variously been identified as prebendal, rentier, predatory, criminalized, privatized, violent, repressive, absolutist, negligent, neopatrimonial and vampirish. Both the individual and the collective dimensions of the postcolonial state in Africa have fostered crises of underdevelopment as reflected in political repression, social and economic malaise, environmental degradation, chaos and instability.

The mission of the neocolonial state is to create an enabling environment in which the international finance capital can privately accumulate and repatriate wealth. The mission of the neocolonial state would need to be changed from serving external interests to empowering citizens so that they can take control over and improve their lives.

The next step would be to conceptualize the core of a new state construct—nature, character and mission. The conceptualization process is analogous to an architectural project in which the desired relevant state construct is designed and mapped out along with its various dimensions.

The reconstitution process would entail the designing of the various dimensions of the state—cultural, environmental, economic, political, religious, security and social. The underlying purpose is to make both the individual and collective elements relevant to the lives of the majority of the people. That is, in their operational dynamics, the various dimensions and their associated elements must positively impact the lives of the majority of the people.

Finally, the state relevance project is pursued through various pathways. Of recent, the sovereign national conference has become a forum where all of the stakeholders in a state assemble to discuss the state's future. However, such a forum must be holistic in its approach: It must not be fixated simply on the change of regime and political democratization. Instead, it must seek to address the myriad dimensions of the state reconstitution process. This is because, although political liberalization is important to the state reconstitution project, it cannot be portrayed as its sole purpose. Another pathway is the holding of a national dialogue at various levels of the society. Again, the purpose of such a dialogue would be to give citizens the opportunity to participate in the discussion and design of the relevant state. The formulation of a process-led constitution is critical to the canonization of the state relevance project. The nature, character and mission of the relevant state must be embodied in the state's constitution. The formulation of the constitution must be an integral part of the state reconstitution process in which all of the various sectors of the society are involved through the making of suggestions. As a complement to the constitution, various statutes should be passed from time to time in continuation of the state reconstitution process. Democratic leadership is pivotal to the state reconstitution process. Such a leadership must be freely chosen by the people and must consist of nationalists and patriots, who have proven records of fostering national unity and integration and development.

The Dimensions of State Relevance

Cultural Relevance

Cultural relevance can be examined at two levels. At the broad national level, the state and its custodians must seek to forge and promote the bonds of nationhood among the disparate sectors of the society. This would entail the creation of a common sense of belonging, affinity and allegiance to the state. The bedrock would be a sense of nationalism and patriotism. In other words, the custodians of the state must ensure that the polity is not beholden to, and dominated by, any particular communal interest and agenda, and must convince the citizens of the state through concrete actions. Instead, the state must be seen as the embodiment of the aspirations and hopes of all of its peoples. Based on concrete actions, the citizens of the state would develop a bond with the state and perceive it as the representative of the totality of its citizenry.

The second, related level involves the promotion of ethnic pluralism in multiethnic societies. That is, the state must provide a conducive atmosphere in which the members of various ethnic groups can maintain their respective subcultures while being respectful of those of other ethnic groups. In other words, each ethnic group must have the right to exist and to pursue its particularistic agenda within the confines of the law and without violating the rights of other ethnic groups.

For the purpose of promoting ethnic pluralism and peaceful coexistence, the state should develop various mechanisms for helping to ensure the inclusion of all groups and equal access to state resources and opportunities. The specifics of such mechanisms would be contingent upon the historical experiences and the objective conditions within each African country. As John Mukum Mbaku aptly notes, "The reconstituted African state should provide mechanisms that do not place any individual or group at a competitive disadvantage or advantage in the competition for resources on the basis of ethnicity."[2]

Economic Relevance

At the base of making the state in Africa relevant must be the transformation of the peripheral capitalist economy and its attendant structures and dynamics. As the repository of evidence shows, since the colonial era, peripheral capitalism, as an economic tapestry, has not engendered development in Africa. Instead, it has, among other things, made African economies the plantations for the production of raw materials and markets for the consumption of manufactured goods. So, Africans produce what they do not consume and consume what they do not produce. Thus, the peripheral capitalist economy must be replaced by an arrangement under which the logic for economic production would be the promotion of internal development.

Similarly, African economies must be transformed from export enclaves that simply produce raw materials to feed the industrial-manufacturing complexes of the developed states. This would entail the creation of an industrial base so that African economies can develop the critical capacity to manufacture goods. This would help to make them competitive in the global marketplace and to reduce, if not eliminate, their total dependence on the industrialized states for manufactured goods. Also, the reconstituted state should have a diversified economy—to include agricultural, industrial, manufacturing and service sectors. This would help militate against the vicissitudes of the global marketplace. The current dependence on a single product—on one primary good or mineral or oil—as the "economic engine" makes African countries vulnerable to the shocks in the international marketplace, which is dictated by the consumer patterns and demands in the industrialized states.

Correspondingly, there should be intersectoral links, so that the introduction of technology in one sector of the economy can benefit all of the other sectors. The dualism of the economy that separates the urban from the rural sector in a fashion akin to the global "core-periphery relations" needs to be addressed. This would entail the full integration of the two sectors into a functioning and holistic national economy. Central to this transformation must be the development of the infrastructure in both the urban and the rural areas, and the concentration of economic activities in the two sectors.

The reconstituted state must be a developmental one. Operationally, it must play a major role in the formulation and implementation of economic policies and activities. Specifically, the state should be involved in the development of the infrastructure—roads, bridges, communication systems, and so on. Also, the state should play a pivotal role in the development of a local patriotic and nationalistic business class that would be engaged in helping to create jobs and contribute to the national revenue base. This can be done, inter alia, by providing local entrepreneurs with training, loans, tax breaks, duty-free privileges and other incentives over a specified period of time.

Also, the relevant state must be a "protective state."[3] Essentially, the state must defend the national interests against marauding multinational corporations and foreign businesses that are singularly interested in the accumulation of profit to the detriment of the society. Multinational corporations and businesses must be made to tailor their activities to the dictates of the national economic strategy of providing for the basic needs of the citizens and improving their standard of living. Also, the state must protect workers from virulent exploitation such as starvation wages and horrendous working conditions.

The challenge of class inequalities must be tackled. Under the current economic dispensation, Africa's peripheral capitalist economies have huge disparities between and among their classes in terms of the distribution of wealth and income. Africa has the second most unequal income distribution next to Latin America.[4] The Gini coefficient for Africa as a whole is 44 percent.[5] The compradorial class, comprising state managers and local merchants, account for a disproportionate share of the national wealth and income in various African states. One of the ways to narrow the gap is to develop and enforce norms that would require public officials to be accountable and transparent in the expenditure of public funds. This is critical because state managers by and large acquire their wealth through plundering and pillaging the state's wealth.

Linked to the issue of class inequalities is the exigency of poverty reduction. Forty-four percent of Africa's population lives below the region-wide poverty line of $39 per capita per month.[6] Significantly, more poor people live in the rural areas.[7] The average income of the rural poor is only $14 per person per month, compared with an average of $27 per month for the urban poor.[8] The state needs to develop and implement various poverty-reduction programs such as economic empowerment through micro-loan programs. The loans could be used to establish farms or other kinds of businesses. The goods sold would then generate income.

Another important issue is job creation. This is because, for example, the unemployment rate in urban areas has increased without abatement over the past two decades; it reached 30 percent by 2000.[9] The state not only needs to create jobs, but good-paying jobs also, which are important because they will help alleviate poverty.

Central to making the state economically relevant is the importance of combating corruption. This is a critical task because the plundering and pillaging of the state's financial resources by state managers siphon off money that could be used on people-centered public programs. Corruption in the public sector is endemic: Public officials have privatized and criminalized the state through an assortment of illegal activities ostensibly designed to foster the crude accumulation of capital. One of the ways to help contain corruption is through a code of conduct for public officials. Such a code could require all public officials, including the president of the country, to periodically declare their assets, including prior to assuming office and when leaving office. In order to succeed by having the desired effect, the code has to be vigorously enforced by an independent body free from political control.

Economic relevance entails that the state must guide against the deleterious effects of neoliberal orthodoxy such as the notorious Structural Adjustment Programs (SAPs) of the Bretton Woods Institutions—International Monetary Fund and the World Bank. Since the 1970s, the IMF and the World Bank have imposed SAPs on various African countries like an albatross. Under SAP conditions, among other things, wages in the public sector were frozen, the social safety net was destroyed and the currencies were devalued and made worthless as instruments of exchange in the marketplace. The resultant effects were increased unemployment and poverty, the reduction of purchasing power and increased external control of the economies of African states. In short, contrary to its vaunted goal of stimulating economic renewal, SAPs have generated debilitating social and economic crises of mammoth proportions in the various African states where they have been employed. Therefore, the relevant state must reject SAPs and their conditionalities. Alternatively, the relevant state can design its own economic management modalities, including the imposition of fiscal responsibility in the public sector.

The related issue is that the current practice of contracting loans to either foster the process of private accumulation by state managers or to invest in conspicuous consumption must be halted and changed. Alternatively, if the state has to contract external loans, these loans must be designed to invest in either revenue-generating activities or projects such as schools that would benefit the state and its citizens.

Environmental Relevance

In the discourse on reconstituting the African state, much attention has not been given to the importance of environmental relevance. This is a critical area because without a healthy environment the survival of the state itself will be in peril. As United Nations Secretary-General Kofi Annan poignantly argues, "If we are to achieve sustainable development, we will need to display greater responsibility for the ecosystems on which all life depends, for each other as a single human community, and for the generations that will follow our own, living tomorrow with the consequences of the decisions we take today."[10] Several issues need to be addressed. The escalating tide of the depletion of arable soil through overcultivation must be contained through the development of new methods of farming that prevent excessive use of the soil. Another area is the development of modalities for dealing with overpopulation and its consequent adverse effects on land use. Also, the broad gamut of pollution—air, land and water—-needs to be addressed through a variety of ways. Effective replanting programs need to be developed to address the vexing problem of deforestation. In terms of toxic waste, effective ways and ideal locations will need to be found to serve as disposal sites. These locations must be isolated from population centers and facilities.

Political Relevance

Political relevance covers an array of issue areas. At the core must be a democratic constitutional order. Such an order must be anchored on a corpus of laws that is nondiscriminatory in terms of its application to all communal, gender and other groups.

The relevant state must respect and protect the human rights of all of its citizens both as individuals and groups—the freedoms of association, of the press, of speech, and so on. These fundamental civil and political rights must be institutionalized, so that the state cannot capriciously abridge them. One of the best ways of institutionalizing the protection of human rights is to guarantee them as inalienable in the state's legal code. This must be linked to effective enforcement mechanisms that would help ensure that if an individual's or group's rights are abridged, they can seek legal recourse and get justice.

The polity must be based on pluralism. That is, individuals and groups must have the right to express their views freely without being muzzled by other groups or the state, even if those views are contrary to state policy or policies. Also, individuals and groups must have equal access to the political process and must have the right to participate free from the control of the state.

The society must be governed by the sanctity of the rule of law. The legal norms of the society must apply to every one without fear or favor, irrespective of the individual's or group's station in society. An independent judiciary that is viewed as fair and impartial must enforce the legal norms. This is critical to the control of the outbreak of violent conflict. The belief by disputants that they will receive a fair hearing in the legal system is crucial to the avoidance of the use of violence as a method for settling disputes. Also, those who are accused of violating the law must be accorded the due process of law, including the presumption of innocence until proven guilty.

State institutions must be efficient and effective in the performance of their respective responsibilities. For example, the legislature must provide oversight over various executive agencies in ways that make these entities accountable and prudent in the use of state resources.

In order to avoid institutional hegemony, there must be a "balance of power" between and among the various branches of the government, irrespective of the system of government—parliamentary, presidential, and mixed. This is quite critical in Africa where there has been the tradition of having "imperial presidencies" with unlimited powers. Under such arrangements, presidents have control over both the legislative and judicial branches of government, hereby creating a dictatorship of the presidency. Using their enormous powers, authoritarian leaders in Africa have established suzerainty over state institutions and resources. Certainly, the institutional "balance of power" would help contain the vagaries of the "imperial presidency."

Politics need to be institutionalized. One way of doing this is the formulation and enforcement of the rules that govern the political process. All actors should be required to comply with the rules without exceptions. The canonization of the norms of the "political game" would, among other things, help to minimize arbitrariness and uncertainty.

The citizens should elect their leaders through regular, free, fair and competitive elections. Individuals and political parties representing various poles of the ideological spectrum should have the constitutional right to contest for the control of state power, as long as these activities are conducted within the confines of the law. The entire electoral process—from the nomination or selection of candidates to the counting of the votes—must be free and fair. This would help ensure that the governors are accountable to the governed. If the governed are displeased with the performance of a governor, they can remove him or her through an orderly process.

The business of the state must be conducted in a transparent manner. That is, in conducting the public's business government agencies and functionaries must operate in an open manner at every stage and level. For example, in the bidding process, the requirements must be cleared and the criteria used in selecting "winners" must be clearly outlined.

The existence of a vibrant civil society is critical to the political relevance of the state. The constituent members of civil society must be free from the control of the state, so that they can be able to act independently. One of the major functions of a vibrant civil society should be to ensure that the government as the agent of the state does not abuse its powers in the conduct of the public's business. Also, civil society would serve as an arena for promoting the participation of various stakeholders in the political process.

Another major issue is the centralization of power in Africa. The prevalent practice has been to concentrate powers in the hands of the central government, while the local areas are relegated to the periphery. Depending on the particular circumstances of each state, an arrangement should be developed between the central and local governments for the devolution of power, irrespective of what system of state exists—federal or unitary. The devolution of power has several benefits. It empowers people at the local level to participate in the conduct of their own affairs. Also, it helps bring local expertise to bear on local problems. That is, since the people in the local areas are closer to and better understand their problems, they are therefore better to play the leading role in addressing them.

Systemic arrangements such as the system of state and system of government must be clearly articulated in the laws of the country and taught to the citizenry, so that everyone would be informed about them. Also, these systems must operate according to the dynamics stipulated in the laws of the country. This is important because it would help to minimize the occurrence of needless conflicts and strifes at all levels of the society.

The state relevance process cannot ignore the importance of the role of the traditional political systems in the national governance structure of the state. Depending on each country's circumstances, ways should be found to integrate the traditional political structures within the body politic. This is significant because the traditional political systems represent significant segments of the population of all of the various African states; hence, the respect for and the incorporation of their views in the national dialogue and the carving out of a role for them in the governance structure would help to promote inclusion.

Security Relevance

Security relevance is anchored on two major premises. The reconstituted state has the responsibility to protect its citizens and their properties from violence and harm. This includes the provision of police protection as well as the punishment of those who jeopardize a citizen's safety and destroys his or her property. The state's responsibility includes the protection of its citizens from the excesses of state security functionaries—like police. Even in the instance in which a citizen's physical well-being is compromised by state security personnel, the state must be willing to take appropriate action, in the event that the guilt of such security personnel is established.

The related premise is that the state has an obligation to provide a peaceful and stable environment in which its citizens can undertake and pursue their legitimate interests and agendas. Accordingly, the relevant state must invest in public safety in terms of personnel, training, equipment and technology. Those who engage in disorderly conduct that pose threats to the safety of others must be dealt with in accordance with the law. Similarly, those who engage in criminal acts such as the theft of property should be apprehended and brought to justice.

Another important aspect of security relevance is the constitutional and democratic control of the military and security establishments. In a relevant state, there must be civilian supremacy over the military and security establishments. This must be enshrined in the constitution. The constitutional provisions should, among other things, make the military's intervention in the political arena as governors illegal. The requisite punitive norms for such interventions must be clearly delineated. Also, the chain of command of both the military and security establishments must be subordinated to civilian oversight and control.

Social Relevance

Social relevance spans a broad gamut of issues. In this section, a few of the major topics will be examined. A relevant state must invest in public education at all levels—primary to tertiary. Efforts must be made to increase the literacy rate to a level where the majority of the citizen of a country can read and write. A highly literate society is indispensable to the functioning of a viable democratic society. That is, literate citizens tend to have much better understanding of their rights and freedoms than illiterate ones. Also, the educational system must teach skills and competencies that would enable citizens to contribute to the development of their countries.

Health care is another major concern. In a reconstituted state, the majority of the citizens should have access to health care at an affordable cost. Also, there must be adequate medical personnel in relation to the population to operate the health care system. The utility of the health care system would be gauged in indices such as high life expectancy and low infant mortality rates.

Also, the majority of the population must have access to safe drinking water. The state should invest in providing safe drinking water for all of its citizens whether they live in the urban or rural areas. The availability of safe drinking water helps to reduce the spread of waterborne diseases.

The provision of decent public housing to the low-income section of the population is a major litmus test of the social relevance of a reconstituted state. Shelter is a critical basic need because it is central to the survival of the individual—the lack of shelter would make the individual homeless and thus vulnerable to the effects of climate changes and the attendant illnesses.

Religious Relevance

The reconstituted state must be secular. That is, religion, irrespective of the sect, must be decoupled from the state. In other words, there should not be an official state religion. This is because such a practice would foster the culture of religious intolerance and exclusion. In short, the state should not be the embodiment of the aspirations of one religious group to the exclusion of others.

Also, all groups should have the right to exist and to practice their faith, so long there is mutual respect and the commitment to peaceful coexistence among all of the religious groups. Operationally, this means that even in those societies in which particular religions and sects draw their memberships from the majority of the population, the rights of minority religious groups and sects must be protected by the state. This includes the right to proselytize.

Gender Relevance

The reconstituted African state must be gender relevant by transcending the narrow confines of male chauvinism, which has dominated every facet of life in Africa. The democratization of gender relations is important because, as Patricia Williams correctly posits, "Women are critical to the democratization and development enterprise in Africa."[11] The centerpiece of the transformation of gender relations in Africa must be a socialization process that teaches, among other things, gender equality and partnership. Africans at various levels must be taught that women are not inferior to men, but rather, women, like men, have the intellect, skills and capacity to be equal partners in the national development enterprise.

Measures should be employed through legislation and concrete practice to promote gender equality. That is, the legal code must clearly delineate the contours of gender equality and the sanctions for violating them. On the practical side, the legal code on gender equality must be vigorously enforced.

Similarly, attention must be paid to the issues of education and health care for women. One of the useful ways would be to make special efforts to provide education and health care for rural women and girls. This is because within the female group, rural women and girls are the most marginalized and exploited.

Conclusion

This chapter has attempted to map out the trajectory of state relevance. Drawing from the various chapters in the volume, we argue that the postcolonial state that was bequeathed to Africa by the European imperialists and colonialists is irrelevant to the lives of the majority of the African peoples. The irrelevance of the African state is reflected in state failure and state collapse. That is, the postcolonial state in every African country has failed and therefore needs to be reconstituted. The chapters in this volume examined the state reconstitution efforts in the various case studies.

Against this background, in order to make the state relevant, the postcolonial state needs to be deconstructed, rethought and reconstituted in its totality—culturally, economically, politically, socially, and so forth. The end product of the reconstitution process must be the creation of a democratic and relevant state. Claude Ake provides an excellent summation of the constituents of the democratic and relevant state thusly:

> A democracy in which people have some real decision-making power over and above the formal consent of electoral choice. . . . A social democracy that places emphasis on concrete political, social and economic rights as opposed to a liberal democracy that emphasizes abstract political rights. It will be a social democracy that invests heavily in the improvement of people's health, education, and capacity so that they can participate effectively.[12]

Notes

1. Omotoye Olorode, "Economic and Political Crises in Africa: Wrong Question, Wrong Answer," in *State Reconstruction in West Africa* ed. Segun Jegede et al. (Lagos, Nigeria: Franked Publishers, 2000), 190–91.
2. John Mukum Mbaku, "Ethnicity, Constitutionalism and Governance in Africa," in *Ethnicity and Governance in the Third World*, ed. John Mukum Mbaku et al. (Aldershot, England: Ashgate Publishing Co., 2001), 95.
3. I am not using the concept of a "protective state" in the neo-mercantilist tradition that is based on wholesale protectionism.
4. United Nations Economic Commission for Africa, *Economic Report on Africa* (Addis Ababa, Ethiopia: United Nations Economic Commission for Africa, 1999), 5.
5. United Nations Economic Commission for Africa, *Economic Report on Africa.*
6. Ousmane Laye, "Socio-economic Conditions in Africa and Risk Management," paper presented at a meeting of the United Nations Economic Commission for Africa, held July 5–9, 1999, Geneva, Switzerland, 2.
7. Laye, "Socio-economic Conditions in Africa and Risk Management."

8. Laye, "Socio-economic Conditions in Africa and Risk Management."
9. See *People's Democracy*, June 18, 1995, 2.
10. Kofi Annan, *Taking Action for Earth's Today* (New York: United Nations Publications, 2001), 1.
11. Patricia Williams, "Woman: The Other Variable in Africa's Development Struggle," in *Preparing Africa for the Twenty-first Century*, ed. John Mukum Mbaku (Aldershot, England: Ashgate Publishing, 1999), 293.
12. Claude Ake, *Democracy and Development in Africa* (Washington, DC: The Brookings Institution, 1996), 232.

Selected Bibliography

Abbay, Alemseged. *Identity Jilted or Re-Imagined Identity?* Lawrenceville, NJ: The Red Sea Press, 1998.

Abdullah, Ibrahim, et al. "Lumpen Youth Culture and Political Violence: Sierra Leoneans Debate the RUF and the Civil War." *Africa Development* 22, nos. 3 and 4 (1997): 171–216.

Abraham, Arthur. *An Introduction to the Pre-Colonial History of the Mende of Sierra Leone.* Lewiston, NY: Edwin Mellen Press, 2003.

Ademoyega, Adewale. *Why We Struck: The Story of the Nigerian Coup.* Ibadan, Nigeria: Evans Brothers, 1981.

Addison, Tony. "Aid and Conflict." In *Foreign Aid and Development: Lessons Learnt and Directions for the Future,* ed. Finn Tarp. London: Routledge, 2000.

African National Congress. *Selected Writings on The Freedom Charter, 1955–1985.* London: 1985.

Ake, Claude. "The State in Contemporary Africa." In *Political Economy of Nigeria,* ed. Claude Ake. London: Longman, 1985.

———. "The Present Crisis in Africa: Economic Crisis or a Crisis of the State?" In *The Political Economy of Crisis and Underdevelopment in Africa: Selected Works of Claude Ike,* ed. Julius Ihonvbere. Lagos, Nigeria: JAD Publishers, 1989.

———. *Development and Democracy in Africa.* Washington, DC: The Brookings Institution, 1996.

Alagappaa, Muthiah, and Takashi Inoguchi, eds. *International Security Management and the United Nations.* Tokyo: United Nations University, 1999.

Anifowose, Remi. *Violence and Politics in Nigeria.* Enugu: Nok Publishers, 1992.

Annan, Kofi. *Action for Earth's Day.* New York: United Nations Publications, 2001.

Assensoh, A.B. *African Political Leadership: Jomo Kenyatta, Kwame Nkrumah, and Julius Nyerere.* Malabar, FL: Krieger Publishing Co., 1998.

Azarya, Victor, and Naomi Chazan. "Disengagement from the State in Africa: Reflections on the Experiences of Ghana and Guinea." *Comparative Studies in Society and History* 27, no. 1 (1987): 106–31.

Barkan, J. D. "The Rise and Fall of a Governance Realm in Kenya." In *Governance and Politics in Africa*, ed. Goran Hyden and Michael Bratton. Boulder, CO: Lynne Rienner Publishers, 1992.

Barkan, J. D., and N. Ng'ethe. "Kenya Tries Again." *Journal of Democracy* 9, no. 2 (1998): 32–48.

Barre Siad. *My Country and My People*. Mogadishu: State Printing Agency, 1974.

Bartlett, John. *Familiar Quotations*. 13th ed. Boston: Little, Brown and Co., 1955.

Baxter, P. T. W. "Ethiopia's Unacknowledged Problem: The Oromo." *African Affairs* 27, no. 308 (1978): 283–96.

Bayart, Jean-Francois. *The State in Africa: The Politics of the Belly*. London: Longman, 1993.

——— et al. *The Criminalization of the State in Africa*. London: James Curry, 1999.

Berman, Bruce. "Ethnicity, Patronage and the African State: The Politics of Uncivil Nationalism." *African Affairs* 97, no. 388 (1998).

Boyce, James. "Beyond Good Intentions: External Assistance and Peace-building." In *Good Intentions: Pledges of Aid for Post-Conflict Recovery*, ed. Shepard Forman and Stewart Patrick. Boulder, CO: Lynne Rienner Publishers, 2000.

Burgess, Michael, and Alain Gagnon. "Introduction: Building on Traditions and Transitions." In *Comparative Federalism and Federation*, ed. Michael Burgess and Alain Gagnon. Toronto, Canada: University of Toronto Press, 1993.

Bwengye, F. W. *The Agony of Uganda: From Idi Amin to Obote*. London: Regency Press, 1985.

Callaghy, Thomas. "The State as a Lame Leviathan: The Patrimonial Administrative State in Africa." In *The African State in Transition*, ed. Zaki Ergas. London: Macmillan, 1987.

Cassanelli, Lee. *The Shaping of Somali Society: Restructuring the History of Pastoral People, 1600–1900*. Philadelphia: University of Pennsylvania Press, 1982.

Central Statistical Authority. *Federal Democratic Republic of Ethiopia*. Ethiopia Statistical Abstract, 1993.

Chabal, Patrick, ed. *Political Domination in Africa: Reflections on the Limits of Power*. New York: Cambridge University Press, 1986.

———. *Power in Africa: An Essay in Politics and Interpretation*. New York: St. Martin's Press, 1992.

Chabal, Patrick, and Jean-Pascal Daloz. *Africa Works: Disorder as Political Instrument*. London: James Curry, 1999.

Clairmonte, Frederick, and John Cavanagh. "Impossible Debt on the Road to Global Ruin." *Guardian* (January 9, 1987): 1–2.

Clapham, Christopher. "Sierra Leone: The Political Economy of Internal Conflict." Working Paper 20. Conflict Research Unit, Netherlands Institute of International Relations, 2003.

———. *Haile Selassie's Government*. London: Longman, 1968.

Clark, Trevor. *A Right Honorable Gentlemen: The Life and Times of Alhaji Abubakar Tafawa Balewa.* Zaria, Nigeria: Hudahuda Publishing Company, 1991.

Clarke, John. "Sierra Leone in Africa." *Sierra Leone in Maps.* London: University of London Press, 1966.

Collier, Paul. "How to Reduce Corruption." *African Development Review* 12, no. 2 (2000): 191–205.

Collier, Paul, and Catherine Pattilo, eds. *Investment and Risk in Africa.* New York: St. Martin's Press, 2000.

"Commentary on Peace and Security in Africa." *Association of African Political Scientists Newsletter* 2, no. 2 (1997): 1.

Conflict Watch. *Conflict Trends.* Pretoria, South Africa: African Center for the Constructive Resolution of Disputes, 2001.

Constitution of the Federal Democratic Republic of Ethiopia. Addis Ababa: Government of the Federal Democratic Republic of Ethiopia, 1994.

Contini, Paolo. *The Somali Republican Experiment in Legal Integration.* London: Frank Cass.

Copson, Raymond. "Peace in Africa." In *Conflict Resolution in Africa*, ed. Francis Deng and I. William Zartman. Washington, DC: The Brookings Institution, 1991.

Corry, J. A. "Constitutional Trends and Federalism." In *Canadian Federalism: Myth or Reality?* ed. Peter Meekinson. New York: Methuen, 1968.

Davidson, Basil. *The Black Man's Burden: Africa and the Curse of Nation State.* London: James Curry, 1992.

Deng, L. A., and E. N. Tonneland, eds. South Africa: *Poverty and Reconstruction.* Bergen: Chr. Michelsen Institute, 1996.

Dollar, David, and Aart Kraay. "Growth is Good for the Poor." In *The Globalization Reader*, ed. Frank J. Lechner and John Bol. Malden, MA: Blackwell Publishing, 2004.

Duchacek, Ivo. *Comparative Federalism: The Territorial Dimension of Politics.* New York: Holt, Rinehart and Winston, 1970.

Dudley, Billy. *Parties and Politics in Northern Nigeria.* London: Frank Cass, 1968.

Edie, Carlene. Politics in Africa: *A New Beginning?* Belmont, CA: Wadsworth/Thomas Learning, 2003.

Elazar, Daniel. *Exporting Federalism.* Tuscaloosa: University of Alabama Press, 1987.

Engedayehu, Walle. "Ethiopia: Democracy and the Politics of Ethnicity." *Africa Today* 40, no. 2 (1993): 29–52.

Eribo, Festus. "Higher Education in Nigeria: Decades of Development and Decline." *Journal of Opinion* 24, no. 1 (1996): 64–67.

Fanon, Frantz. *Toward the African Revolution.* Harmondsworth, UK: Penguin Books, Ltd., 1970.

Fatton, Robert. *Predatory Rule: State and Civil Society in Africa.* Boulder, CO: Lynne Rienner Publishers, 1992.

Fisher, Humphrey. "Elections and Coups in Sierra Leone, 1967." *Journal of Modern African Studies* 7, no. 4 (1989): 611–36.

Francis, David. "Diamonds and the Civil War in Sierra Leone." *The Courier* (July–August 2001): 73–75.

Freedom House. *Survey of World Freedoms*. New York: Freedom House, 2003.
Friedrick, Carl. *Trends of Federalism in Theory and Practice*. New York: Frederick Praeger, 1969.
Freund, Bill. *The Making of Contemporary Africa: The Development of African Society since 1800*. London: Macmillan Press. 1984.
Furedi, F. *The New Ideology of Imperialism*. London: Pluto Press, 1994.
———. "The African Crowd in Nairobi: Popular Movements and Elite Politics." *Journal of African History* 14, no. 2 (1973): 275–90.
Fyfe, Christopher. *A Short History of Sierra Leone*. London: Longman Group Ltd., 1962.
Geoffrey, Tukahebwa. "Contradictions in the Democratization Program under the National Resistance Movement." Paper presented at a conference organized by the Faculty of Social Sciences, Makerere University, Kampala, Uganda, October 25–27, 2000.
Gedda, George. "Diamond Trade in Africa Fuels Insurgencies, National Conflicts." *Atlanta Journal Constitution* (October 17, 1999): A20.
Gibrill, Hashim. "War and Recovery in Africa: Getting Beyond the Bitter Lessons." *Endarch* (Spring 2000): 7–18.
Gillett, Nicholas. *The Swiss Constitution: Can It Be Exported?* Bern: Yes Publication, 1989.
Hadjar, Kofi. *On Transforming Africa*. Trenton, NJ: Africa World Press, 1987.
Halliburton, Warren. *Africa's Struggle for Independence*. New York: Crestwood House, 1992.
Harbeson, John. "A Bureaucratic Authoritarian Regime." *Journal of Democracy* 9, no. 4 (1998): 62–69.
Harrington, John A. "Between the State and Civil Society: Medical Discipline in Tanzania." *Journal of Modern African Studies* 37, no. 2 (1999): 207–39.
Hashim, Alice. *The Fallen State: Dissonance, Dictatorship and Death in Somalia*. Lanham, MD: University Press of America, 1997.
Hassen, Mohammed. "Ethiopia: Missed Opportunities for Peace Democratic Process." In *State Building and Democratization in Africa: Faith, Hope and Realities*, ed. Kidane Mengisteab and Cyril Daddieh. Westport, CT: Greenwood Press, 1999.
Hayward, Fred. "Political Leadership, Power, and State: Generalizations from the Case of Sierra Leone." *African Studies Review* 27, no. 3 (1984): 19–39.
Henze, B. Paul. "A Political Success Story." *Journal of Democracy* 9, no. 4 (1998): 55–61.
Herbst, Jeffrey. "Responding to State Failure in Africa." *International Security* 21, no. 3 (1997): 120–24.
Heritage Foundation. *Preserving American Security Ties to Somalia*. No. 745. Washington, DC: The Heritage Foundation, 1989.
Hicks, Ursula. *Federalism: Failure and Success*. Oxford: Oxford University Press, 1978.
Hintjens, Helen. "Explaining the 1994 Genocide in Rwanda." *Journal of Modern African Studies* 37, no. 2 (1999): 241–86.
Holmquist, F. W., et al. "The Structural Development of Kenya's Political Economy." *African Studies Review* 37, no. 1 (1994): 76–98.
Hountondji, Paulin. "Producing Knowledge in Africa Today." *African Studies Review* 38, no. 3 (1995): 1–10.

Ibrahim, Jibrin. "A Political Analysis of the 1999 Nigerian Constitution: Its Problems and Prospects." *Legislative Mandate* 2, no. 2 (1999): 18–24.

———. "Democratic Transition in Africa: The Challenge of a New Agenda—Concluding Remarks." In *Democratization Processes in Africa: Problems and Prospects*, ed. Eshetu Chole and Jibrin Ibrahim. Dakar, Senegal: CODESRIA, 1995.

———. "Religious and Political Turbulence in Nigeria." *Journal of Modern African Studies*. 29, no. 1 (1991): 115–36.

Ihonvbere, Julius. "Avoiding Globalization: The State and Depolitization in Nigeria." In *Globalization and the Dilemmas of the State in the South*, ed. Francis Adams et al. London: Macmillan Press, 1999.

———. "Where is the Third Wave? A Critical Evaluation of Africa's Non-Transition to Democracy." *Africa Today* 43, no. 4 (1997): 343–68.

———. "Political Pluralism and the Crisis of Development in Africa: The Case of Zambia." *Hemispheres*, no. 10 (1995): 59–76.

Indangasi, H. "In the Company of Democrats." In *Writers Speak: Essays on Literature and Democracy*, ed. K. King'ei and H. Indangasi. Nairobi: Writers' Association of Kenya, 1997.

International Crisis Group. *Burundi: The Issues of the State, Political Parties, Freedom of the Press and Political Prisoners*. ICG, Africa Report No. 23. 2000.

Jackson, Robert. *Quasi State Sovereignty: International Relations and the Third World*. Cambridge, UK: Cambridge University Press, 1990.

Jorgensen, J. J. *Uganda: A Modern History*. London: Croom Helm, 1981.

Joseph, Richard. *Democracy and Prebendal Politics in Nigeria: The Rise and Fall of the Second Republic*. Ibadan, Nigeria: Spectrum Books, 1991.

———. "Oldspeak vs. Newspeak." *Journal of Democracy* 9, no. 4 (1998): 55–61.

July, Robert. *A History of the African People*. Prospects Heights, IL: Waveland Press, 1992.

Kandeh, Jimmy. "Ransoming the State: Elite Origins of Subaltern Terror in Sierra Leone." *Review of African Political Economy* 26, no. 8 (1999): 349–66.

Karp, Mark. *The Economics of Trusteeship in Somalia*. Boston: Boston University Press, 1960.

Kasfir, Nelson. "State Magendo, Class Formation in Uganda." *The Journal of Commonwealth and Comparative Politics* 21, no. 3 (1983): 84–103.

"Katalikawe, the Freedom of Association, the 'Museveni' Movement Political System, and the Referendum 2000: The Great Debate." Paper presented at a conference organized by the Faculty of Social Sciences, Makerere University, Kampala, Uganda, October 25–27, 2000.

Kenyatta, Jomo. *Suffering Without Bitterness: The Founding of the Kenyan Nation*. Nairobi: East African Publishing House, 1968.

Khapoya, Vincent. *The African Experience: An Introduction*. 2nd ed. Upper Saddle River, NJ: Prentice Hall. 1998.

Kieh, Jr., George Klay. "The Crisis of the Neo-Colonial State and the Sierra Leonean Civil War." *African Strategic Review* 1, no. 1 (2006), 47–62.

———. "Democratization and Peace in Africa." *Journal of Asian and African Studies* 31, nos. 1–2 (1996): 99–111.

———. "Democratization in Africa: A Balance Sheet." In *Preparing Africa for the Twenty-first Century*, ed. John Mukum Mbaku. Aldershot, UK: Ashgate Publishing, 1999.

———. "Constitutionalism and the Reconstitution of Collapsed States in Africa." Paper Presented at the International Conference on Constitutionalism and Society, University of Ohio, Athens, Ohio, November 6–8, 2000.

King, Preston. *Federalism and Federation.* Baltimore: Johns Hopkins University Press, 1982.

Kirsten, Adele. "Stopping Gun Violence in South Africa." *Africa News* (South Africa) (June 1997). www.freeworld.it/peacelink/afrinews.html.

Kiyaga-Nsubuga, John. "From 'Communists' to Neo-Liberals: The Transformation of the National Resistance Movement Regime's Economic Policy, 1986–1989." Departmental Seminar Paper No. 5, Department of Political Science and Public Administration, Makerere University, 1997.

Kukah, Matthew. "Religion and Politics of National Integration in Nigeria." In *The State of the Nation and the Way Forward*, ed. Mahadi Abdullahi et al. Kaduna: Arewa House, 1994.

Kulick, D. Gilbert. "Ethiopia's Hollow Election: Observing the Forms." *Foreign Service Journal* 69, no. 4 (1992): 41–45.

Kup, A. P. *Sierra Leone: A Concise History.* New York: St. Martin's Press, 1975.

Lata, Leenco. "The Making and Unmaking of Ethiopia's Transitional Charter." In *Oromo Nationalism and the Ethiopian Discourse*, ed. Asefa Jalata. Lawrenceville, NJ: The Red Sea Press, 1998.

Latin, David, and Said Samatar. *Somalia: Nation In Search of a State.* Boulder, CO: Westview Press, 1987.

Laye, Ousmane. "Socio-economic Conditions in Africa and Risk Management." Paper presented at meeting of the United Nations Economic Commission for Africa, Geneva, Switzerland, July 5–9, 1999.

Lemarchand, Rene."Uncivil State and Civil Societies: How Illusions Become Reality." *Journal of Modern African Studies* 30, no. 2 (1992): 177–91.

Levine, Donald. *Greater Ethiopia.* Chicago: University of Chicago Press, 1974.

Lewis, I. M. *A Modern History of Somalia: Nation and State in the Horn of Africa.* Boulder, CO: Lynne Rienner Publishers, 1988.

———. "The Politics of the 1969 Somali Coup." *Journal of Modern African Studies* 10, no. 3 (1972): 383–408.

———. *A Pastoral Democracy.* Oxford: Oxford University Press, 1961.

Lewis, Peter M., et al. *Stabilizing Nigeria: Sanctions, Incentives, and Support for Civil Society.* New York: Council on Foreign Relations and The Century Press, 1998.

Longman, Timothy. "State, Civil Society, and Genocide in Rwanda." In *State, Conflict and Democracy in Africa*, ed. Richard Joseph. Boulder, CO: Lynne Rienner Publishers, 1999.

———. "Rwanda: Chaos from Above." In *The African State at the End of the Twentieth Century: Parameters of the Critical Juncture*, ed. Leonardo Villalon and Phillip A. Huxtable. Boulder, CO: Lynne Rienner Publishers, 1998.

Lonsdale, J. "The Political Culture of Kenya." In *Political Culture, Local Government and Local Institutions*, ed. Frederiksen and K. Westergaard. Occasional Paper No. 7. International Development Institute Roskilde University, 1993.

Low, D. A. "The Dislocated Polity." In *Uganda Now: Between Decay and Development*, ed. H. M. Hansen and Twaddle. London: James Currey, 1998.

Luke, David Fashole, and Stephen P. Riley. "The Politics of Economic Decline in Sierra Leone." *Journal of Modern African Studies* 27, no. 1 (1989): 133–41.

Ly, Frank. "Sierra Leone: The Paradox of Economic Decline and Political Stability." *Monthly Review* 32, no. 2 (1980): 10–26.

Lyons, Terrence, and Ahmed Samatar. *Somalia: State Collapse, Multilateral Intervention and Strategies for Political Reconstruction.* Washington, DC: The Brookings Institution, 1995.

Mafeje, Achie. "Theory of Democracy and the African Discourse: Breaking Bread with My Fellow Travelers." In *Democratization Processes in Africa: Problems and Prospects*, ed. Eshetu Chole and Jibrin Ibrahim. Dakar, Senegal: CODESRIA Book Series, 1995.

Mahadi, Abdullahi, et al., ed. *Nigeria: The State of the Nation and the Way Forward.* Kaduna: Arewa House, 1994.

Makinda, S. M. "Democracy and Multiparty Politics in Africa." *Journal of Modern African Studies* 34, no. 4 (1996): 555–73.

Makumbe, John M. *Democracy and Development in Zimbabwe: Constraints of Decentralization.* Harare, Zimbabwe: SAPES Books, 1998.

Mamdani, Mahmood. "Preliminary Thoughts on the Congo Crisis." *Social Texts* 17, no. 3 (1999): 53–62.

———. *Citizen and Subject: Contemporary Africa and the Legacy of Late Colonialism.* Princeton, NJ: Princeton University Press, 1996.

Mandaza, Ibbo. "The One-Party State and Democracy in Southern Africa: Towards a Conceptual Framework." In *The One-Party State and Democracy: The Zimbabwe Debate*, ed. Ibbo Mandaza and Lloyd Sachikonye. Harare: SAPES Books, 1991.

Markakis, John. "Ethnicity and Conflict with Reference to Ethiopia and Sudan." In *Social Science and Conflict Resolution Analysis*, ed. Arvi Hurskainen and Mohammed Sallih. Uppsala: Nordiska Afrikainstitutet, 1993.

Markovic, Mihailo. "The Federal Experience in Yugoslavia." In *Rethinking Federalism: Citizens, Markets and Governments in a Changing World*, ed. Karen Knop et al. Vancouver, Canada: University of Vancouver Press, 1995.

Mbaku, John Mukum. "Ethnicity, Constitutionalism and Governance in Africa." In *Ethnicity and Governance in the Third World*, ed. John Mukum Mbaku et al. Aldershot, UK: Ashgate, 2001.

Mbembe, Achille. *On the Post Colony.* Berkeley: University of California Press, 2001.

Mengisteab, Kidane, and Cyril Daddieh. "Why State Building Is Still Relevant in Africa and How It Relates to Democratization." In *State Building and Democratization in Africa: Faith, Hope and Realities*, ed. Kidane Mengisteab and Cyril Daddieh. Westport, CT: Greenwood, 1999.

———. "New Approaches to State Building in Africa: The Case of Ethiopia's Ethnic-Based Federalism." *African Studies Review* 40, no. 3 (1997): 111–37.

Mitchell, Peter, et al. "Sierra Leone." *Africa South of the Sahara.* 32nd edition. London: Europa Puiblications, 2003.

Mkandawire, T., and C. C. Soludo. *Our Continent, Our Future: African Perspectives on Structural Adjustment.* Dakar, Senegal: CODESRIA. 1999.

Morton, A. Moi. *The Making of an African Statesman.* London: Michael O'Mara Books, Ltd., 1998.

Mudoola, Dan. "The Problems of Institution Building: The Case of Uganda." In *Beyond Crisis: Development Issues in Uganda,* ed. Paul D. Wiebe and Cole P. Dodge. Kampala: MISR/Cross Roads Press, 1987.

Munene, G. M. "Cold War Disillusionment and Africa." In *The United States and Africa: From Independence to the End of the Cold War,* ed. M. Munene et al. Nairobi: East African Educational Publishers, 1995.

Munro, William. "Power, Peasants and Political Development: Reconsidering State Construction in Africa." *Comparative Studies in Society and History* 38, no. 1 (1996): 112–48.

Murunga, Godwin. "Globalization and the Politics of Selective Blame in Kenya, 1963–1990." Paper presented at the International Conference on Mainstreaming Democratic Governance in the Social Sciences, Humanities and Universities for the 21st Century, Dar es Salaam, Tanzania, September 29–October 1, 1999.

Museveni, Yoweri. *What Is Africa's Problem?* Kampala: NRM Publications, 1992.

Mutua, Makau. "Breaking Barriers: Radical Constitutionalism in the Next African Century." Paper presented at the International Conference on Constitutionalism in Africa, Kampala, Uganda, October 5–8, 1999.

Nabudere, D. W. "External and Internal Crisis in Uganda's Continuing Crisis." In *Uganda Now: Between Decay and Development,* ed. H. B. Hansen and Michael Twaddle. London: James Curry, 1988.

Nafziger, Wayne, and Juha Auvinen. "The Economic Causes of Humanitarian Emergencies." In *War, Hunger and Displacement: The Origins of Humanitarian Emergencies,* ed. Wayne Nafziger et al. Vols. 1 and 2. Oxford: Oxford University Press, 2000.

Nasong'o, S. W. "Democratization and Human Rights Issues in Kenya: The Role of American Ambassadors William Attwood and Smith Hempstone." Revised edition of a paper presented at the Sixth Regional Conference on American Studies in Eastern Africa, July 8–12, 1997.

Ndikumana, Leonce. "Institutional Failure and Ethnic Conflicts in Burundi." *African Studies Review* 41, no. 1 (1998): 29–47.

Ngaruko, Floribert, and Javier Desire Nkurunzizix. "An Economic Interpretation of Conflict in Burundi." *Journal of African Economics* 9, no. 3 (2000): 370–409.

Nkrumah, Kwame. *Axioms of Kwame Nkrumah.* London: Panaf Books, 1972.

Nnoli, Okwudiba. *Ethnicity and Development in Nigeria.* Aldershot, UK: Averbury, 1995.

———. *Ethic Politics in Nigeria.* Enugu: Fourth Dimension, 1980.

Nyamnjoh, Frances. "Cameroon: A Country United by Ethnic Ambition and Difference." *African Affairs* 98, no. 390 (1999): 101–18.

Nzongola-Ntalaja, George, ed. *The Crisis in Zaire: Myths and Realities.* Trenton, NJ: Africa World Press, 1986.

Ogot, B. A., and W. R. Ocheing', eds. *Decolonization and Independence in Kenya, 1940–93.* Nairobi: East African Educational Publishers, 1995.

Okali, Agwu. "Accountability and Africa's Renaissance." *West Africa* (February 14–20, 2000): 19–20.

Okumu, Washington. *The African Renaissance.* Trenton, NJ: Africa World Press, 2002.

Olorode, Omotoye. "Economic and Political Crises in Africa: Wrong Question, Wrong Answer." In *State Reconstruction in West Africa,* ed. Segun Jegede et al. Lagos: Franked Publishers. 2000.

Olukoshi, Bayo. "State, Conflict and Democratization in Africa: The Complex Process of Renewal." In *State, Conflict and Democracy in Africa,* ed. Richard Joseph. Boulder, CO: Lynne Rienner Publishers, 1999.

Olukoshi, Adebayo. "The Politics of Structural Adjustment in Nigeria." In *Between Liberalization and Oppression: The Politics of Structural Adjustment in Africa,* ed. Tthandika Mkandawire and Adebayo Olukoshi. Dakar: CODESRIA, 1995.

Olukoshi, Adebayo, and Lisa Laakso, eds. *Challenges to the Nation State in Africa.* Uppsala: Nordiska Afrikainstituet, 1996.

Omara-Otunnu, Amii. "The Dynamics of Conflict in Uganda." In *Conflict in Africa,* ed. Oliver Furley. London: Tauris Academic Studies, 1995.

Osaghae, Eghosa. "Federalism and the Ethnic Question in Africa." In *Ethnicity and Governance in the Third World,* ed. John Mukum Mbaku et al. Aldershot, UK: Ashgate Publishing, 2001.

Ottaway, Marina. "Ethnic Politics in Africa: Change and Continuity." In *State, Conflict and Democracy in Africa,* ed. Richard Joseph. Boulder, CO: Lynne Rienner Publishers, 1999.

———. *Democratization and Ethnic Nationalism: African and Eastern European Experiences.* Washington, DC: Overseas Development Council, 1994.

Palmberg, Mai. *The Struggle for Africa.* London: Zed Press, 1983.

Pankhurst, Richard. *Economic History of Ethiopia, 1800–1935.* Addis Ababa: Haile Selassie I University Press, 1968.

Paz, Octavio. "The Philanthropic Ogre." *Dissent* 26, no. 1 (1979): 43–52.

Posthumus, Bram. "In Conte's Fortress." *West Africa* (February 20–22, 2000).

Ramsey, Jeffress. "Africa: The Struggle for Development." In *Africa.* 8th ed. Guilford, CT: McGraw-Hill/Dushkin, 1999.

Reno, William. *Corruption and State Power in Sierra Leone.* New York: Cambridge University Press, 1995.

Republic of South Africa White Paper on Reconstruction and Development. *Government Gazette* 353 (1994).

Republic of Uganda. *Constitution of the Republic of Uganda.* Entebbe: Government Printer, 1995.

Rodney, Walter. *How Europe Underdeveloped Africa.* Washington, DC: Howard University Press, 1982.

Rotberg, Robert. *A Political History of Tropical Africa.* New York: Harcourt, Brace and World, Inc., 1965.

Rothchild, Donald. "Hegemony and State Softness: Some Variations in Elite Responses." In *The African State in Transition*, ed. Zaki Ergas. London: Macmillan, 1987.

Samatar, Abdi. *The State and Rural Transformation in Northern Somalia, 1884–1986.* Madison: University of Wisconsin Press, 1989.

Samatar, Ahmed. *Socialist Somalia: Rhetoric and Reality.* London: Zed Books, 1988.

Samura, Sorious. *Cry Freetown: A Documentary on the Sierra Leonean Civil War*, 2000.

Sauser-Hill, George. *The Political Institutions of Switzerland.* Bern: Swiss National Tourist Office Publishing Department, 1946.

Sawyerr, A. *The Political Dimension of Structural Adjustment Programs in Sub-Saharan Africa.* Accra: Ghana Universities Press, 1990.

Seidman, Ann, and Frederick Anang, eds. *Twenty-first Century Africa: Towards a New Vision of Self-Sustainable Development.* Trenton, NJ: Africa World Press, 1992.

Senteza-Kajubi, W. "The Historical Background to the Ugandan Crisis, 1966–1986." In *Beyond Crisis: Development Issues in Uganda*, ed. Paul Wiebe and Cole Dodge. Kampala: MISR/Cross Road Press, 1987.

Sisk, Timothy. *Power Sharing and International Mediation in Ethnic Conflicts.* Washington, DC: United States Institute of Peace, 1996.

Smillie, Ian, et al. *The Heart of the Matter: Sierra Leone, Diamonds and Human Security.* Ottawa: Partnership Africa Canada, 2000.

South African Institute of Race Relations. South Africa Survey, 1999/2000. Millennium edition. Johannesburg: SAIRR, 2000.

Teka, Tegegne. "Amhara Ethnicity in Making." In *Ethnicity and the State in Eastern Africa*, ed. M. A. Salih and John Markakis. Uppsala: Nordiska Afrikainstitutet, 1989.

Throup, D., and C. Hornsby. *Multi-Party Politics in Kenya.* London: James Currey, 1998.

United Nations Development Program. *Human Development Report.* New York: Oxford University Press, 1991.

United Nations Economic Commission for Africa. *The African Debt Crisis.* Addis Ababa, Ethiopia: UNECA, 1999.

———. *Economic Report on Africa.* Addis Ababa: UNECA, 1999.

Villalon, Leonardo, and Phillip Huxtable, eds. *The African State at the End of the Twentieth Century: Parameters of the Critical Juncture.* Boulder, CO: Lynne Rienner Publishers, 1999.

Walker, Roselyn. "The Paramount Chieftaincy in Sierra Leone: Introductory Essay." In *National Museum of African Art, Smithsonian Institution. Paramount Chiefs of Sierra Leone: Photographic Portraits by Vera Viditz-Ward.* Washington, DC: The Smithsonian Institution, 1990.

Wamba-dia-Wamba, E. "Democracy, Multi-partyism and Emancipative Politics in Africa: The Case of Zaire." *Africa Development* 18, no. 1 (1993): 95–118.

Wamwere, K. Wa. *The People's Representative and the Tyrants of Kenya: Independence Without Freedom.* Nairobi: New Concept Typesetters, 1992.

Werbner, Richard. "Multiple Identities, Plural Arenas." In *Post-Colonial Identities in Africa*, ed. Richard Werbner and Terence Ranger. London: Zed Books, 1996.

Whitaker, C. S. *The Politics of Tradition, Continuity and Change in Northern Nigeria, 1946–1966.* Princeton, NJ: Princeton University Press, 1970.

Williams, Patricia. "Woman: The Other Variable in Africa's Development Struggle." In *Preparing Africa for the Twenty-first Century*, ed. John Mukum Mbaku. Aldershot, UK: Ashgate Publishing, 1999.

World Bank. *Reducing Poverty in South Africa: Options for Equitable and Sustainable Development.* Washington, DC: The World Bank, 1994.

Young, Crawford. *African Colonial State in Comparative Perspective.* New Haven, CT: Yale University Press, 1994.

Young, John. "Ethnicity and Power in Ethiopia." *Review of African Political Economy* 23, no. 70 (1996): 531–42.

Zack-Williams, A. "Child Soldiers in the Civil War in Sierra Leone." Paper presented at the Development Studies Association Conference, University of Bath, September 12–14, 1999.

Zartman, I. William, ed. *Collapsed States.* Boulder, CO: Lynne Rienner Publishers, 1995.

Index

About the Editor and Contributors

Pita Ogaba Agbese is Professor of Political Science at the University of Northern Iowa and Senior Fellow in the Program in Ethnic and Federal Studies at the University of Ibadan, Nigeria. Previously, he served as Acting Chair of the Department of Political Science at the University of Northern Iowa. His research interests are in the areas of civil-military relations, African politics, democratization, constitutionalism, and political economy. He has authored, coauthored and coedited books, monographs, book chapters, and articles in various scholarly journals. His most recent publication is a coedited volume with George Klay Kieh Jr., *The Military and Politics in Africa: From Engagement to Democratic and Constitutional Control* (2004).

Hashim Gibrill is Associate Professor of Political Science at Clark Atlanta University (CAU). Previously, he served as Chair of the Department of Political Science as CAU. His research interests are in the areas of conflict, African international relations, and politics and political economy.

Alice B. Hashim is a former Assistant Professor of Political Science at the University of Louisville, Kentucky. Her research interests are in the areas of African government and politics, Middle Eastern studies, international organizations, women and leadership in the developing world, and violence and the law. She is the author of *The Fallen State: Dissonance, Dictatorship and Death in Somalia* (University Press of America, 1997).

Toure Kazah-Toure is Lecturer and Researcher in the Department of History at Ahmadu Bello University, Zaria, Nigeria. His research interests are Africa's colonial and postcolonial history, nationalism, conflict, interethnic relations, citizenship, and the national question. His most recent publication is *Ethno-Religious Conflicts in Kaduna State* (HRM, 2003).

George Klay Kieh Jr. is Professor of Political Science and African Studies at Grand Valley State University, Allendale, Michigan, and Senior Fellow, Program in Ethnic and Federal Studies, University of Ibadan. Previously, he served as Dean of International Studies at Grand Valley State University, and Chair and Professor of Political Science at Morehouse College. His research interests are in the areas of peace and conflict studies, security studies, African politics, international cooperation, American foreign policy, and political economy. He has authored, coauthored, edited, and coedited books, monographs, book chapters, and articles in various scholarly journals on topics dealing with his various research interests. His most recent publication is a coedited book with Pita Ogaba Agbese on *The Military and Politics in Africa: From Engagement to Democratic and Constitutional Control* (2004).

Kidane Mengisteab is fomer Chair and Professor of African and African-American Studies at Pennsylvania State University. He has authored, coauthored, edited, and coedited books, book chapters, and articles in scholarly journals on various issues including state-building, democratization, conflict, development, and political economy. Previously, he served as Chair and Professor of Political Science at Old Dominion University.

Godwin Murunga is Lecturer of History at Kenyatta University, Kenya. Currently, he is completing his doctoral study in history at Northwestern University.

Musifiky Mwanasali is currently Special Assistant to the Assistant Secretary-General for Political Affairs of the United Nations. Previously, he served on the faculty of Sarah Lawrence University, as an Analyst in the Conflict Management Bureau of the African Union, and Advisor on Good Governance for Central Africa for the United Nations Development Program. He has written extensively on issues relating to the state in Africa, governance and democratization, conflict, and political economy.

Leonce Ndikumana is Associate Professor of Economics at the University of Massachusetts at Amherst. His research interests are in the area of applied macroeconomics, economics and conflict in the Great Lakes Region of Africa, and economic development. He has written extensively on various issues in these areas.

Paul Omach is Lecturer of Political Science at Makerere University in Uganda. His research interests are in conflict, peacekeeping, foreign policy, and the state in Africa. He is the author of "The African Response Initiative: Domestic Politics and Convergence of National Interest," *African Affairs* (2000).

Owen Sichone is Lecturer in the Department of Social Anthropology at the University of Cape Town, South Africa, and a Tate and Lyle Cambridge Scholar and Fellow of the Cambridge Commonwealth Trust. He has taught at various universities in South Africa, Tanzania, Zambia, and Zimbabwe. His recent publications include two edited volumes on *Democracy in Zambia: Challenges for the Third Republic and the State and Constitutionalism in South Africa.* Both books were published by SAPES Books. His current research interests are on xenophobia, the informal sector, and globalization with special focus on the lives of African immigrants in Cape Town.

www.ingramcontent.com/pod-product-compliance
Ingram Content Group UK Ltd.
Pitfield, Milton Keynes, MK11 3LW, UK
UKHW012036150926
475560UK00001B/35

9 780739 108925